STORES MANAGEMENT

STORES MANAGEMENT

Dr. Reuben Ray

GDMM (IIMM); PGBM;
M.A. (Philosophy, Political Science, English and Linguistics);
Master of Fine Art (Acting);
Doctorate of Fine Art (Films and Documentaries)

Himalaya Publishing House

MUMBAI • NEW DELHI • NAGPUR • BENGALURU • HYDERABAD • CHENNAI • PUNE • LUCKNOW • AHMEDABAD • ERNAKULAM • BHUBANESWAR • INDORE • KOLKATA • GUWAHATI

First Edition : 2010
Reprint : 2015

Published by	:	Mrs. Meena Pandey for **Himalaya Publishing House Pvt. Ltd.,** "Ramdoot", Dr. Bhalerao Marg, Girgaon, **Mumbai - 400 004.** Phone: 022-23860170/23863863, Fax: 022-23877178 **E-mail: himpub@vsnl.com; Website: www.himpub.com**
Branch Offices	:	
New Delhi	:	"Pooja Apartments", 4-B, Murari Lal Street, Ansari Road, Darya Ganj, New Delhi - 110 002. Phone: 011-23270392, 23278631; Fax: 011-23256286
Nagpur	:	Kundanlal Chandak Industrial Estate, Ghat Road, Nagpur - 440 018. Phone: 0712-2738731, 3296733; Telefax: 0712-2721215
Bengaluru	:	No. 16/1 (Old 12/1), 1st Floor, Next to Hotel Highlands, Madhava Nagar, Race Course Road, Bengaluru - 560 001. Phone: 080-22286611, 22385461, 4113 8821, 22281541
Hyderabad	:	No. 3-4-184, Lingampally, Besides Raghavendra Swamy Matham, Kachiguda, Hyderabad - 500 027. Phone: 040-27560041, 27550139
Chennai	:	New-20, Old-59, Thirumalai Pillai Road, T. Nagar, Chennai - 600 017. Mobile: 9380460419
Pune	:	First Floor, "Laksha" Apartment, No. 527, Mehunpura, Shaniwarpeth (Near Prabhat Theatre), Pune - 411 030. Phone: 020-24496323/24496333; Mobile: 09370579333
Lucknow	:	House No 731, Shekhupura Colony, Near B.D. Convent School, Aliganj, Lucknow - 226 022. Phone: 0522-4012353; Mobile: 09307501549
Ahmedabad	:	114, "SHAIL", 1st Floor, Opp. Madhu Sudan House, C.G. Road, Navrang Pura, Ahmedabad - 380 009. Phone: 079-26560126; Mobile: 09377088847
Ernakulam	:	39/176 (New No: 60/251) 1st Floor, Karikkamuri Road, Ernakulam, Kochi – 682011. Phone: 0484-2378012, 2378016; Mobile: 09387122121
Bhubaneswar	:	5 Station Square, Bhubaneswar - 751 001 (Odisha). Phone: 0674-2532129, Mobile: 09338746007
Indore	:	Kesardeep Avenue Extension, 73, Narayan Bagh, Flat No. 302, IIIrd Floor, Near Humpty Dumpty School, Indore - 452 007 (M.P.). Mobile: 09303399304
Kolkata	:	108/4, Beliaghata Main Road, Near ID Hospital, Opp. SBI Bank, Kolkata - 700 010, Phone: 033-32449649, Mobile: 7439040301
Guwahati	:	House No. 15, Behind Pragjyotish College, Near Sharma Printing Press, P.O. Bharalumukh, Guwahati - 781009, (Assam). Mobile: 09883055590, 08486355289, 7439040301
DTP by	:	Megha
Printed at	:	M/s. Aditya Offset Process (I) Pvt. Ltd., Hyderabad. On behalf of HPH.

Preface

When we're on an adventure hardly anyone of us look into time. Uncertainty, hazards and risk are imminent at any instance resulting to calamity at any hour of our adventurous odyssey. Still the mission continues with thrill and camaraderie for reaching to our destination. The resolve in unison is firm amongst us; "Fortune favors the brave." Such an analogy equally applies to the working and operation in Stores by any employee at any level, right from a helper even to a manager. The onus of working in stores is equally on everyone's shoulder. These are most cumbersome and onerous necessary to be complied at every level of operation, with a few essential functional aspects are briefed below.

At every process, by permitting entering of a truck on the weighbridge platform, loading or unloading of material manually or through material handling equipment, entry into inward register, preparation of GRI note, processing of inspection, recording of shortages, identifying defective and damaged goods, acceptance of material by the indenting department, and other series of transaction culminating toward issue of material to the consuming department, for example, we may take this to shop floor, Steel Melting Shop (SMS) in a Steel Plant.

The issue of material to the shop floor in one lot at a time or daily issue in small lot depending upon the quantum of consumption of material and melting program being processed for the day (Number of heats by SMS).

All such multiple handlings and series of transactions processed, aforesaid described fall within the purview of functions of the Stores department monitored and controlled by a storekeeper or a stores manager, depending upon the magnitude of operations. Every minute lost or delayed for reasons of slackness and inefficient handling of material by any of stores' staff or operators ultimately ensures increasing overheads and carrying cost of material. By efficient and systematic storing and handling of material prevent such adverse impact on company's profitability. All such functional aspects of Stores Management have been covered in this book by providing both theoretical and pragmatic explanations and examples.

The text and study material substantiating the aforesaid functional and operational aspects are covered under chapters 1-5, 8 and 10.

'Inventory" in Stores includes major categories like consumable stores, spares, raw material, building material, explosives, timber, oil and lubricants, and even WIP and saleable finished goods for dispatch to the customers. All such inventory holdings accrue carrying cost and require safe handling, preservation and safety keeping away from likely pilferages, damages and obsolescence. The handling and carrying cost of inventory in our country range between 20-30%. Sloppy turnover of stocks, unusual stock outs, overstocking, frequent breakdown and immobilization of MHE [Material Handling Equipment], excessive carrying of non-moving spares, wastage and damage of material during handling process, all such pitfalls and irregularities result to adverse repercussions on the working capital of the company, thereby reflecting loss to the company's balance sheet for the current financial year, as on 31st March. These related areas of stores operation and workings including its processing and responsibilities are covered under chapters 6, 7, 9, 11and l2.

By tradition, "Inventory" or "Stores", we call this to **be locked up capital,** accounting people term this to be **part** of working **capital,** and in layman's language it is consumable stores. Every item occupying space in store or awaiting issue by the consuming department entails cost both in term of carrying and handling, apart from procurement and actual cost of the product.

By reduction of carrying cost by 10% by the stores manager, can bring about increase in profit of the company by 25%. This is certainly possible by the stores department ensuring the system is organized based on.

(1) Integrated approach pursued with other departments of the company

(2) Automation of stores by implementing ERP system

(3) Standardization of stores procedure and determination of inventory norms

(4) Achieving high inventory turnover, JIT for shop floor requirements

(5) Computerization of stores accounting system

(6) Establishing mechanized material handling system for transshipment of material to the consuming departments, loading and unloading of material from trucks and trailers

(7) Formulating codification system making it conversant to the employees of the company for compliance.

Though many of such processes are incumbent to ERP system, still every store strives for achieving cent percent service level, low carrying cost, efficient handling of material, ensuring economy in the transportation of goods and removing all barriers of operation resulting to speedy disposition of material to the consumers.

When automation of stores is fully established and operational in league with the existing manpower, the benefits from the system are rewarding and profit oriented for the company. The working modules of ERP system corresponding to stores and materials management appears in chapter 13.

Most of companies have realized that implementation of ERP system is a necessity for any professionally managed and automated stores. Though huge investment is required for the system implementation still the ROI and cost reduction and benefits are tremendous over the period of time.

An old adage reminds me here, "Penny wise pound foolish". When such systems are set aside simply pursuing the traditional methods and processes of storekeeping, then the losses are inevitable resulting to serious crisis in terms of management of material by the stores officials and staff. The vision of ERP system in stores management can transform the existing warehousing and materials management function into profit centers, service outlets and feeders for the consuming and users departments.

Now stores in every organization is identified more to be a profit center, a selective tool for cost control and cost reduction, and pragmatic applications focusing on value analysis, value added process, inventory control, operation research, business process reengineering, and realizing economy of cost on the handling and transportation of material.

- Author

CONTENTS

1

Chapter

STORES FUNCTIONS

Objectives

After studying this chapter, you should be able to understand:

- Importance of stores management
- Stores functions
- Objectives for excellence in stores management

Structure:

1.1 STORES FUNCTION

The function of stores in modern times is more focused toward profitability of the company and even oriented to improving the service provided to the indenting departments and consumers.

It is true that storekeeping does not add to the value of a product. But focused storekeeping reduces costs, restricts downtime, increases customer satisfaction through timely deliveries and thus has a positive impact on firm's bottom line. Storage provides critical connecting link to suppliers, manufacturers and customers.

Too often, executives view their operations merely as a link in the chain of the manufacturing and marketing process and consider only the single connection between themselves and their suppliers or customers. But managers should assess the impact of their specific actions upon the overall business operation. To do this, information on part and product availability is essential. While information systems for controlling production processes have reached a high degree of accuracy and reliability, unfortunately the same cannot be said for storage systems.

Waiting Time

Most of the time, parts and products sit in storage awaiting picking, packing, and shipping. The relative inefficiency of the storage function is indicated by the fact that the inventory turnover for products in, our country, averages about two times a year. Individual firms show much higher turnover, but there are long marketing chains in virtually all industries that require multiple storage levels to reach a single end market.

One reason for stores being assigned a low place on the corporate totem pole is that it usually is taken for granted as a single source of supply. But stores usually have many of their own supply sources that are geographically diverse, product differentiated, bound by various lead times, and affected by many other uncertainties.

Similarly, on the outbound side for finished products, the Sales and Marketing functions place a different set of demands on the store creating a crisis in its processes.

Despite the complexity, the careful application of relatively simple principles to stores management can greatly improve the productivity of the **storage function** and bring down associated revenue capital and expenses.

1.2 MODERN CONCEPTS

Basic Elements of Stores

The operating efficiency of stores revolves around line control over inventories. Efficient line operations of inventory in turn depend upon appropriate store keeper's design and operating procedures. Any stores consists of three basic operations: (1) reserve storage of product to serve future manufacturing or sales needs, (2) order picking of unitized loads to fulfill immediate manufacturing and customer needs, and (3) order picking of broken lots of less than case lot size, These three requirements mean that three separate operations must converge into all overall plan to achieve maximum efficiency.

The three basic cost centres requiring control of stores include (1) space for storage and order picking, (2) equipment, and (3) labour. In today's environment, labour is by far the most important consideration. The amount of land required depends upon the final store design. The business impact of stores from an accounting point of view is its impact on operating cost and the balance sheet.

The **modern stores** usually is a single-storey building between 10 to 15 meters high from floor to ceiling and with main travel aisles and bypass routes. The emphasis is upon labour productivity to enhance output. In such store, handling 500 to 2,000 or more cases per man-hour is easily achievable if the stores is properly designed. The productivity of labour depends upon the inter-relationships of the three **basic factors of space, equipment, and labour**. The space required is a function of materials handling equipment. It ranges from four meters aisles when using the standard sit-down counter balanced truck to two meters aisles for a typical turret-type lift truck. This reduces unproductive aisles space by 50 per cent and also reduces capital expense for space by a similar ratio. Capital costs will increase as more sophisticated equipment is purchased. However, space costs typically are depreciated over 30 years, while equipment costs generally are depreciated over about five to 10 years. This results in a more favourable cash flow and tax rate as equipment is substituted for space.

In addition, narrower aisles increase labour productivity by reducing travel time and distance due to smaller total area and shortened distance per trip. Dividing the aisle width by one half and adding the space required for pallet storage yields the number of square feet required for each storage floor position. Each floor position, however, may hold a number of storage locations above it. When they rise to more than one level, racks are required for easy entrance and exit of product.

Operations and Control

The final layout of the physical parts of the stores is the easiest job in store keeping. The more difficult task is to establish an operating procedure to assure smooth physical product flow. As indicated earlier, the key to store keeper's operational control revolves around the inventory. Only five events concerning inventory are essential for proper control. (1) What product is scheduled to come into the stores and when? (2) What product do we actually have in the stores (3) What orders need to be filled today? (4) Do we have the product? (5) Where is it?

Functionary Aspects of Stores

(1) Controlling Costs: Controlling warehousing costs depends upon: (1) material handling equipment selected; (2) amount and type of floor space (3) storage equipment and storage aids; (4) work methods, and (5) handling of records, documents and materials. To control costs, it's necessary to separate the store keeper's functions, then determine the sequence in which they are being performed. If they're not being handled in the order listed below, chances are that the store keeper's operation is in trouble.

(2) Inventory Control: It is essential that records show the amount of inventory on hand and ready for shipment when orders are entered. If this is not done, orders will not match product availability, resulting in wasted travel time in the stores, crew interference, back orders, scratching of orders, and other wasteful practices, all orders must be checked for product availability before sending them to the store floor.

(3) Purchasing: While this isn't a store keeper's function, it nevertheless has tremendous impact on the store keeper's. An open vendor receiver file should be installed to facilitate identifying purchase orders and authorised customer returns. Frequently store keeper's employees must spend time trying to figure out what they are to receive. The presence of a purchase order or receiver properly describing items, size, pack, colour, and so on will not only reduce store keeper's wasted time, it also can greatly help in processing the transactions through record keeping and accounting. Ideally, the store keeper's should have a document to serve as the store keeper's receiving record. This document should be designed to facilitate the correct identification of and accurate counting.

(4) Order Entry: Orders must be entered before the receipt of the product and for its allocation to customer order prior to dispatch. These orders must be modified when there are revisions to customer requirements. In absence of this important information store personnel may take their own decisions which can turn harmful to customer service and result in significant losses.

(5) Receiving: Store keeper's managers who can not receive inventory efficiently and correctly identity the material, will pay dearly later on when they attempt to find out what really happened. This is also the ideal place to get control of inventory allocated to back orders. If back orders are filled as goods are received, the inventory will be used as intended. In addition put-away and storage costs will be saved and chances for fouling up the back order system will be minimised.

(6) Inspection: If goods must be inspected the receiver document should provide the necessary instructions. Inspection should be done as quickly as possible so inventory can be put away and become available to fill orders.

(7) Put-away: Put away is an important function. Location and reporting errors will foul up the inventory control system. When prime locations are used the location is incorporated in the catalogue description. It is only necessary to keep track of bulk reserve. However, failure to have an efficient locator system can cost you a lot of non-productive time.

(8) Storage: Floor space generally is one of the cheapest ingredients in the store keeper's cost formula. But it is the most difficult resource to add to an existing store keeper's location. Therefore, it is essential to make the best possible use of this valuable resource. Storage (aids tracks and shelving) can do much to alleviate space shortages. For these resources to work at maximum efficiency, you must match the storage space allocated to each item with the volume that needs to be stored.

(9) Replenishment: This function is frequently necessary when a prime location is assigned to each item. Often, there is not enough room at the prime location to accommodate all of the inventory, so excess inventory must be stored in a temporary location. If you use a peelable label to chain the reserve location to the prime location, inventory can be found and transferred easily. Without an efficient locator system, you can lose reserve inventory, and when it can't be found you may purchase more stock than is actually needed. This inevitably will raise the cost of carrying the inventory.

(10) Order Selection: This is the primary function of the store keeper's. The document used for order selection should be a model of clarity, contain all essential information and contain no information that is not required in order to ensure rapid and accurate order fulfillment. Using the sixth copy of an invoice to fill orders is not a model of clarity. An order picking document and not an invoice or shipping order designed for accounting on transportation, is needed for this purpose.

(11) Checking: Provide good documentation and a machine-written original copy for order selection and many of your checking problems will disappear.

(12) Packing and Marking: Frequently orders are received several days in advance of shipment. But regardless of when received, it is wise to expedite all orders that involve picking and packing to the floor as soon as possible. This will result in better control over scheduling. Marking is an important function that is often neglected. Use of properly designed adhesive labels and quality stencil can do much to eliminate errors in checking and counting.

(13) Staging and Consolidation: Many store keeper's don't have enough room to stage orders. However where orders are assembled on pallets, labelled boxes can help. Transport by carts used to fill orders however should not be used in staging. Heavy-duty forklift truck or non-storage trucks can be used to sort out large number of small orders. As orders are received at the shipping dock for staging, the order assembly pallets or boxes can be removed. Then the orders can be staged and the documents labelled with the staging locations. The orders now can be delivered to the tailgate of the route truck as they are needed.

(14) Shipping: Routing orders in advance of pulling them permits the orders to be assembled for shipping in a sequence that approximates your routing requirements.

(15) Clerical and Administration: Much of the clerical and administrative effort performed in many firms is made necessary by failure to design an efficient warehousing system. In short, clerks are often hired to compensate for the errors of omission and commission that take place in performing all of the preceding functions.

(16) Computerisation: It has been pretty well demonstrated that you can't achieve the improvements described without a computer. The alternative is a highly labour intensive operation with more people than can be economically justified. The computer is necessary to achieve cyclic control and economies of scale. To justify the computer, it is necessary to engineer the system and provide the software necessary to achieve operating goals.

(17) Front End Control: Warehousing as practiced by most firms regardless of size, is essentially a small business. Many store keeper's have fewer than ten store keeper's employees. All too frequently operations are labour intensive due to lack of front-end control.

Front-end control means that management is in control of the store keeper's especially the inventory otherwise the store keeper's is being managed by your order fillers.

Non-productive time is an item of expense that few accounting systems take into account. Instead, it gets buried in one or more of the cost accounts, and it is ignored because there is no real measure of it.

1.3 MODERN CONCEPT OF MATERIALS MANAGEMENT

Visionary Managers have the power to redically rationalize costs and lead times in their stores and materials networks. Infact, pursuit of enormous improvements in the production pipeline has become a way of life for all major manufactueres. Reduction goals of 90 percent of pipeline inventories and lead times are now relatively common, especially among the most dynamic industry leaders. Nor must the customer service, product value or quality of life be sacrificed on the altar of productivity. Magnificent strides in adopting the best productivity methods has proved that magnificent strides can be made simultaneously in productivity improvement and in customer and employee benefits and *vice-versa*. Goal-settling is a vital milestone on the trip in the 21st Century of Stores Management. Executive Management, determined to excel and willing to support every action required to turn goals into self-fulfilling prophecies, must initially set new goals far above those of the past. Recent laudable achievements fall in the range of the following improvement percentages.

- 50% customer service lead time
- 50% space occupied by store keeper's and distribution facilities.
- 25% personnel costs
- 50% inventory investment in the stores and production pipe lines
- 25% stores transaction (receipts and issues, for example) processing costs
- 75% better inventory record accuracy
- 75% fewer damaged and defective goods

Unfortunately, hampered by seemingly insurmountable barriers such as demand seasonality, inaccurate forecasts, and suppliers convinced that they must have long lead times, progress in overall distribution improvement has been less dynamic than in the production operation stores network. Dogmatic acceptance of the conditions that dictate modes of operation only perpetuates inefficient operation, the costs of which are passed on to the consumer.

The Materials and Stores vision, spanning decades or even centuries, as shown in Exhibit-1, encompasses dreams that go far beyond the practical scope of a business's or government's immediate action agenda. Therefore, strategies that flow from the vision are actionable, major initiatives that require several years to come to fruition. For example, materials and stores vision would encompass long-term creation of national and international clusters of suppliers, production

EXHIBIT 1: VISION-STRATEGY-TACTIC

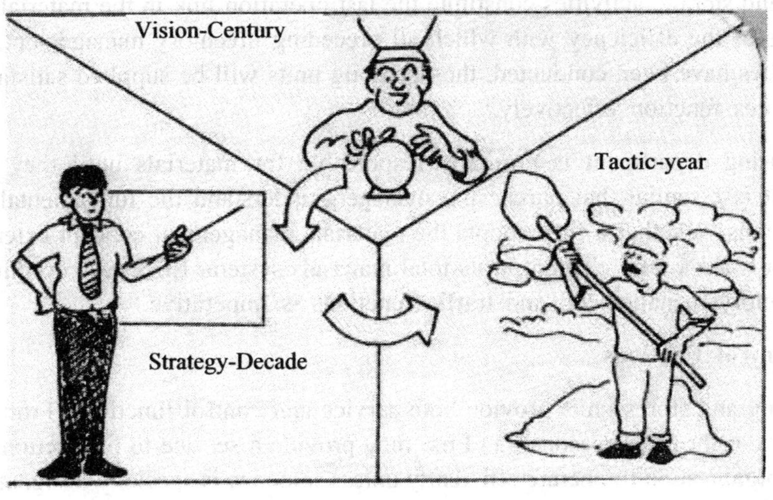

and distribution facilities in every regional markets area. A practical strategy would be to concentrate work in early years on achieving near-ideal clusters in one or two of the largest market regions. However, the managers need more specific goals and objectives to drive their tactics in the coming years. Their tactics, therefore, would be to locate local supplier in the target region for some vital goods/and or components, to work with distant supplier to establish production facilities in the region, and to start building the new distribution and production facilities appropriate for the cluster.

This is not to say that some feasible strategies will not come to full fruition beyond the decade time frame. In fact, the business will take a more active role in government and industry associations. The most worthwhile pursuits of industry associations will be those directed at making visions come to pass.

1.4 STRATEGIES FOR TWENTY-FIRST CENTURY

Most store keeper's and Storerooms are much larger than they need to store the present levels of inventory. This may be hard to understand when one sees pallets stocked in aisles and every other available nook and corner. However, the more important issue for strategic planning purposes is to recognise that radical improvements in the supply, manufacturing, stores and distribution pipe line will revolutionize the amount of store keeper's space required to meet significantly improved levels of customer service. Therefore, the challenge to executive management will be to move forward or to stay in front of the leading edge by implementing vendor, factory, and store keeper's improvement programs for adopting new technologies that will achieve those ends. Given these improvement programs management can start to develop strategies for reducing the excess stores and store keeper's capacity, and those strategies will evolve continuously as improved programs progress throughout the distribution, supply and stores network.

1.5 WHAT IS STORES?

Receiving and storage activities constitute the last operation link in the materials management chain. Regardless of the efficiency with which all preceding inventory management, procurement, and traffic activities have been conducted, the operating units will be supplied satisfactorily only if receiving and stores function effectively.

The purchasing department is normally responsible for materials until they are ready for production use, it is essential that purchasing managers understand the fundamentals of receiving and stores operations. Whether a firm adopts the materials management concept extensively or not, receiving and stores are a vital element in its total materials system. Effective coordination with the purchasing, inventory management, and traffic functions is imperative.

Service and Control Fnctions

The receiving and stores units provide both service and control functions. From a managerial viewpoint, they exist for three reasons, (1) First they provide a service to production. It is difficult for a production organization to operate efficiently unless someone is specially designated to organize and control the flow of materials into the operation. (2) Second, the stores organization acts as a custodial and controlling agency. It is responsible for the safety and physical control of a substantial portion of a firm's current assets. (3) Third, the existence of stores permits quantity buying and the attendant savings in price, paper-work, and handling.

Stores Systems

Two basic systems can be used in physically controlling stores materials: (1) a closed stores system and (2) an open stores system. A single firm often employs both systems. The application of each system depends on the nature of the production operation and the way in which materials are used in it..

Closed System

As its name indicates, a closed stores system is one in which all materials are physically stored in a closed or controlled area. Wherever possible, the general practice is to maintain physical control by locking the storage area. As a rule, no one other than stores personnel is permitted in the stores area. Material enters and leaves the area only with the accompaniment of an authorizing document. This system is designed to afford maximum physical security and to ensure tight accounting control of inventory material.

Today, most firms maintain centralized perpetual inventory records independent of storeroom stock cards. Receipts are posted to the perpetual record from suppliers' invoices or from the firm's receiving reports. Withdrawals from stores are normally authorized and posted from one to two sources. The most common source is the stores requisition, which is made out by the user and signed by an authorized supervisor. The central record provides a running balance for each major inventory item.

Another commonly used source of withdrawal authorization is the engineering bill of materials These lists of materials are developed along with the design drawings. After the design engineering work for a job has been completed production control schedules the job and arranges for the release of the required materials to the shop instead of preparing a set of stores requisitions for these materials, Production control may simply reproduce the engineering bill of material and send a copy to stores as the document authorizing release of the materials. 'For effective use, this system requires clear and complete identification of all materials on the engineering bill of materials. For the materials involved a single companywide inventory numbering system is a necessity when this system is used.

When the materials required for a job are to be withdrawn from stores over a period of time, using bills of material as withdrawal authorizations, presents a problem. Unless a daily report of withdrawals for the job is prepared it is difficult for the central inventory record section to keep its records current because the stores department must retain its copy of the bill of materials until all withdrawals are made.

This problem can be circumvented, however, by using a material apportioning system. Under this system, the bill of materials goes first to the inventory record section, where the total requirement for each material needed on a job is deducted from the current inventory balance. The required amount is set aside, or apportioned (on the perpetual record) so it will not be allocated for use on another job before the current requirement materializes in the shop. When the apportioned material is actually used, the apportioned quantity, on the inventory record is charged off to the job. The apportioning system, of course, can be used to assure material availability for specific jobs regardless, of the method used to authorize stores withdrawals. The system is widely used among firms job-shop-type operations.

Every firm uses many low-value inventory items. To maintain a perpetual inventory record for all low-value items may cost more than the control provided by such a record is worth. To obtain a record of approximate usage, it is much cheaper to have the stores clerk record all receipts on a bin tag. To indicate when an item should be ordered, a bin level mark or some form of the two-bin control system can be used. Many firms simply place the reorder quantity of small items in a plastic bag, when the clerk has to use stock from the bag, he knows it is time to reorder. This method is frequently used for nuts, bolts and other low-value hardware. If the accounting charge can be determined at the time an order is issued, the accounting department can pick up the proper distribution code from the purchase order. If not, the accounting department usually develops a method by which the expenditure can be allocated equitably among the users.

Physical Inventory

Physical Inventory can be conducted in one of three ways:

(1) Fixed Annual Inventory: Many companies take physical inventory annually at the close of the fiscal year. This necessitates shutting down the production operation and organizing a special crew for the inventory job.

(2) Continuous Inventory: At the beginning of each year some firms divide their inventory into fifty-two equal groups and assign one of the fifty-two groups to be physically counted each week. Thus, the physical inventory operation goes on continuously without interrupting the production operation or upsetting storeroom activities.

(3) **Low-point Inventory:** Some companies take physical inventory irregularly, whenever the stock level of an item reaches its lowest point.

All three methods are widely used; the selection of the appropriate one depends largely upon conditions in each individual business. The fixed annual inventory can be troublesome because it is a major task which must be accomplished in a short period of time. However, it is ideal for seasonal businesses or for businesses that completely close down for an annual vacation.

The continuous inventory approach possesses two important advantages. It can be planned and worked into scheduled activities without a shutdown. And it can be conducted in an orderly and relaxed manner, which is conducive to accurate work. This approach also facilitates efficient utilization of stores personnel. In many storerooms, withdrawals are heavy early in the day and are much lighter later on. Thus, when the stock clerks' normal work slacks off, they always have a backlog of inventory work to do.

The low-point approach minimizes the time required for actual inventory work because of the small quantities of materials involved. However, it has the disadvantage of producing an irregular inventory schedule, which tends to peak the work load for stores personnel.

Finally, before developing the details of any physical inventory method, a company should consult the accounting firm that audits its books. A company must be able to demonstrate to auditing firms. and to local and federal tax officials that the method finally selected is capable of producing accurate inventory reports.

Storeroom Location In laying out a manufacturing operation, a layout engineer attempts to develop an efficient work flow that minimizes the transportation and handling of materials. This means that materials should be stored as close to their point of use as is feasible. Hence, the use of decentralized storage facilities frequently reduces manufacturing cost

On the other hand, the centralization of storage facilities also yields significat benefits. From a managerial point of view the major advantage of centralization is that it facilitates control of the total stores operation, manpower, materials, space utilization, and equipment Whenever an activity is divided and conducted as a number of separate subactivities, supervision and coordination of the total operation become more difficult. Up to a point the larger the storage area, the more efficiently space and equipment can be used. Similarly, a larger operation facilitates the balancing of individual work loads and permits more efficient utilization of personnel.

A firm normally attempts to use both centralized and decentralized locations in its total stores operation. The objective is to secure the major advantages of both approaches to the extent possible in a particular situation. Most plants attempt to centralize as much material as is practical. The result, for example, may be two or three large storerooms strategically located near different manufacturing areas, the exact number depending upon the size and nature of the production operation. When possible, heavy or bulky materials that are costly to handle should be stored adjacent to the point of use. For example, in a processing plant it is quite common to find one or two large centralized storerooms handling small production items, packaging materials, tools, and MRO supplies. Located throughout the plant adjacent to the point at which they are used in the process are numerous stacks of large bags and drums containing such things as chemicals and additives.

Open System

The open system represents the second major type of stores system. It finds its widest use in highly repetitive, mass production types of operations that exhibit a continuous and predictable demand for the same materials.

In plants using the open stores system, no storeroom as such exists. Each material is stored as close to its point of use as is physically possible. Materials are stored in bins, on shelves, in racks, on pallets, in tote boxes, and so on, much as they would be stored in a storeroom. However, the storage configuration at each work station is arranged to fit the available space. Storage facilities are completely open, and any worker has access to any storage facility.

After material is received, stores personnel are usually responsible for its delivery to the production areas They are further responsible for working out satisfactory physical storage arrangements with the production supervisors. After the material has been delivered, production supervisors assume responsibility for materials stored in their areas.

The open system is designed to expedite production activities. It places little emphasis on the physical security of materials In ideal applications, there is considerable justification for this approach because the material is used relatively quickly, and it is not subject to a high rate of deterioration, obsolescence, or theft.

An automobile assembly plant offers the clearest example of an open stores system. Here, daily production is high and purchased parts. and subassemblies flow into the plant in a steady stream. or higher-cost, bulky items, deliveries from suppliers are scheduled at frequencies as high as several times per day. As a result, average inventory is extremely low relative to plant output. Such systems place unusually exacting demands for close cooperation on production control, purchasing, and suppliers' personnel.

The open system also places less emphasis on the accounting control of materials. Materials are usually put into production without the use of a requisition or a control document. No perpetual inventory records are kept in an open system. To determinc the *actual* usage of a material during a given period, it is necessary to take a physical count of the material at the end of the period and to compare this figure with the similar beginning-period figure (which has been adjusted for material receipts during the period). Hence, accounting charges are determined indirectly rather than directly. As a result the system provides control over material usage only if it is used in conjunction with an accounting system employing "standard cost" techniques.

To conclude, the open system is most applicable in situations where repetitive production operation produces standardized products. Materials handled in an open system should not be subject to pilferage, nor should they be easily damaged. If production requires delicate or pilferable items, they should probably be controlled in a closed storeroom. Generally speaking, an open system is more likely to function successfully if it is not applied to a large number of items. Firms applying such a system to several hundred items typically experience better results than those applying it to several thousand items.

Random-Access Storage System

The random-access storage system is a unique type of closed stores system, used by a relatively small number of large firms. In this system, no material has a fixed storage location. When an item enters the storeroom, it is stored in the first available bin or shelf suitable for its storage requirements. When the item is withdrawn from stores, the storage space available for any other incoming item having similar physical storage requirements. All materials are thus stored at random locations throughout the storeroom. This means, for example, that a stock of nine 20-horsepower electric motors may be located at nine different locations.

Requisites of Stores Responsibilities

The receiving department is responsible for the receipt, identification and general inspection of all incoming materials. Receiving is also responsible for notifying all interested parties of the arrival and condition of incoming material.

The stores department is responsible for safe and technically sound storage of all production materials, some in-process inventory, and most MRO items.

The stores department must protect materials in its custody against pilferage, unauthorized usage, and unnecessary damage or deterioration. It must also classify, mark, and locate all materials in a manner which permits ready accessibility. Finally, the stores department must control the physical issuance of materials in a manner that provides effective service for the production operation and, at the same, protects against unauthorized withdrawals.

Cost Implications

Receiving and stores activities *indirectly* influence product costs in several ways. Inventory carrying costs stemming from deterioration and pilferage of materials, as well as indirect stores labor, are controllable to a great extent by these organizations. Moreover, an alert stores organization can help reduce the costs of obsolescence by developing systems to detect inactive materials. Similarly efficient use of scarce storage space can further reduce inventory carrying costs.

The stores operation also exerts a strong influence on *direct* labor costs.

1.6 RECEIVING OF MATERIALS

Receiving is essentially a clerical operation. Because many clerical activities are regarded as "routine" however the importance of the receiving function is often underrated. It is only at the receiving desk that the purchasing control documents meet the physical materials themselves

The receiving report which the clerk completes upon receipt of a shipment is the only document a firm possesses which details the material it has actually received. This document is used as the basis for invoice payment, for continued purchasing negotiation and for closing the order. Accuracy is therefore essential.

Receiving is an important control point in a firm's materials system. The receiving clerk can detect those suppliers who meet only the minimum standards of quality and service. Receiving records show which suppliers are consistently late in their deliveries which have the maximum number of rejects and which deliver the greatest number of split shipments. Any of these supplier failures is costly to the buyer; hence, close coordination between purchasing and receiving usually pays dividends.

Receiving Procedure

A typical receiving procedure consists of four steps:

(1) **Unloading and Checking the Shipment:** The number of containers unloaded from the carrier's vehicle should be checked against the carrier's manifest (freight bill) to make certain the full consignment has been delivered.

(2) **Unpacking and Inspecting the Material:** A receiving clerk is held responsible for count verifications.

(3) **Completion of the Receiving Report:** In most companies, a document known as a receiving report" is prepared as a by-product of the purchase order, for the quantity received.

(4) **Delivery of the Material:** In the case of non-stock materials, the receiving department is usually responsible for delivering them to the requisitioner or for releasing them to an internal delivery service that transports them to the requisitioner.

Receiving Paperwork

The paperwork system used in the receiving operation varies substantially among firms. In a majority of cases, the receiving department is notified of an impending shipment by a copy of the original purchase order.

1.7 IDENTIFICATION OF MATERIALS

Stores activities involve the physical aspects of materials handling and storage. However, management is concerned not only with the physical operations, but more importantly with the design and control of the systems utilized in conducting these activities. Developing a system for effective identification of materials is the first responsibility confronting a stores manager.

Consequently, a firm with a sizable production and MRO inventory is compelled to develop its own numerical identification system for its materials. The inventory catalog often is arranged and indexed by the *purchaser's* own part numbers. It should also include the supplier's part number along with a concise verbal description of each item. The catalog can be cross-indexed in alternative ways; certainly it should be cross-indexed by generic name of the items and perhaps also by suppliers and their part numbers.

The objective is to develop an unambiguous identification system that facilitates clear internal communication. Ideally, this system should be designed so that it can be used effectively by all departments in the firm. Clearly, the purchasing, inventory control, and stores departments are critical areas where the system must provide consistent and unambiguous identification of materials. If the system can also be integrated with the operations of design engineering, production, and cost accounting, improved communication plus simplified clerical activities are almost certain to result.

Sytem Design

Three basic approaches may be used in developing an identification system: (1) the arbitrary approach (2) the symbolic approach, and (3) the use of engineering drawing numbers. Using the arbitrary approach, inventory items are simply assigned arbitrary numbers in sequence as they are added to a stores account.

The symbolic approach to system design is commonly used in Industry. Symbolic systems can be either *numerical* or *mnemonic:* A numerical system assigns a six-to ten-digit code number to each item. The first several numbers usually indicate the classification to which the item belongs, the next several numbers typically indicate the subclass, and the last three numbers are usually uncoded. The following example illustrates the concept:

2	137	019	508
General Class	Generic Class	Sub-Class	Specific Item Number

This ten digit code number is one firm's stock number for a 1/4 by 3/4-inch stainless steel square-neck carriage bolt. The first digit indicates that the item is a purchased part, in accordance with the following general classification:

(1) Raw materials

(2) Purchased parts

(3) Manufactured parts

(4) Work in process

(5) MRO supplies

Physical Identification

Even though a satisfactory identification system is developed, physical identification of material in the storeroom may still be a problem. The first step in minimizing identification problems is to record the storage location of all items in an inventory catalog. When a storeroom is properly laid out, every storage location has a numerial designation. Each inventory item should be assigned a specific storage locator index so that anyone should be able to locate any material with ease.

1.8 OBJECTIVES FOR EXCELLENCE IN STORES MANAGEMENT

Physical improvements alone are usually not enough to reap the bountiful returns of the fully reinvented store. It is vital simultaneously to upgrade the paperwork and computer systems that must mesh with radically improved store operations. In fact, many store operations need modern modes of logical systems and procedures every bit as much as they need new storage, receiving and shipping methods. The objectives of new systems and procedures should be simple and clear, and they must lead to improved operations. The most important of these objectives are as follows.

(1) Reduction of the time required to enter and ship new and changed customer requirements.

(2) Lowering the inventory levels in the entire pipeline, thus slashing not only the required investment but also the lead time through the pipeline.

(3) Increasing the productivity of **all** company assets, with emphasis on reducing payroll costs by eliminating bureaucratic procedures in favour of streamlined, computer supported white-collar operations.

Distribution and manufacturing managers must know how to evaluate their store operations and systems against a new standard of excellence. The following manager checklist presents the beginnings of the new standard.

(1) Accounts receivable and payable sections of accounting organizations will virtually vanish following the establishment of long-term price agreements for use by common customer and suppliers systems for electronic funds transfers between their bank accounts.

(2) Laborious item-by-item check-ins at the receiving dock and the generation of a receipt transaction for every individual item will be eliminated.

(3) Since inspection of incoming goods will no longer he required, systems and transactions to move and track receipts through inspection and into stock will also disappear.

(4) Picking, sorting, packing and shipping customer requirements still constitute a far costlier operations than it needs to be, especially when done the old fashioned way, one order at a time. Newer systems must provide exciting new modes of batch order picking, sorting and shipment staging (or synchronisation) to make their contribution to the spectacular improvements that physical changes in **store layout** and operations will effect.

(5) Productive **utilization** of store space is the most important aspect of controlling all other store costs.

(6) Two vital keys to efficient store space utilization are the use of standard containers for each item stocked and a standard quantity per container. Superior companies will devote more attention to capturing item information in their data bases. This will not require significant time and expenditures since modem software features will support low-cost data capture and maintenance.

(7) Cubic volume and weight per stocked item calculated by user-friendly maintenance aids and stored in the data base, will enable the system to plan truck load shipments that fit the cubic trailer size and permissible load weight.

(8) Store replenishment **Inventory Management Systems** that routinely require planners to review computer action notices add unnecessary cost to operations.

(9) The **safety stock** component of inventories is far too liberal to satisfy the ensuing real demand especially in light of exciting new methods for achieving supplier delivery and quality improvements. New system must provide simpler data for setting safety stock and continuously reducing it, as warranted by improvements in the stores network.

(10) Traditional **budgeting and reporting** systems will be the nucleus of twenty-first century management systems. But they need to be modified to include target and measurement of budget items as a percentage of revenues.

(11) In the most perfect stores of the future, inventory quantity discrepancies will still occur, albeit with a lower rate of error than in the past. Lightning-fast checks to verify location accuracy in specified bays will be supported by system reports designed for that purpose.

(12) The best disposition is to add the out-of-stock items to the next scheduled shipment after their receipt.

(13) Kanban, **card** or electronic form, will be adopted to pull deliveries of repetitive items through the network of vendors, factories and distribution stores.

1.9 SUMMARY

(1) Stores function does not add value to the product, but has direct impact on firm's bottom line.

(2) Stores has three basic cost centres-space for storage, equipment and labour.

(3) Significant improvement must be achieved by implementing modern concepts in stores management.

(4) Closed stores and open stores are two important systems for physical control of stores.

(5) Scientific materials identification system has to be designed and implemented.

(6) Management need to set objectives for achieving excellence in stores functions.

1.10 SELF ASSESSMENT QUESTIONS

(1) How does stores function impact earnings of a firm?

(2) Describe open stores system? When can it be employed?

(3) Describe closed stores system? Enumerate conditions under which it can be applied.

(4) List any three objectives to bring in excellence in stores management.

2 Chapter

STORES ORGANIZATION

Objectives

After studying this chapter, you should be able to understand:

- The role of stores organisation and its impact on income of the organisation.
- Relationship of stores with other departments in the organisation.
- Stores operations.
- Centralised and decentralised stores with their merits and demerits.
- Factors to be considered in location and layout of different stores.

Structure:

2.1 INTRODUCTION

In a small firm the stores function may be operated from a single office run by one storekeeper but, in a large organization, it is necessary to apportion the various duties to separate sections, e.g.:

(i) Identification or vocabulary section.

(ii) Standardization section.

(iii) Storehouse section.

(iv) Stockyard section.

(v) Stock control section.

(vi) Records section.

(vii) Accounts section.

The importance of the stores function is being increasingly recognized in industry and public undertakings and, in most large concerns. Nowadays, the person in charge of it occupies a senior supervisory position of managerial status, and is described as the stores controller, stores manager, stores superintendent or stores officer. A specimen organization chart for a large department is shown below.

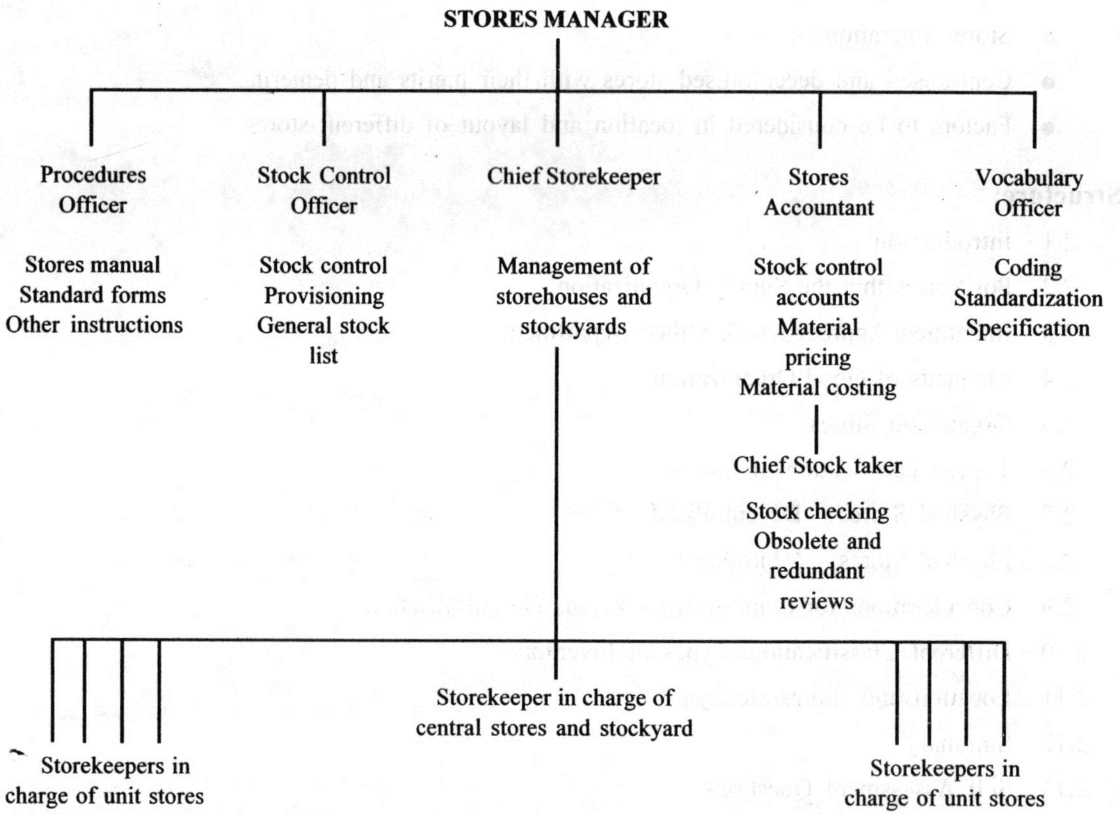

2.2 POSITION WITHIN THE SUPPLY ORGANIZATION

In the industrial field particularly, the specialization of production and the increasing complexity of modern products and machinery requires a very high standard of organization and performance in stores work, as the range of materials, components and spares is continually expanding. Stores and Purchasing are largely inter-dependent, and any inefficiency or lack of co-operation on either side is soon reflected in the other. To cope satisfactorily with the whole supply problem in modern conditions, a complete 'dovetailing' of these two functions is essential.

There are occasionally special circumstances in an industry which would justify some split in control, but the more progressive concerns show an increasing tendency to set up a completely integrated purchasing and stores department responsible for all these activities, bringing the following work under one responsible departmental manager:

PURCHASING AND STORES DEPARTMENT

Purchasing Branch	**Stores Branch**
Tendering	Stores coding and vocabulary
Quotations	Materials specifications
Commercial negotiations	Materials standardization
Agreement of prices	Stock control
Order placing	Maintenance of stock records
Supply contracts	Stores accounting
Erection contracts	Stock checking
Sales of scrap and obsolete materials	Review of obsolete and surplus stock
Market research for buying	Co-ordination for Inspection of goods delivered from suppliers
Purchasing statistics	
Progressing of orders	Operation of storehouses
Clearance of invoices for prices, discounts, carriage and purchase conditions	Operation of stockyards
	Certification of invoices for quantity

An arrangement of this kind has obvious advantages, the chief of which are outlined as follows:

(i) One Department head only reports to the line management and his responsibility for the price and availability of materials is clear and unavoidable.

(ii) A single departmental control eliminates friction and ensures the maximum co-operation of each section.

(iii) It is easier to give a more comprehensive training to the staff, and improve promotion prospects,

(iv) It avoids duplication of records and activities.

2.3 INTEGRATED APPROACH WITH OTHER DEPARTMENTS

To discharge its responsibilities adequately, the stores department must actively co-operate with other departments, not only to provide a service, but to give and receive information so that the service is efficient. The nature of the other functions involved varies in different organizations, so does the scope and responsibility of the stores function. It is difficult to be precise about the relationships unless each case is considered separately. By way of example the following notes indicate the position as it is normally found in production factories.

Production Department

This department is the main stores 'customer' and it is therefore of the first importance that the services to production are satisfactory in all respects. The closest co-operation is essential not only on the provision of materials but also on the stock levels to be maintained in accordance with the policy for inventory control and production schedules.

The stores department provides materials, tools and other shop supplies at the required times and in the required quantities to meet the factory programme, advises anticipated difficulties or failure in supply, and notifies any substitute or surplus materials available from stock. The storehouses are ready to accept work in progress and finished goods at any time and to receive scrap, off-cuts, rejected items and salvaged or reclaimed materials as they arise, so that the shop floor may be promptly cleared.

The production department sends to the appropriate storehouses work in progress and finished goods, as well as any excess materials, tools, fixtures and equipment not currently required. It further notifies as soon as possible any impending changes in the production schedule.

Design and Engineering Departments

It is most desirable to have a close contact with these departments, particularly from the point of view of specifications, standards and obsolescence. Arrangements are made to see that, before any new design, modification or technique is put into production, due note is taken of materials available or on order to the old design, so as to avoid obsolescence. Whenever possible, new items and modifications are introduced to coincide with the running down of existing stocks. The design or engineering departments are consulted when obsolescent or obsolete items are being listed for disposal, to see if they can be used in current production with some modifications.

Inspection Department

Accommodation for inspection personnel may be provided in store houses, and they are notified of all receipts. The stores department is responsible for holding goods received in 'quarantine' and submitting samples to inspection promptly. In return, the inspection department inspects and tests deliveries without delay, and indicates acceptance or rejection together with advice on whether doubtful consignments can be put into use subject to a discount in price, or whether they should be returned to suppliers as totally unacceptable.

Maintenance Department

The stores service in this case consists in holding appropriate materials and machinery spares and being in a position to issue them as and when required. To facilitate this work, the maintenance department advises details of the forward programme on repairs and overhauls as far as possible, particularly where planned maintenance is in operation, and advises on the initial quantities of spares to be provided when any major new plant or machinery is installed.

Finance Department

There is a continuous exchange of information covering verification of book entries and physical stock, clearance of invoices both inwards and outwards, revision of prices, supply of material-cost information, and control of working capital allocated to the financing of stock. Procedures are organized to work together effectively to control the value of inventory and cost of materials. The finance department usually provides regular periodic detailed statements of the cost of operation of the stores services.

Transport Department

The stores department is itself sometimes responsible for transport but, where there is a separate transport department, it is essential that the two work together harmoniously. The stores function reports details of loads, pick-up locations and discharge points, makes facilities available for the speedy, safe loading or discharge of goods, and provides a weighbridge service. The transport department is responsible for the ready availability of vehicles and for advising any circumstances which may delay deliveries or collections, such as breakdowns, strikes or adverse weather.

Sales Department

The service provided is normally the acceptance, storage, packing and dispatching of finished products. The sales department co-operates by advising of any appreciable fluctuations in the demand for finished goods which may affect storage accommodation, and is also responsible for giving instruction on the quantities of spare parts or other materials to be held for servicing sales already made.

2.4 ELEMENTS OF GOOD ORGANIZATION

The stores and receiving jobs are closely related hence the receiving activity is often placed under jurisdiction of a store-keeper.

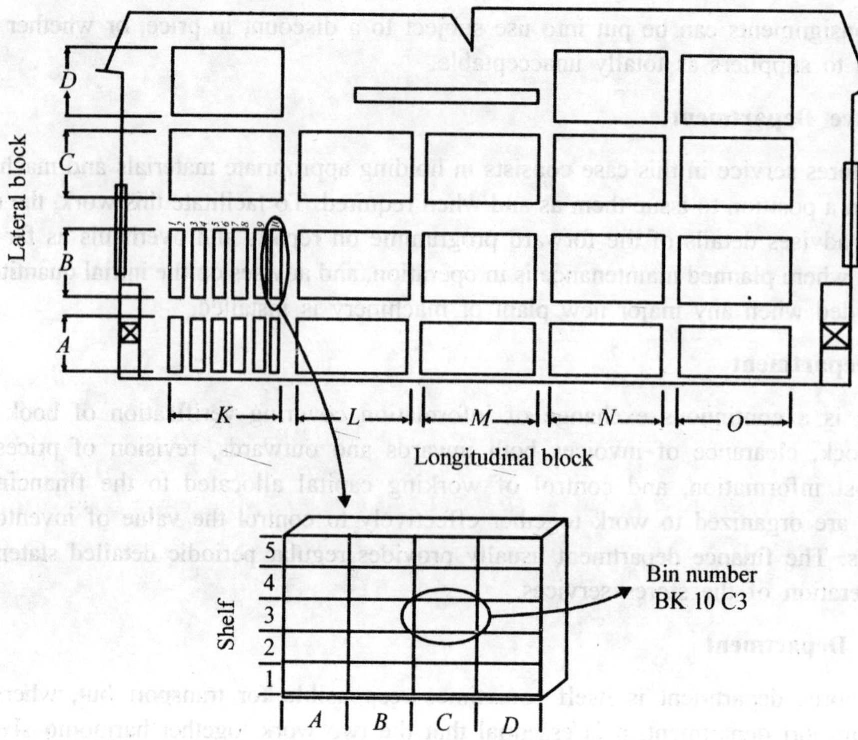

Fig. 2.1: A Common System Used in Addressing Storage Locations

There are two strong arguments for such an organizational arrangement:

(1) The stores activity is a materials-oriented activity; therefore, it should report to a department whose primary interest also lies in materials and supply operations. Supervisory personnel thus will recognize and be equipped to deal with the materials and supply problems encountered in receiving and stores.

(2) Receiving is the last step in the material acquisition process, and stores is the last step in the material supply process. From the standpoint of the *total control of materials* these activities should be included with the rest of the materials activities. From an operating point of view, such a materials organization facilitates coordination among the related materials activities. Specifically, it ensures that the relationships between stores, inventory control, and purchasing will receive proper attention, as will the important factor of indirect material costs.

Some firms place the stores activity under the production department. In a few cases, it is placed under a factory superintendent; in others, it reports to the production control manager; and in still others, it reports to the general production manager. Two common justifications for this form of organization are:

(1) Production management is responsible for running the production operation smoothly and for meeting product delivery dates. Production should therefore have control of its immediate

material supply group to ensure smooth delivery of material to the production work stations.

(2) Receiving and stores disbursement activities should not be supervised by the department that buys and authorizes payment for the same materials. Collusion and embezzlement possibilities are eliminated when stores and receiving personnel report to a manager outside the purchasing department.

In making the organization decision, management's primary concern should be the fulfillment of three basic objectives. First, materials must be stored and managed so that they are immediately available and in good condition when the production organization needs them. Second, the order-filling and delivery system must efficiently supply the production organization in accordance with production schedules. Third, these and related activities must be accomplished at an optimum cost.

Receiving and stores activities constitute the final link in the materials acquisition chain. Receiving is responsible for expeditious receipt and general inspection of materials, as well as for a thorough review and comparison of all relevant documentation with the materials. Stores is responsible for identification and safe, efficient physical handling and storage of material.

The receiving operation is an important control point in a firm's materials system. This is the only point at which the purchasing control documents actually meet the materials themselves. Subsequently, a store assumes responsibility for the physical care and control of the firm's inventory. Since this material represents from 15 to 30 percent of the organization's total invested capital, this responsibility is a significant one, to say the least.

In addition to the custodial and material control aspects of the responsibility, these functions directly influence costs. The manner in which receiving and stores activities are conducted clearly influences inventory carrying costs and, to some extent, the direct labour costs of production.

2.5 ORGANISING STORES

Stores procedure involves the receipt, inspection, storage and issue of materials. Stores department is to be organised in such a way that the above purposes are achieved and it is equipped for handling of materials coming and going out. The location of the stores department should be carefully planned in order to achieve the maximum efficiency. It should be situated in a position where it is nearer to the road and railway siding so that the handling charges are also minimum. It should also be conveniently located in a place which is readily accessible from any production department so that the cost of internal movement of the materials is kept at minimum. Good location of stores will reduce the cost. The lay-out of the department depends on the class and quantity of the materials to be stored and the general nature of the business. Shelves, racks, bins, etc., should be situated in such a way as to make the flow of materials follow the minimum distance traversed, with minimum handling and maximum speed. Cold storage is to be provided for storage of special materials which are affected by atmospheric condition and this will avoid losses due to evaporation and deterioration of such materials.

Central Stores and Sub-stores

There are three main types of stores as follows:

(1) **Central Stores:** Centralised buying and centralised handling of stores

(2) **Central Stores with Sub-stores:** Centralised buying and decentralised handling of stores

(3) **Independent Stores in Production Department:** Decentralised buying and decentralised handling of stores.

A Storehouse is a building or room where materials ate kept, and storekeeping involves the proper receipt, safe custody, preservation and issue of the materials to various users or customers and also the physical and financial accounting of the stocks kept in the Warehouse.

The warehouse renders a "service" to the organisation and the fundamental objective is to make available, in an efficient and economical manner, a balanced flow of materials, components, tools, etc., for manufacture, operations or maintenance, and the receipt and issue of finished goods.

The responsibilities of stores personnel would inlcude the following:

(i) Identification of all materials stored.

(ii) Receipt of incoming goods.

(iii) Inspection of all incoming goods.

(iv) Storage and preservation of materials in stock.

(v) Materials handling.

(vi) Packaging.

(vii) Issue and Despatch.

(viii) Maintenance of stock cards.

(ix) Stores accounting.

(x) Inventory control.

(xi) Stock taking

Research has shown that about 35% of the covered area in a factory is usually utilised for storage of raw materials meant for production, and of finished goods. Storage costs account for as much 6 to 8% of the sales rupee realisation. Every paisa that can be saved in terms of storage cost can add to profitability and while every extra rupee spent on storage is a direct charge on the profits of the Company. A Stores Manager has, therefore. a very great responsibility on his shoulders as none of the operations for which he is responsible adds anything to the value of the product manufactured by the Company. On the other hand, all the expenses that he incurs come directly from the profits of the Company.

Responsibilities of Stores Officer

Stores Department should be under the control of the Stores officer and he is responsible for receipt, storage and issue of materials. His duties and responsibilities are as follows:

(1) Receiving the materials, arranging for the inspection thereof and accepting the materials as per the specification given in the purchase order and the accepted quantity mentioned in the Goods Receipt and Inspection Note.

(2) Storing the accepted quantity in the respective bins, in a proper manner so that deterioration is avoided.

(3) Maintaining the stores in a tidy manner and the storage space is to be utilised to the advantage by placing the bins, shelves, racks and other containers in a convenient manner.

(4) Issuing correct materials against authorised stores requisition.

(5) Checking the bin card balances with the physical quantities in the Bins.

(6) Requisitioning of general items of stores for purchases by the purchasing department, when the re-order level is reached.

(7) Entering the receipts, issues, return on materials in the bin cards and maintaining the bin cards and other material records.

(8) Reporting on the obsolete stock, waste, scrap, slow-moving and non-moving materials.

(9) Taking back surplus materials returned from jobs or processes as per the material return notes

(10) Preventing unauthorised persons entering the stores.

(11) Furnishing the following information to the Cost Accounting Department:

   (a) The job numbers, process, operations or departments to be debited for all the materials issued by and to be credited for all the good materials returned to him.

   (b) A record of finished parts and products delivered by the production departments

   (c) A record of scrap received, disposed and balance of stock of scrap.

   (d) A record of number of all vouchers relating to goods receipt and inspection note, stores requisitions, material return notes and stock verification vouchers for shortages and excesses. This ensures that these vouchers are verified in the Cost Accounting Department as to their receipt, posting and reconciliation.

Receipt and Inspection of Materials

A. After receipt of the consignments, store keeper has to prepare goods receipt and inspection note and arrange for inspection of the materials by the technical personnel. The materials which are in accordance with the specification only will be accepted and entered in the "Quantity accepted" column. It is entered in the "Receipt Column" of the Bin card. Goods Receipt and Inspection Note are signed by the Store Keeper and Inspector respectively. Most of the organisations are preparing the combined voucher named as Goods Receipt and Inspection Note in order to avoid the duplication of the work. The number of copies will be prepared as per the requirement of the organisation. The details as to the payment of freight and demurrage charges, etc., paid but to be recovered from the supplier are also to be furnished in the Goods Receipt and Inspection Note so that the recovery from the supplier is not missed at a later stage.

B. Rejected materials are to be kept separately and the supplier is to be informed for the replacement of those materials if they are still required. If necessary, these rejected materials are to be returned to suppliers by booking them on *"To-pay"* freight basis. This will enable the storekeeper to avoid the congestion in the Rejection Material Cell. Inspector has to record the reasons for rejection of materials.

2.6 TYPES/CLASSIFICATION OF STORES

Functional and Physical Stores

Stores fall into broadly two categories contingent on following considerations:

(a) Functional: depending on the use to which the material is put — chemicals, tools, raw materials stores, etc.

(b) Physical: depending on its size and location — central stores, sub-stores, transit stores, site stores, etc.

(a) Functional Stores

(i) Raw Material Store: This is where raw materials used in the factory are stored. Usually, this is the largest kind and its location should be such that it is situated alongside a railway, canal or river. Where the deliveries are by road, there must be adequate space for trucks to move, turn and park.

(ii) Production Store: Production also requires a large number of materials, generally called "consumables", — eye-shields, cutting oils, abrasives, gloves, aprons, bigs, small tools, etc. A store stocking such items is called a Production Store.

(iii) General Store: Various kinds of miscellaneous items like paints, brushes, cleaning materials, wood and spirit are kept here. In some cases where there is no Production Store, the materials mentioned in (ii) are kept in the General Store.

(iv) Tools Store: All kinds of tools like files, measuring instruments, saws, small tools like hammers, pliers, etc., or special tools required in the factory are kept here.

(v) Salvage Store: Here materials rejected on the factory floor are stored either with a view to salvage them or to sell them as scrap. Steel scrap is usually kept separately, preferably in the open.

(vi) Packing Store: Packing materials are kept in here and these include wood for making crates, cardboard cartons or bottles, drums as in a pharmaceutical company, or empty cylinders.

(vii) Spare Parts Store: These spares are usually required by Maintenance for repair or overhauling of equipment and machinery in the factory. These spares and components are either manufactured in plant or purchased from outside.

(viii) Receipt Store: This is where goods are received from vendors or those cleared from the railway station, airport or the docks. The materials arriving here have to be retained until they are inspected. Once they are accepted they are sent to the respective places for storage, or directly to where they will be used.

(ix) Quarantine Store: Here materials received from outside awaiting inspection are stored. This is usually part of the receipt store. The term quarantine is used because often inspection may not be completed in a day; e.g., a lab test may be required for specific items. In such cases, until inspection is complete material are placed in the Quarantine Store, as they are not to be issued for use.

(x) Finished Goods Store: Finished products of the company meant or despatch to Customers or for transfer to another stock point or distribution centre are kept here.

(xi) Work-in-progress Store: In many cases a particular shop may produce an item in batches, e.g., 1000 units. The other shops might not be able to reach this figure or the actual quantity required might only be 200. Here, the rest of the 800 units in semi-finished form are kept in the WIP Store for future use. This is neither raw material nor finished goods. It is in an intermediate state.

(xii) Stationery Store: Keeps office stationery for issue to various departments of the company.

(xiii) Bonded Store: This is a store which keeps goods on which customs or excise duty has not been paid. These goods are not available for use.

(xiv) Flammable Materials Store: This is used for the storage of highly combustive material like oil paints, etc. This store consists of separate compartments partitioned by fire walls, which is done with a view to prevent movement of flames from one area to another in the event of a fire. These fire walls will normally have a four hour fire resistance rating. The main dependence for fire protection is placed on an automatic deluge type sprinkler system connected to an adequate water supply.

(xv) Shed Storage: A shed is a roofed structure without complete side and end walls, and is used for the storage of materials that require maximum, ventilation or those that do not require protection from weather. This type of building is a compromise between a yardstore and a closed stores building, because it offers more protection to materials than the former but less than the latter. If necessary, tarpaulins can be used on the sides for protection during the monsoon. It is built at ground level with a concrete floor

(xvi) Open Yard: This is used for storing bulk items which do not require specialised storage. Even though there is no protection from sun and rain, the surface of the open yard is normally levelled and is covered, by sheets or steel mats.

2.7 PHYSICAL STORES – DECENTRALISED

The new wave of visionary, revolutionary change is most likely to be founded in the way products are designed and in solving such thorny distribution and retail problems as peak and valley sales. Chief among the new manufacturing concepts related to storage and warehousing is the decentralization of inventories into small subplants throughout a factory. The executive checklist is a convenient tool for comparing the characteristics of the outmoded central or remote manufacturing store to that of the focussed store of the twenty-first century facility.

The manufacturing store of the twenty-first century will be incredibly smaller than traditional stores and warehouses. The most important aspect of the newly highly efficient store is that components and materials will be received and stored as close as practical to their point of use in production. Following are additional important operating practices that companies aspiring to be superior must adopt.

(1) Containers and receiving equipment must be designed to virtually eliminate forklift trucks from the receiving and inspection process for all but the largest components and heaviest materials.

(2) Inspection must be eliminated as a step in the receiving process. Supplier programs can teach vendors how to produce perfect quality and can help them to achieve it.

(3) Counting and weighing components and materials received is a wasteful procedure that must be discontinued. Errors in counts, which will probably slip through forever, can best be trapped by infrequent low-cost or free physical counts.

(4) The production teams in small cells and on assembly lines might incorporate receiving, storage and issue activities into their work routine, as long as this does not disrupt the production flow or lower equipment utilization in selected instances in which high utilization is vital.

(5) Bar coded, kanban- type receiving documents should be scanned to record receipt until such time as they can be replaced by electronically transmitted load manifests. All components entire truckload can then be recorded via a single transaction.

(6) Recording of issues must be discontinued in favour of automatic deduction from inventory of material and components based on reported production of the product. Progress to this level will require stringent control of unrecorded floor loss and quality at the level of parts-per-million defect rates.

(7) Reusable containers, designed to optimize production efficiency and minimize personnel injury and fatigue, should flow directly from the supplier's last factory operation, through shipping, to receiving and storage at the customer's factory, to the production operation, and back to the supplier. Through out this continuous flow, it should be unnecessary to repackage or to count the contents of any container.

(8) Focussed storage space utilization should be every bit as high as it would be in conventional stores. Therefore, every trick of storage space savings should be employed.

(9) Most new, focussed sub plant stores will be too small to warrant a full-time employee. Since it is not practical for the production team to take over the function, a fulltime-person might be assigned to take care of all the stores for a cluster of subplants.

2.8 PHYSICAL STORES – CENTRALISED

In new, smaller factories-within-a factory, virtually all support functions are decentralized and moved into the small subplants. All resources necessary for successful operation are directly at hand, enabling relatively small production and support teams to work cooperatively and continuously to improve the efficiency and quality of operations.

The history of manufacturing storage in most big companies has been one of avoiding real solutions to the basic problems caused by suppliers. Instead, companies have added layers of store bureaucracy (count verification, inspection and tracking of incoming goods) between material receipt and its use in machining or assembly. When companies were small, the factory received a few materials and components and stocked them, as close to the operation needing them, as was practical. The office where the materials and components where ordered and where inventory records were maintained was a few steps away from operations. **Inventory management** personnel were in the factory, sight checking inventory levels and conferring with production people about the latest schedules in order to update material priorities. As factories got bigger, their increased size and complexity started to cause problems. It was no longer practical for the dozens of people responsible for inventory records and purchasing to maintain control the best way possible by direct involvement in and observation of manufacturing operations. The office was now too far from most operations, and there were too many factory operations to make visiting all of them a practical option. As a result, inventory errors became rampant.

Finally, some one hit on the idea of gathering up all the materials and components in a factory and putting them under lock and key in a **central store**. Since the using departments could no longer simply use what they needed it, new formal procedures for kitting issues and replenishing live stocks were developed, and requisitions were required to withdraw any components from stock in excess of demands (e.g., scrap and floor loss replacements). The new central stores added days, even weeks, to the processes of stocking and issuing. In addition, new fleets of lift trucks were needed to make the long delivery trips from **central stores** to the places around the factory that used centralized materials and components, as indicted on the schematic on the left side of Exhibit-2.1.

It didn't occur to more people that the real problem was simply that factories had become too large to be as superbly manageable as when as they were small. A much better solution to the problem would have been to reorganise the big factory into small factories-within-a factory, called subplants. Now that many companies have seen the benefits of doing so, they are subdividing their factories into subplants and moving materials and components out of **central storage** into the subplants that use them as the small subplants on the right side of the Exhibit 2.1. One not so inconsequential benefit is that fork lift truck travel is slashed, because, the delivery distance form focussed receiving and stores is a fraction of what it was when stored centrally.

EXHIBIT 2.1: DECENTRALIZE — STORAGE

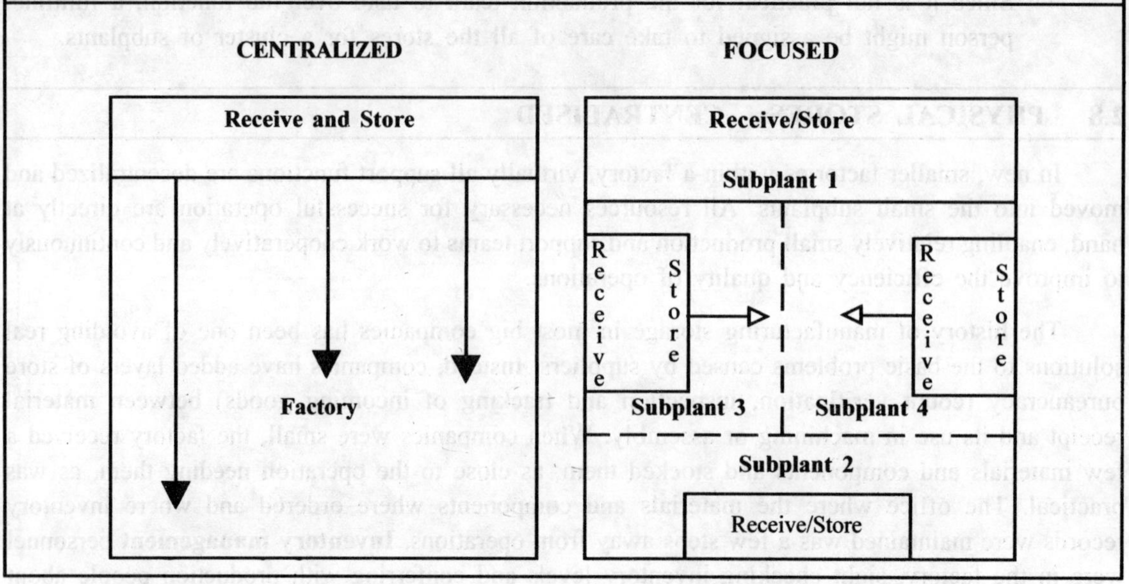

For big companies, the worst decision was not simply to centralize storage but to move it to an entirely separate, offsite store, as illustrated in Exhibit 2.2. In many instances, such stores have been located miles from the factories they were intended to service. As a result, management of the remote stores became an even greater abstraction. Instead of being able to see first hand the size of piles of stored containers in the factory, **inventory management** relied on computer status information. On a computer screen, differentiating the investment and space occupancy resulting from an inventory of a thousand brackets and those of the same quantity of engine blocks is difficult! In big factories, all too often, storing, purchasing and inventory management functions were moved out of the manufacturing executive's organization and into a **central materials management** organization. This fragmented the responsibilities for inventories in such a way that it became impractical for a single individual to control the investment and to provide required service level.

Infact, the establishment of central stores did not necessarily shift all inventory permanently from factory to store. The factory usually continued to maintain formal and informal plant floor inventories to buffer it from delays in receiving materials and components from the store.

EXHIBIT 2.2: COSTLY CENTRALZED STORAGE

The traditional store of the giant (or even medium size) factory epitomises worst of the centralized world. It has the following short comings.

(1) The distance between the store and the departments it serves, is long, necessitating long trips between the two points.

(2) Centralized store employees come to feel that they are members of a business apart from the production areas they serve. It is not uncommmon for them to act over burdened when asked for an expedited delivery of parts to the factory, for example.

(3) The bureaucracy of the central store becomes stifling. Lines of production people often form at locked windows of the store to obtain one or two replacement parts for lost or defective components. Each such request must be accompanied by a paper work transaction.

(4) A hierarchy of specialities is created within the central store. The cycle counters often become an elite group, with other store men specializing in receiving, others in issuing, and still others in paper work processing.

(5) Surprise shortages and deliveries that arrive too late at the assembly line have often caused line stoppages. As a result, the store routinely schedules kit preparation far in advance of actual need, adding store processing time and inventory to the manufacturing pipeline. Large sections of store are dedicated to storing kits prepared in advance but still awaiting arrival of shortage items. The advance kitting procedure, not only identifies shortages, it causes them. A much smaller area is occupied by complete kits ready for issue but not yet required by the production department.

(6) Eventually the store empire builders hit upon the idea of making their business even more important. They move their operations to a separate, remote store location. Separation of the factory from its store increases the already excessive store process lead time and further complicates communication and cooperation between the "separate businesses".

Receiving Stores

The superior manufacturers of the world are hard at work breaking down communication, distance and physical barriers between stocks of material and components and the production workers, who, through their labour, transform them into higher value products. They recognise a revolutionary new receipt, storage and issue concept that, when carried to its ultimate end eliminates teams of nonproductive store workers and monstrous automated storage and retrieval systems from the pipeline.

The concept is simple. Receipts should be delivered to the immediate vicinity of production operation and stored there, then picked up and used at the same spot. However, few companies, if any, have reached this ultimate goal, because to do so requires that components be produced and delivered in small, frequent lots, This requires that the supplier's set up and change over costs be near zero, that his factories be in the local cluster of company and that the transport systems between supplier and user be superbly organized, with small trucks continuously shuttling between customer and supplier through out the day. Further, it requires receiving points adjacent to every production area. The present state of art in most supplier networks is not advanced enough to support the ideal. Nor is it likely that the receiving points can ever be directly adjacent to every production operation in most factories. The required number, size and shape of the most productive cells and lines dictates a relatively low ratio of exterior wall length (potential receiving points) to factory floor space. Therefore, the practical alternative in most cases will continue to be mini stores located as close as practical to the cell or line, with a capacity for much smaller amounts of inventory.

2.9 CONSIDERATIONS FOR CENTRALIZATION VERSUS DECENTRALISATION

For this purpose it is necessary to consider the following in order to evolve the best possible organisation:

(1) The magnitude and variety of operations; efficiency of communication.

(2) The various specialised functions.

(3) Locations of plants, projects and operating units and so on.

(4) Various types of products manufactured or various types of projects/operations undertaken.

(5) The various stages of manufacture or operations.

(6) Major categories of materials; major commodities purchased.

(7) The major markets for purchase.

It should also be remembered that what may be regarded as a good organisational set-up this year, may need considerable change in 3/5 years as the above factors and management techniques and policies change.

Let us now consider the above points. The magnitude and variety of operations may indicate decentralisation in case of a large industrial establishment with more than one plant, each plant producing, say, products worth more than ₹ 5 crores per annum, although all the plants may be in the same neighbourhood. On the other hand, efficiency of communications and use of electronic data-processing may indicate that centralisation is the correct policy.

Then there are specialised functions which comprise Materials-Management, such as Purchasing, Stores keeping, Materials Control or Stores Inventory Control. In most establishments, separate sections or wings of the Materials Department will deal with these functions in co-ordination with each other. Value Analysis and Operations Research for Materials-Management may in some organisations come within the orbit of the Materials Department, whereas in other organisations these may be 'Staff' functions with which the Materials Department will be closely associated.

Locations of the various plants (or projects or operating units) will largely influence decisions regarding centralisation and decentralisation of operations. Units within a small radius may come largely under the central control, whereas geographically remote units will naturally require decentralised operation. In some cases, on account of the magnitude of the operations in terms of total output in rupees, geographical distance, and production of dissimilar products, the outlying units may have to be made virtually autonomous, with only "Staff Control" from the centre or headquarters.

Finally, the major markets for purchase have to be considered in organising the-Materials Department when there are large scale purchases of a particular commodity or commodities for which the market is concentrated in a particular town or part of India, e.g., Jute and Jute Manufactures in Calcutta; certain types of oils in Kerala.

In addition to the above, there are also "Administrative" reasons favouring centralisation or decentralisation and indicating necessary compromises. Let us consider some of the advantages and disadvantages of centralisation and decentralisation.

Advantages of Centralisatfon

(a) It takes advantage of the volume of purchases of all plants.

(b) There are advantages of standardisation and variety reduction.

(c) Specially trained staff at Headquarters can deal more efficiently with problems of Value-Analysis and Operations Research.

(d) There is better control of stocking points and the volume and categories of stocks to be held at different points.

(e) There is often reduction of paper-work and increase in flexibility.

(f) There is overall economy and better control of the entire materials management operations of the company.

Disadvantages of Centralisation

(a) If all purchases are made from the headquarters, it is likely to be uneconomical for many items and the lead-time for purchases and replenishments will increase unnecessarily.

(b) It often deteriorates "Service" and lowers over-all efficiency of operations of the branches.

(c) It may often lead to too rigid control and delays in decision-making.

(d) It may hinder better "buyer-seller" relations.

(e) It may make more difficult to pin-point inefficiency in Materials-Management and production.

Advantages of Decentralisation

(a) Better control and speed in purchasing dissimilar items required specially by the branches/ plants away from the headquarters.

(b) Greater flexibility in purchasing and stock control.

(c) Better 'buyer-seller' relationship.

(d) Decision making in relation to price, quality, delivery, local problems and so on takes less time.

(e) It pin-points responsibility for Materials-Management and Production.

(f) There is greater economy.

Disadvantages of Decentralisation

(a) Duplication of effort; dangers of competing against one self in the market; higher overall costs of purchasing and re-ordering.

(b) Quantity discounts may not be obtained on account of smaller purchases.

(c) Loss of efficiency in regard to control of operations; extra-paper work.

(d) Dangers of lack of standardisation.

(e) Dangers of higher over-all inventory.

(f) Difficulty in keeping up with improvement at the headquarters and other divisions/branches.

No fixed role for Centralisation versus Decentralisation

It will be seen that some of the arguments in favour of or against centralisation apply equally to decentralisation. There can, therefore, be no standard formula. From complete centralisation with limited local responsibility to virtual autonomy of the divisions/branches have been tried by various organisations with almost equal success.

Merging of different profit centers into one makes centralisation more desirable. On the other hand separation of profit centers calls for greater decentralisation.

Finally, the answer is very often a compromise between centralisation and decentralisation varying from organisation to organisation and in accordance with prevailing policies and circumstances.

In some organisations major items of purchase are dealt with at the headquarters, minor purchases and local purchases being done at the divisions and branches. On the other hand in certain organisations where each unit is autonomous there are only policy and procedural directions from the headquarters, the divisions and branches being free to act on their own or through the headquarters according to their discretion.

In general, wherever centralisation with decentralised operations is in force, there are staff and line supervisions of the materials departments at the divisions and branches by the headquarters and their own branch/division respectively. In other words, at the branch/division level the Materials Department is answerable as regards line relationship to the General Manager or Administrative head of the unit concerned; whereas it is responsible as regards Staff relationship to the head of the Materials Department at the headquarters.

2.10 DIFFERENT CLASSIFICATIONS/TYPES OF INVENTORY

The primary function of inventory is to make supplies available when needed to maintain continuous operation. The primary objectives of inventory control are :

(1) To have a stock of goods when needed by production and by sale

(2) To keep capital investment at the lowest level possible

(3) To institute controls for the protection and distribution of inventory

To achieve these objectives, inventory control must have the cooperation of the production and purchasing and coordinate activities with them. When considering the goal that inventory control seeks to achive — the lowest cost and the minimum inventory necessary for continuous operation — one must define the different classifications of industrial inventory assets (inventory is a company asset), which include:

(1) Production Inventory: this includes raw-materials, purchased parts and components that enter the finished product.

(2) Work-in-progress Inventory: this is composed of all production processes at various stages of production prior to being incorporated into the finished product. Also includes any material released from stores.

(3) Finished-product Inventory: this is the end product ready for shipment to the consumer.

(4) Maintenance, Repair and Operating Supplies (MRO): this includes all expendable items that are required for the manufacturing operation but which do not enter the finished product.

2.11 LOCATION AND STORES/STOCKYARD

Storeroom Location: In laying out a manufacturing operation, layout engineering attempts to develop an efficient work flow that minimizes the transportation and handling of materials. This means that materials should be stored as close to their point of use as is feasible. Hence, the use of decentralized storage facilities frequently reduces manufacturing costs.

On the other hand, the centralization of storage facilities also yields significant benefits. From a managerial point of view, the major advantage of centralization is that it facilitates control of the total stores operation — manpower, materials, space utilization, and equipment. Whenever an activity is divided and conducted as a number of separate subactivities, supervision and coordination of the total operation become more difficult. Up to a point, the larger the storage area, the more efficiently space and equipment can be used. Similarly, a larger operation facilitates the balancing of individual workloads and permits more efficient utilization of personnel.

A firm normally attempts to use both centralized and decentralized locations in its total stores operation. The objective is to secure the major advantages of both approaches to the extent possible in a particular situation. Most plants attempt to centralize as much material as is practical. The result, for example, may be two or three large storerooms strategically located near different manufacturing areas, the exact number depending on the size and nature of the production operation. When possible, heavy or bulky materials that are costly to handle should be stored adjacent to the point of use. For example, in a processing plant it is quite common to find one or two large centralized storerooms handling small production items, packaging materials, tools, and MRO supplies. Located throughout the plant adjacent to the point at which they are used in the process are numerous stacks of large bags and drums containing such things as chemicals and additives.

Location of Stock Yard

A large volume of materials, especially, various non-perishable goods that is materials that will not easily deteriorate, are generally stored in open storage areas. The materials that are usually in bulk like steel plates or coils, castings, timber, coal, steel barrels, cable drums, piping, lamposts, lorries, tractors, cranes, scrap materials and so on are also stored in open areas.

Mechanical handling is usually employed and materials are usually taken to the work centre directly from the yard. If the yard contains production items, for example, as in an engineering company, because of, various costs, security and other factors storage yards are located near the production building as a covered Store. Otherwise stockyards are set aside in one corner of the factory complex and connected by a good link road. In some cases, e.g., a cable drum Store of an Electricity Department may have a yard at an independent location. In some cases, e.g., in the case of SAIL's steel stockyards it may be part of the distribution system. There are a number of factors which will have to be evaluated in deciding upon the location of the stockyard/stores.

(1) **Cost of Land:** If the cost inside a city is prohibitive, it may mean looking for land outside the city limits. One fact to be remembered in yard storage is that everything has to he stored on the ground.

(2) **Adequacy of the Space Available:** Within the factory complex.

(3) **Transport Connections and Accessibility:** Transport links by road are of prime importance. In many cases, a railway siding is required.

(4) **Nature of Goods Stored:** Inflammable, items may require special storage conditions.

The first, question that needs to be answered is the size of the stockyard. This will of course depend on the type of materials to be kept there and the, volume of each. Take for example the

Telephone or Electricity Departments who would want to store huge cable drums or a steel re-rolling mill wanting to keep several hundred tonnes of scrap or a barrel making plant wanting to store steel coils used for the manufacture of drums. In each such case, it is necessary to have a proper assessment of the space required to meet needs. It would also be necessary to have an idea about the expansion that would be required as the company grows in size and to plan yard requirements for future needs also.

The second problem is a stock layout. The yard must have access to bulk transport and the truck or mobile crane must reach upto the point of storage. This means that accessibility by road upto the point of storage must be ensured. Materials handling equipment like fork lifts, straddle carriers, cranes, etc., will also generally be used. Increasing use of long wheel-base, semi-articulated vehicles necessitates large turning areas. Adequate provision must be made for all these requirements.

Uneven road surfaces can create jolts which can damage the material hauled. Road surfaces should also be skid-proof. It will be most unwise to depend upon gravel surfaces. The layout and road systems need to be very carefully planned.

Thirdly, the material must be retrievable on the basis of the FIFO (first in first out) principle, which means that the arrangement of material must be such that all the material stored must be accessible easily.

The fourth factor is that more often than not, materials are stacked on the gound. This would mean that the ground itself should be strong enough to bear the load. Quite often, concreting may have to be done. It would also be necessary to provide proper water proofing to prevent seepage of moisture from the ground and attack by insects. Proper sanitation in the form of good drainage would also be necessary. A water-logged yard can often not only cause nasty operational problems but can be highly dangerous to the materials stored.

Where the materials arc inflammable, a stockyard, if properly laid out, can give a good security against the spread of fire.

Some of the main advantages of yard storage are:

(1) It is cheaper than storage in covered buildings.

(2) Ideal for heavy or bulky materials and for vehicles.

(3) Enables use of heavy material handling equipment.

(4) Low overheads like lighting, cleaning and upkeep, repairs and maintenance, etc.

Security is an important factor. This means high perimeter walls and good yard lighting.

It should also be ensured that grass, weeds, debris, etc., are cleared frequently as these can encourage the presence of snakes or other reptiles. Fires in stockyards are usually started, by combustible waste materials such as old wooden packing cases dry grass, paper, etc.

Where the materials stored are by thcmsclves flammable, strict precautions should be taken against unauthorised entry of outsiders. Fire is a hazard which calls for utmost security precautions to be exercized.

The yard should have adequate **material handling equipment** as necessary. These may be fork lifts, pallet trucks and manual handling equipment. Fire fighting equipment is another necessity.

PROJECT SITES: Perhaps one of the most neglected areas in Stores management relates to materials arriving at Project sites. Quite often, the Project manager gives the storage of such materials, the least priority. Often, there is nothing more than a small temporary structure and this will hardly be sufficient to hold all the materials. The balance is kept in the open, often without any proper flooring, and the utmost protection offered will be some tarpaulins. For security, there may he some temporary watchmen whose sense of responsibility may perhaps better be left unsaid.

2.12 SUMMARY

More progressive concerns show an increasing tendency to set up completely integrated purchasing and stores departments. Stores department has to adopt an integrated approach with production, design and engineering, inspection, maintenance, transport, sales and finance departments.

The stores and receiving jobs are closely related hence the receiving activity is placed under jurisdiction of a storekeeper.

The stores activities cover receiving materials, arranging their inspection, storing accepted materials, issuing materials against authorsations, checking physical quantities, maintaining records for transactions, furnishing required information to cost accounting department, etc.

Stores can be maintained in centralised or decentralised locations. Each has its own advantages and disadvantages. World Class manufacturing systems use decentralised. Different combinations of centralized and Decentralized stores have been tried by various organizations with almost equal success.

Great care has to be exercised in deciding location and layout of stores as they have direct impact on income of an organisation.

2.13 SELF ASSESSMENT QUESTIONS

(1) What are the functions of a storekeeper?

(2) Describe the role of stores in an organisation.

(3) What is centralised stores? What are its merits and demerits?

(4) Why do modern manufacturing systems prefer decentralised stores?

(5) What factors need to be considered in location and layout of a stockyard?

3

Chapter

STORES BUILDING AND LAYOUT

Objectives

After studying this chapter, you should be able to understand:

- Factors to be considered while locating warehouses.
- Principles of stores design and layout.
- Different storage facilities to ensure full utilization of storage space.
- Mechanical/manual material handling equipment.

Structure:

3.1 Location System – Ware house

3.2 Principles of Stores Building Design

3.3 Store Layout

3.4 Storage Facilities

3.5 Location System Stores

3.6 Materials Handling Equipment

3.7 Manual Handling Equipment

3.8 Summary

3.9 Self Assessment Questions

3.1 LOCATION SYSTEM – WARE HOUSE

A company planning to establish regional warehouse or store would be well advised to consider the selection of one or more of the areas, taking into account the following additional basic factors.

(1) The central warehouse should normally be located near the largest production facility to facilitate communications and co-operation with the supplying factory.

(2) The business strategy alternatives for new regional facilities should be either to serve an established base of customers better or to win customers in a new, unpenetrated region. Some companies need to consider warehousing in an area of high market penetration to protect their market share in that region.

(3) If a company's overall strategy is to protect existing market share, facility locations should be selected in the regions of highest sales volumes. If alternatively, the main strategy is to penetrate new customers in regions of little or no sales volume, the new locations should be prioritized according to the population of the regions.

The cubic volume of existing or potential market is also an important criterion to use in locating warehouses. If the products warehoused are small and lightweight, warehouses could be located almost anywhere with little cost penalty for less-than-truck-load shipments. Conversely the primary decision criterion would be to establish warehouses in regions in which the practical, achievable market share would be equal to or greater than one truckload (or economical shipment) per day. The rule of thumb would help to miximize customer service. It would also help to minimize **safety stocks** and total inventories. A second rule of thumb would be to limit warehouse locations based on a projected need for a warehouse staff of no less than three or four.

Business interested in maintaining or, better yet, improving market share must continuously strive to reduce operating costs and investment. To fail to do so runs the risk of losing ground to fierce competitors who should be working every bit as hard to achieve the same ends. The most important costs and investments of a warehouse are not an infinite array. Among costs of greatest importance are transport to and from the warehouse; the building, equipment, people and inventory investment; and the operating expense. Of these, controlling building and equipment design stands out as a vital key to success because of the designs' impact on other operating costs. The distribution center-warehouse-store-room with the lowest cost per unit of space occupied will have the best potential for reducting all others costs and investments. For example, in building that are larger than necessary, people and automations spend more time in motion. The result? Higher pay roll and equipment expenses and capital investment than would be a necessary in a smaller building in which better space utilization makes it possible to store and process the same business volume. Mundane expenses such as utilities are also often proportionate to the degree of store space utilization.

Although the ideal warehouse is no warehouse at all, even the most visionary seer has difficulty foreseeing complete elimination of distribution warehousing of slowmoving, inexpensive and small parts and products. However, this should not deter superior companies from pursuing continuous reduction of warehousing through vendor programs designed to upgrade their supplier's ability to fill customer orders directly from the end of the production process. In the long transition period during which distribution inventories are continuously being reduced and warehouses are still a practical reality, it will behoove companies to reorganise their facilities to yield superior results.

3.2 PRINCIPLES OF STORES BUILDING DESIGN

Following is a short list of some of the key ingredients of the new store environment. This represents a fundamental framework for most companies' vision of the principles and goals for future operations.

(1) New stores must be designed in improved modular form to allow for future growth of products and product lines if it is reasonable to anticipate increases. However, provision of "Just-in-case" extra space would be fool hardy in the new era in which drastic inventory reductions will finally become practical for most superior companies. Preplanned future store or a warehouse modules should be added only when needed and with minimal disruption to the logic and flow of the previously constructed modules.

(2) Most stores and warehouses operate best with a blend of high-tech automation, semi-automation, low-cost automation and manual storage for the range of high-medium, and low-demand items and their various container sizes and shapes. Therefore, the best store and warehouse plans will be based on the most logical match of families of stocked items to various storage, transport and conveyance equipment alternatives. The typical store will have more than one family of items of like characteristics and, thus, a variety of equipment types.

(3) Wise, thorough utilization of the store's cubic space is vital to maximising the use of the capital while minimizing operating expenses and payroll. Storage spaces that precisely match the size of full containers destined to be stored in them slash wasted space by 50 percent, as compared with container sized that are one-half of the size of the space or containers that are one-half full. Both situations are found in a fairly high percentage of all stores, thus most stores have huge potential for improvement.

(4) Virtually every store can benefit from physically reorganising and shrinking the space it occupies. One reorganisation target should be to establish or improve the zones of activity frequency. By locating the fastest-moving items in one area and equipping them for high-volume processing, a store can greatly increase the productivity of stocking and shipping/issuing the relatively few items that account for the largest volume of activity.

(5) Wherever practical, long-range plans should include slashing store inventories to the bone while maintaining or improving customer service. This will be accomplished by continuous improvement, overtime, through company and vendor programs that will dramatically reduce resupply lead time and increase frequency of smaller store deliveries. A vendor program to achieve that end can reduce the supply lead time, through the entire production and distribution pipeline, by as much as 90 percent. In addition many companies can and should achieve immediate large reductions by simply reexamining safety stocks and delivery quantity policies and judiciously lowering them.

(6) Stores that are designed to receive, ship and pick orders twenty-four hours a day will best utilize the investment in building and equipment. In contrast to these facilities, stores designed for and operating only one shift are at a great competitive disadvantage. Their investment in building and equipment must be significantly greater than competitors' facilities that operate around the clock, seven days a week.

(7) Extra store space, provided for just-in-case, long term future growth and seasonal peaks, often cause the store to have capacity far in excess of its usual need, especially in the early years. Modular store designs that incorporate features for fast, nondisruptive building additions as growth actually occurs and temporary leasing arrangements during peak storage seasons are two valuable key options for minimizing this type of waste.

(8) Straight-line flow through a store is almost always a poor layout alternative. The best layout usually have entrance and exit at the same docks, with high volume items closest to the point of receipt and shipment.

(9) Drastically reduced aisle sizes is one method for reducing movement and increasing the storage density.

(10) Many, stores have a wealth of unoccupied space in receiving, packing and shipping areas. Some even waste overhead space in storage areas. The best stores will use every cubic centimeter of space for either vertical storage or ovehead offices. The reduction of space occupied pays large dividends in terms of reducing overhead costs and improving the productivity of store personnel.

(1) Initial Design: A very narrow segment of an entire organisation is studied in great depth, and a very in-depth design of proposed changes is sketched. For example, a team studied one warehouse bin/bay and all of the items stored in it in great detail. The results are used to design and illustrate improved storage methods based on using better equipment, containers, layout and low-cost semi-automation and full automation and computer support.

EXHIBIT 3.1: OVERVIEW PLANNING CHART

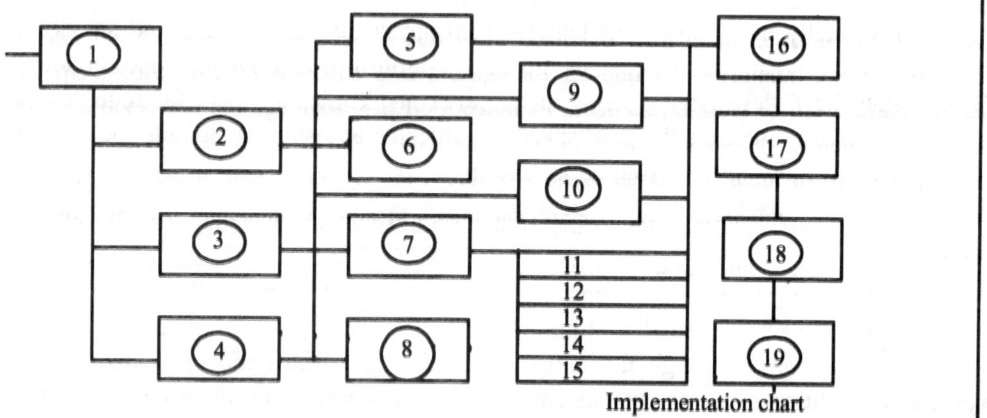

1. Entrance and Administration
2. Review Operations
3. Establish Project Standards
4. Initiate Equipment Vendor Assistance
5. Design Storage Zones
6. Design Packing/Shipping
7. Design Receiving/Shipping
8. Design Procedures and Systems
9. Design Wave Pick Sorting
10. Design Production Subplant
11. Organisation issues
12. Strategic Issues
13. Personnel issues
14. Supplier Program
15. Customer Program
16. Design integration
17. Cost Benefit Analysis
18. Implementation planning
19. Management Review

The detailed results then be projected into order-of-magnitude costs and benefits for the entire warehouse. The indepth design sketches make it easy for all management and employees to know precisely what changes will be made, their cost, and how long it will take to pay for improvements before committing to starting the next phase.

(2) Design: The *breadth* of the work performed is expanded, Detailed design, in this phase, encompasses many more bin/bay locations, perhaps even an entire warehouse. Operating personnel are heavily involved in this phase.

(3) Implementation: The detailed conversion and operating procedures are finalised and training is conducted. New equipment is ordered constructed and installed; the physical reorganisation is performed.

(4) Follow-up: After successful implementation, the team monitors the results, not only to tweak the design as much as necessary to achieve the desired results but also to ensure the perpetuation of benefits and to outline additional changes for the next improvement project.

One purpose of the above project segmentation is to divide the overall program into small manageable phases. Management should view the end of each phase as an opportunity either to approve or to cancel continuation. Management commitment to a program means *full* support of an initiative that all agreed *will have the desired benefits, at reasonable cost.* It may be necessary for management to break a program into multiple projects, the starting points of which are spread over time, in order to schedule payout and pay back into more manageable bites, or else, management may need to direct the project team to pursue lower-cost methods. However, management would have been at fault if it were to abandon the program after initially supporting it.

3.3 STORE LAYOUT

Smith and Tomkins have sagely identified the ideal shape of a store (from an efficiency stand point) as circular However, they envisioned shipping and receiving docks all round its perimeter, that would be highly inefficient. A round store or warehouse alone would not take full advantage of the fact that a few items have very high demand, while a very large percentage of items have very low demand. The even more ideal round warehouse in Exhibit 3.2 solves this short-coming with a drive-through lane. As the exhibit indicates, the average distance from the combination drive-through receiving and shipping lane to the storage location is shorter than in square or rectangular alternatives.

EXHIBIT 3.2: WAREHOUSE IDEALS

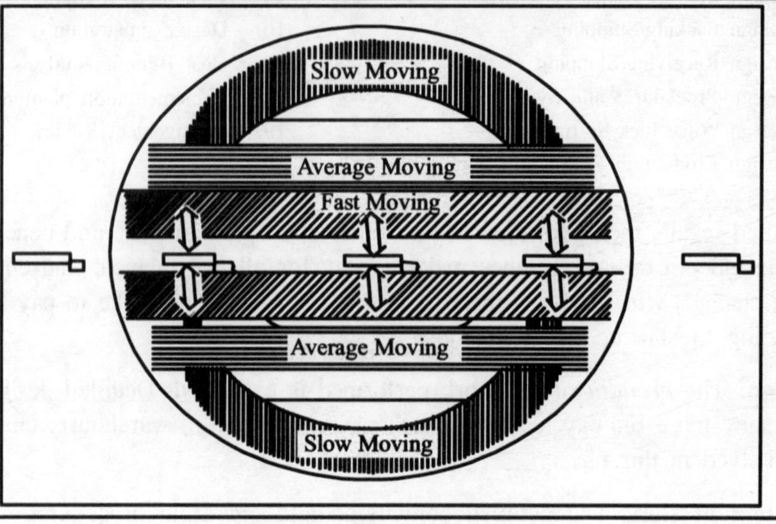

Fast-moving items are stocked closest to the truck lane, so inbound trucks can be rapidly unloaded and reloaded with outbound shipments with a minimal amount of travel. Slower moving items are stocked further from the truck lane, and the slowest-moving in the most remote warehouse locations.

If all trucks were open-sized, a store team could speedily load and unload from both sides of the truck, greatly reducing the time required as against the use of trucks from which loads can be accessed only through the rear doors. Each truck could then move rapidly from one "dock" to another, unloading and reloading the items stocked in that area of the warehouse.

Endorsing the straight-through warehouse form as applicable for factories is not intended to be an endorsement for factories of the past, which were designed with giant **central store** rooms. The factory of the future will have docks and storage all around its perimeter. As exhibit 3.3 indicates, each such dock and storage area will be located as close as possible to the subplant point at which the items received are used. It has been found that in most factories in which such docks have been designed for just-in-time delivery, the required storage depth, adjacent to the dock, is so shallow and small that the question of storage shape becomes largely academic.

EXHIBIT 3.3: MULTIPLE SUBPLANT DOCKS

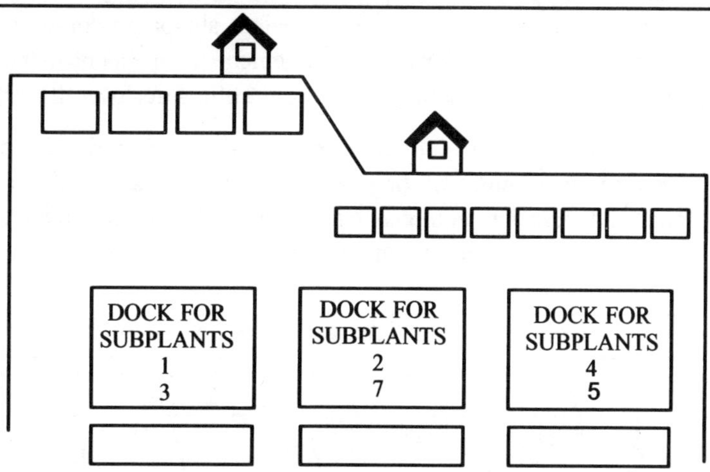

Practical ware house designs will, in reality, be rectangular in shape, as are the two examples in Exhibit 3.4. This illustration addresses the issue of where to locate receiving and shipping docks.

Two — options shown are localting them on opposite sides or both on the same side of the building. In the straight through option, trips from either receiving or shipping to a storage location will average 50 meters in the warehouse in Exhibit 3.4, with one half of all trips transporting nothing. Further, the straight-through layout makes it virtually impossible to reduce the transport travel average by organising zones of storage on the basis of customer demand volume. In the **u**-form warehouse, the logistics of inbound and outbound transport to and from storage can be designed and managed so that almost every trip into storage will first transport products received into storage and then pick up products to be shipped. (In light of their high cost, automated storage and retrieval systems must be designed and computer-controlled to achieve this objective). With the highest-volume products closest to the docks, the majority of trips to and from storage are much shorter than 50 metre.

EXHIBIT 3.4: DOCK LOCATION ALTERNATIVES

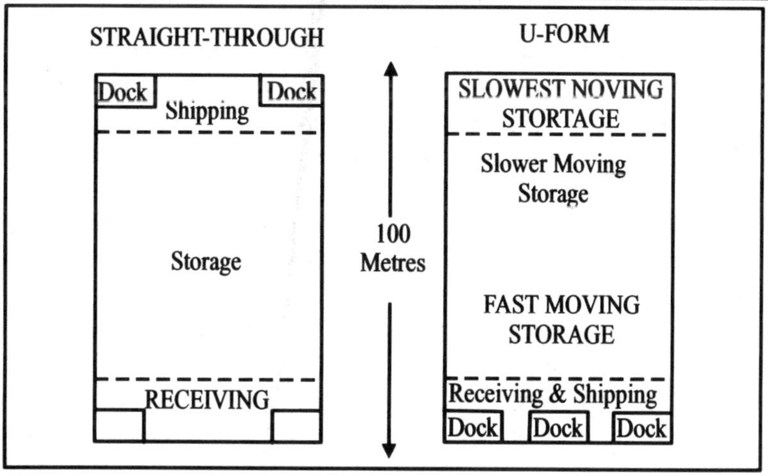

Most large stores are designed to operate as one huge business, with different specialists operating within separate departments, such as receiving, shipping, storage and packing. The sheer size of the entire store requires unreasonable management involvement if the responsible executive is expected to play an active participating role in controlling its overall performance.

With its several different types of storage racks and shelving for the different sizes of containers, the warehouse in Exhibit 3.5 begins to get closer to a realistic layout for a warehouse. Storage, conveyance, and transport equipment that match the size of items stored and the volume of demand are of the utmost importance in minimizing labour and investment costs.

EXHIBIT 3.5: STORAGE RACKS AND SHELVING

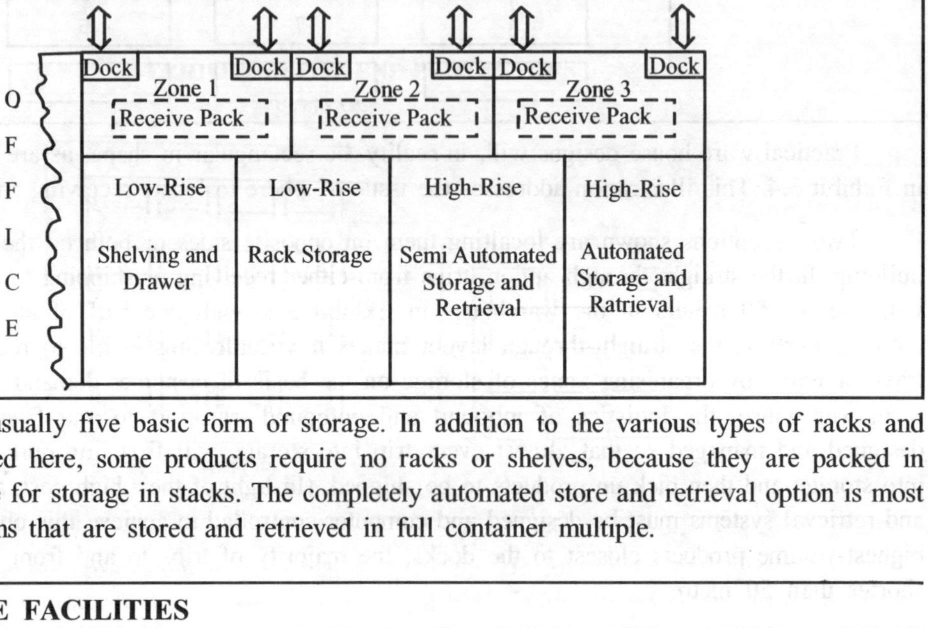

There are usually five basic form of storage. In addition to the various types of racks and shelving illustrated here, some products require no racks or shelves, because they are packed in a manner suitable for storage in stacks. The completely automated store and retrieval option is most applicable to items that are stored and retrieved in full container multiple.

3.4 STORAGE FACILITIES

Maximizing Space Utilization

Paying to store air sounds foolish, but that is exactly what many companies do The wasteful use of space is foolish in terms of the capital investment in the building surrounding it. Further, larger-than-necessary facilities cause personnel and equipment costs to be much higher than in more compact stores. The main reason is that larger facilities require more movement by people, transport equipment and conveyors than smaller facilities despite having equal storage and throughput capacity. Therefore, careful attention to maximising store space utilization pays handsome dividends in the form of lower total operating costs and capital investment per unit of goods received, stored, picked, sorted, packged, and shipped (or issued). For Less Even the most sophisticated, automated stores often utilize the available cubic space far less effectively than they should. Stores managers usually have over looked simple but important reasons for wasted space. The first reason is that container and storage space sizes for various items have been inconsistent with the minimum cubic volume needs for individual items to be stored, considering their various sizes, shapes and demand levels. The second reason has been deliberate provision of space in excess of average need, to meet either future growth or periodic fluctuations of demand or both.

When one can attempt to assimilate three factors whenever taking a first fast tour of a storeroom or a warehouse: (1) the per centage of the space of storage racks occupied by inventory; (2) the average per centage of space on the racks used for storage; (3) the ratio of aisle space to storage space versus the minimum feasible aisle space. It is easy to fall into the trap of believing that inefficient space utilization can be found only in small or poorly managed companies. That is far from reality. There is huge opportunities in companies both large and small, successful and teetering on the brink of bankruptcy. Thus, it is vitally important for every store executive to be able to make a rapid assessment of his own facility, analysing factors and then advise his company's top management of the approximate space saving potential of its stores.

Exhibit 3.6 illustrates what one so often sees on store. In this typical example of one storage space, close examination reveals that as much as 50 percent of the cubic volume of the storage location is wasted. Further, if the containers in the location were found to be one-half full, it would mean that the real space utilization would be only 25 percent. In this example, part numbers are stored in approximate part number sequences, but more than one part number can be stocked in one storage slot (bin). Thus, cubic space utilization is much better than it would be if one space were to be allocated to each part number stocked. However, one penalty of such a storage method is that order filling of part number 12 requires extra labour (part 11's containers may be shuffled to the back of the bin, making them hard to find.) This often causes the order filler to conclude that the item is out of stock.

In other storerooms and warehouses one often sees storages like that illustrated in Exhibit 3.7.

EXIHIBIT 3.6: STORAGE WASTE

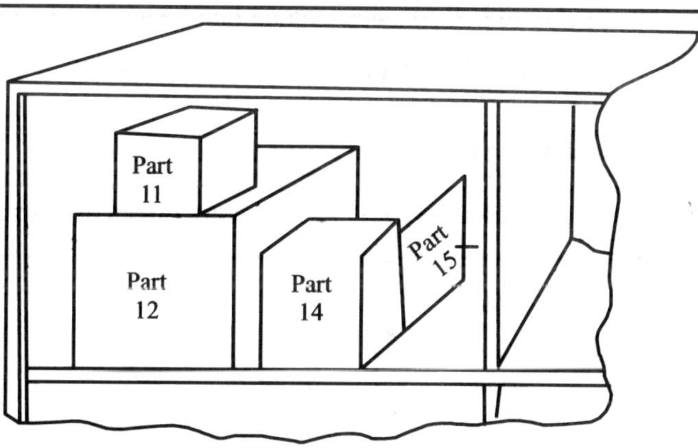

- Stacking
- Hiding
- Variable container size

In this example, storage bins for plastic caps of vairous sizes were designed and constructed to store loose, unpackaged caps. Caps received in containers would be emptied into the open front bins. While this eliminates opening and closing containers each time an order was filled, the open-face construction made it impossible to fill the bin space to its cubic capacity since caps would spill out of the open space. Infact, the amount of caps stored averaged well under one-half of the space occupied by the rack. Further, the bin design was responsible for several inefficiencies. first, parts received in inbound containers could not be simply poured out but had to be laboriously emptied into the bins handfuls since the inbound containers were too large to pour into the bin opening. Second, because the bins were some-what difficult to get into, picking parts entailed a large amount of time and motion to reach into the bin's far corners. All of this contributed to much higher than necessary labour costs.

A new storage rack with smaller drawers enabled the company to reduce the floor space occupied to less than one-half the previous area and cubic space utilization to one-quarter of the old bins. The smaller area cut the walking time, and it became easy to place stardard-size containers in the drawers of the same size, further reducing waste labour.

EXHIBIT 3.7: PIPE END PROTECTORS

STORAGE

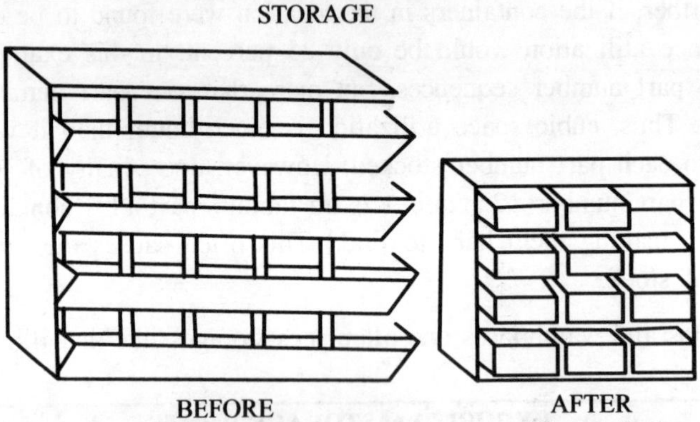

BEFORE 20 Square Feet | AFTER 9 Square Feet

Thus, the storage space savings is of major importance in improving total storage costs and stocking and order filling efficiency. Hence, even low labour savings were great enough to justify new storage containers and racks.

EXHIBIT 3.8: ELIMINATE COUNTING/PACKAGING

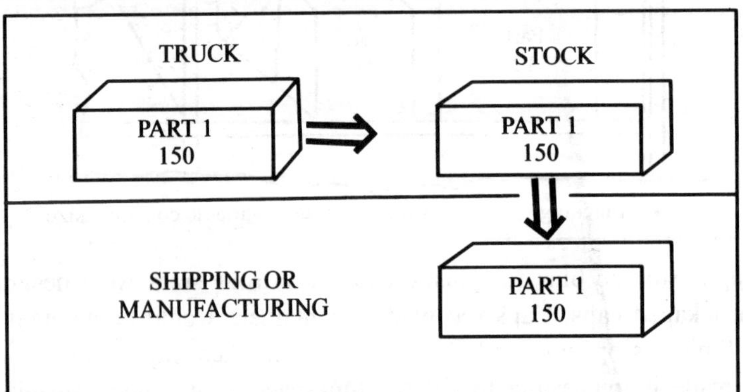

Exhibit 3.8 illustrates one ideal container design and usage objective. In this example, a truck delivers part number 1 in containers that hold 150 pieces. The containers stored are the same ones received, so repackaging and count verification are no longer part of the receiving process. Since, the container quantity specified is the same as, or in multiples of, picking/issue requirements, full containers or multiples of containers can be picked from stock and sent to shipping without counting or repackaging.

When a company finds the long-term goal of eliminating counting and repackaging to be a practical objective, prodigious amounts of storing labour and packaging material costs can be slashed.

After storage container sizes have been determined for each item, storage racks, shelving and bins can be modified or obtained to match the containers selected, as illustrated in Exhibit 3.3.

The costs of modification or procurement are usually far less than expected, because of storage equipment needed is drastically reduced. Further, a large number of existing racks and shelving can continue to be reused, with modifications. Avoiding investments for new equipment is often vitally important for maximising return on investment. Savvy professional will strive to avoid purchasing new equipment until every lower-cost possibility has been explored. For example, as illustrated in Exhibit 3.4, many low-cost modifications can be made to existing equipment by adding shelves, dividers or even bin inserts.

EXHIBIT 3.9: CONTAINER BIN SIZE

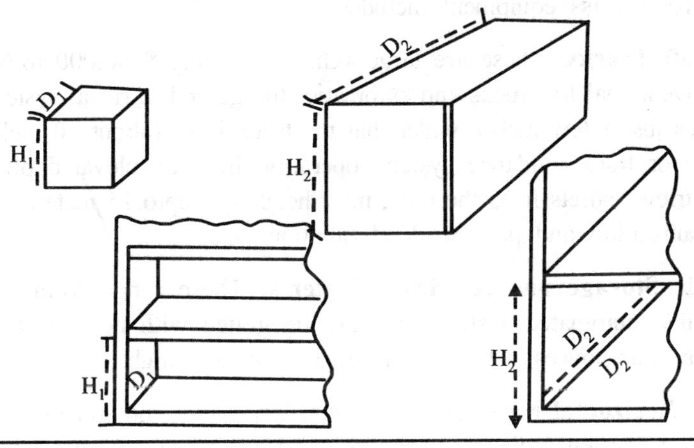

3.5 LOCATION SYSTEM – STORES

The evolution of storing and distribution in companies that have grown from small, entrepreneurial businesses to large national on international enterprises is accompanied by changes in their store methods, materials and distribution networks. Simple, easy-to-manage warehouse store businesses have grown to the point where they involve multiple giant facilities and complex networks of national and international distribution stock locations. At the same time, methods for finding stocked items have evolved from simplest level to one of greater complexity as follows: (1) Personal knowledge (2) Logical sequences of storage (like items are stored together or in part number or product code sequence) (3) Random sequence, requiring that a stock location information system be developed. (4) National and international sites, with or without location control, and centralized or local systems of location control.

Most stores authorities give too little credit to the effectiveness of personal knowledge and logical sequences of storage as valid, efficient and effective methods for small, focused stores that are still small or simple enough for "personal responsibility" management of stock location.

The fact is, storage location methods should be designed to match the equipment used and the complexity of the storage problem. For example, one cannot imagine a completely automated storage system that would function without a computer location control system. However, in the rack and shelving environment of focused warehouse-in-a warehouse, manual or computer locator systems add an often unnecessary layer of complexity to management. For example, in the relatively small stores in retail and dealer environments, simple personal knowledge and logical groupings of stocked items are usually the most suitable methods and can operate problem- free for years. Further, the strongest argument in favour of random storage systems may lose most of its logic in the twenty-first century, when deliveries into and out of the store should be **"Just-in-time"**.

3.6 MATERIALS HANDLING EQUIPMENT

Rapid innovation in warehousing process has brought new technology in the materials handling equipment. Some world class equipment includes.

(1) Hybrid Lift Trucks: These are large vehicles, costing $ 60,000 to $ 100,000, that are a cross between conventional lift trucks and automatic storage and retrieval systems. This equipment will operate in aisles just a few inches wider that the truck itself (about 60 inches). Extra features may include a wire or track guidance system, operation from an elevated platform, a mast that swivels at 90^0 to retrieve pallets from the rack, mast heights of upto 15 meters and microprocessors for two-way communication and paperwork elimination.

(2) Automatic Storage and Retrieval Systems: These range from manually controlled stacker cranes to fully automated systems that are integrated with horizontal movement devices. Most ASRSs require warehouses with bays at least 15 meters high.

(3) Improved Horizontal Movement Systems: Driverless and sometimes with automatic or semiautomatic loading and unloading features, these systems use wire-guided carts or electronic guidance devices. They can pause at programmed locations or switch to temporary holding areas. The route of travel can be easily modified.

(4) High-speed Sorting/Scanning Systems: In high-volume distribution centers, these systems use scanning and check-weight devices to permit rapid sorting of packages. The product of laser and other high-speed reading technology, they may be designed to read industry wide coding such as the food industry's Universal Product Code. Scanner technology allows a computer communication interface, which in turn permits instantaneous inventory file updating. This technology could forge sophisticated data linkages between customer and supplier.

(5) Item-picking Systems: In some applications, such as replacement parts or item production replenishment systems, new materials-handling devices will bring the item to the order picker. Vertical and horizontal carousel system controlled by computer bring substantial productivity improvement in certain types of order picking.

(6) Accumulating Conveyor: A conveyor which is used for, allow cartons to build up prior to an operation or to take care of peaks of throughout without need to stop the flow.

(7) Automatic Depalletiser: A machine capable of automatically resolving a unit load, not necessarily palletised, back into a stream of single cartons.

(8) Automatic Dispenser: A device containing a number of cartons of cases which it is able to release singly in accordance with signals received.

(9) Automatic Height Selection Device: A system of limit switches which enables the fork truck to raise its fork to one or more predetermined levels at the push of a button.

(10) Automatic Palletiser: A machine capable of automatically forming a unit load from a number of cartons fed into it singly. The unit does not necessarily have to be on a pallet.

(11) Automatic Sorting: The electronic recognition of cartons by size or code enabling these to be sorted into groups.

(12) Carton Clamp: Hydraulically operated blades which can be attached to fork-lift trucks to enable unit loads of cartons to be handles without the use of pallets.

(13) Circulting Conveyor: An endless accumulating conveyor which will permit goods to be stored and removed in any order.

(14) Coding Keys: Mechanical trips which allow remote routing of elements of a system.

(15) Dock Leveller: A device installed to over come the difference in height between a loading bank and the vehicle floor so that goods may be moved from one to the other on wheeled vehicles.

(16) Driverless Truck: A truck which will without the need for an accompanying driver follow a predetermined route guided either by rails or electronically.

(17) Fork Truck (Pedesteian Controlled) Cantilver: Exactly as fork truck (rider controlled) except that the driver does not ride on the truck.

(18) Fork Truck (Rider Controller) Cantilever: A three or four wheeled counterbalanced powered truck, with the driver standing or seated on the truck, which is fitted with a mast which may be telescopic. Forks are attached to the carriage on the mast which can be raised or lowered within the limits of the mast design. The mast, together with the forks, is generally designed to tilt forward or backward.

(19) Hardware: An expression referring to the mechanical handling equipment in an automatic warehouse.

(20) Lowerater: A device for lowering cartons one at a time, the return of the mechanism being accomplished by the energy given up from the carton which is being lowered.

(21) Magnetic Grab: An electro-magnetic attachment to cranes or fork trucks which can be used to handle suitable goods in cartons.

(22) Ordet Picking Dicking Display: An optical device which displays information to guide an order-picker.

(23) Order Picking Truck: A truck with a platform on which a man can stand and control his vertical and horizontal position to enable him to select items for an order from a picking space.

(24) Oberhead Converyor: A conveyor designed to carry goods at a height and so leave the floor area below, free for other operations.

(25) Pallet Truck-power Operated: A truck with three elevating fingers for insertion of below the top deck of a pallet, the elevating motion and traction being power operated. This truck may be designed for pedestrian or rider control.

(26) Powered Conveyor: Any conveyor in which the goods would not move without the input of power.

(27) Powered Through Racks: Live storage in which cartons or pallet loads are mechanically propelled along horizontal conveyors.

(28) Reach Trust: A fork truck for use in narrow aisles, which has forward-mounted load wheels enabling the fork carriage to move horizontally within the wheelbase, so that the forks can extend (or reach), for picking up or depositing the load. In the picking-up position, the load is counterbalanced by the weight of the truck and in the carrying position the centre of gravity of the load is within the wheelbase.

(a) Reaching Carriage Type: forks and load move forward, mast remains stationary.

(b) Reaching Must Type: mast, forks and load move forward together.

(29) Release Gate: The device which allows individual units to be released from live storage.

(30) Remotely Controlled Order Picking Platform: A platform on which a man stands and is automatically positioned in front of those items in a picking face which are required for a given (order(s). The positioning is controlled by signals from punched card, paper or similar device.

(31) Remotely Controlled Stacker Crane: A stacker crane which is controlled by signals from punched card and paper tape readers, or an on-line computer or similar device.

(32) Semi-Automatic Paletiser: A machine capable of producing a unit load from layers of cartons manually arranged. The unit does not necessarily have to be on a pallet.

(33) Software: An expression referring to the non-mechanical equipment involved in an automatic warehouse, e.g., data processing and electronic controls, etc.

(34) Stacker Crane: An overhead crane-type system with a suspended fork-lift mast capable of handling pallet loads. They are mostly but not invariably used in conjunction with pallet racking. The operator may be located in a cabin near the forks or control movement by a pendant switch whilst walking.

(35) Telescoping Conveyor: A cantilever conveyor used in vehicle loading which can be retracted at the push of a button as the vehicle load is built up.

(36) Vechicle Tipper: A device which will bodily tilt a vehicle in connection with its loading or unloading.

3.7 MANUAL HANDLING EQUIPMENT

(a) Box Pallet: A pallet with or without a lid having a superstructure of at least two fixed, removable, or collapsible vertical sides, solid, slated or mesh, which permit stacking.

(b) Buffer Storage: The part of a warehouse in which products are stored awaiting transfer into active storage.

(c) Gravity Conveyer: Any conveyor in which the source of the force used to convey the cartons is only that of gravity.

(d) Gravity Through Racks: Live storage in which cartons or pallet loads move down inclined rollers under the influence of gravity.

(e) Load Restraining Destraining Device: Any method of preventing the movement of loads resting on wheels or roller conveyors in the vehicle during transit.

(f) Pallet: A load board with two decks separated by bearers constructed with a view to transport and stacking with the overall height reduced to a minimum compatible with handling by fork-lift trucks and pallet trucks.

(g) Pallet Truck-Hand Operated: A truck with two elevating fingers for insertion below the top deck of the pallet, the elevating motion being manually operated by mechanical leverage or hydraulic pump, to enable the load to be raised just clear of the ground for movement. Lateral movement is by manual propulsion.

(h) Stillage: A load board comprising a single deck supported on bearers or legs, with an uninterrupted space between the bearers or legs for the entry of a stillage truck. If required, the deck may be fitted with a superstructure.

Note: There is a close similarity between stillage and certain types of pallets. Stillages, however, are not normally intended for stacking. Whilst a pallet truck might be suitable for moving a stillage, a stillage truck cannot enter a pallet with centre bearers or a bottom deck.

(i) Tote Box: An open topped rigid box for holding component or documents.

3.8 SUMMARY

(1) The cubic volume of existing and potential markets, marketing strategy for the future and optimization of operating costs are three factors that are considered in determining location of warehouses.

(2) Stores design and layout should maximize the use of capital and minimize operating expenses. This objective can be achieved through the best utilization of stores space and the least movements of men and materials in receipt, storage, issue and despatch of materials.

(3) Stores layout and storage facilities can increase efficiency of business operations significantly.

(4) Wide range of automatic, mechanical and manual equipment is available for materials handling.

3.9 SELF ASSESSMENT QUESTION

(1) How do large companies determine location of their warehouses?

(2) How does stores design and layout affect business expenses of an organisation?

(3) Suggest various means for optimum utilization of stores space.

(4) Describe five types of mechanical and manual materials handling equipment.

Chapter

4 STORES IDENTIFICATION SYSTE

Objectives

After studying this chapter, you should be able to understand

- **Need for stores identification**
- **Stores identification systems**
- **Variety reduction and standardisation**
- **Codification of materials**

Structure:

4.1 Introduction

4.2 Internal System Design

4.3 Need for Identification

4.4 Stores Vocabulary

4.5 Simplification or Variety Reduction

4.6 Standardization

4.7 Codification System

4.8 Summary

4.9 Self Assessment Questions

4.1 INTRODUCTION

In a broad sense, there are two types of material identification systems-those designed primarily for *external use* and those designed for *internal use.* The systems designed for external use have as their objectives, the facilitation of sales transactions (buyers and suppliers using common identification codes) and material reporting activities required in international trade. As the name implies, internal systems are designed with enough detail to communicate unequivocally the identification and description of materials to all using departments within the organization-from design engineering to operations to purchasing and supply to accounting.

The basic difficulty is that most firms want their internal systems to contain as much detail as possible to fulfill their own unique needs. And systems used for external purposes tend to be somewhat more attenuated, focusing on product and material *types,* rather than on specific items, detailed characteristics, and so on.

Stores operations involve the physical aspects of materials handling and storage. From a management perspective, however, the stores manager and the materials manager are concerned first with the design and control of the systems utilized in conducting stores activities. Developing a system for effective identification of materials carried in stores is a major responsibility confronting these managers.

A firm's stock catalog, prepared by the inventory management group, lists and describes every item normally carried in inventory. These descriptions, however, usually are somewhat imprecise and awkward for use in identifying materials during daily operations. Although all standard purchased items can be identified by suppliers' part numbers, different suppliers use vastly different numbering systems. Consequently, a firm with a sizable production and MRO inventory is compelled to develop its own numerical identification system for its materials. When the system is complete, the inventory catalog usually is arranged and indexed by the *purchaser's own* part numbers, and includes a reference to the supplier's part number for each purchased item.

The objective is to develop an unambiguous identification system, with adequate item description, that facilitates clear communication among all users.

4.2 INTERNAL SYSTEM DESIGN

Literally hundreds of similar but unique internal material identification systems are used in American industry today. However, most firms follow some common systems like

- The Harmonized Commodity. Description and Coding System
- The Export Commodity Control Numbers (ECCN) system.

The *Harmonized* system provides a set of descriptions and six-digit codes for commodity identification, description, and reporting. It also contains an option for the addition of four more digits to provide more local detail. This is perhaps the most widely used of the two international systems.

The *Export Commodity Control Numbers* system consists of product numbers that take the form of a five-character alphanumeric code. This system is used primarily for security-sensitive materials requiring export control.

For readers interested in other standardized coding systems, it should be noted that two government-oriented systems exist in the United States. The National Institute of Governmental Purchasing (NIGP) has developed its Commodity/Service Code System that is designed for public purchasing operations. Additionally, the General Services Administration has developed the Federal Supply Classification system for use in identifying and coding materials commonly used by federal government agencies.

4.3 NEED FOR IDENTIFICATION

The normal way of identifying an article is by simple description, but this by itself is not entirely satisfactory for stores purposes. Several different names may be used for the same thing, e.g., a 'dustbin', 'refuse container' or 'rubbish receptacle'. Again, in order to identify some articles accurately, a very long and complicated description is required. Everyone knows what is meant by a chair, but there are many kinds of chairs and, to identify only one of them properly, it is necessary to say that it is an armchair, with frame made of beech, polished carved walnut legs, spring seat, back and arms, stuffed with horsehair, finished in sage-green moquette and fitted with two foam-rubber cushions; even this is not the whole story, for nothing has been said about the quality of the materials or the dimensions of the various parts. It is necessary to have some logical basis of identification which is more precise and less cumbersome. This can be done by using letters or figures or a combination of both in the form of a stores code.

The code is then employed to identify all stores items exactly - the chair mentioned above being indicated by a number such as 70/15/8234, or a combination of letters and numerals such as CH8234.

Part numbers, rather than part descriptions, are more amenable to computerisation of materials management.

There are many different kinds of stores codes in use, and most of them are specially designed to suit the needs of the business they serve. They may be based upon the nature of stock items, the purpose for which items are employed, or on any other basis which is regarded as suitable according to local circumstances.

4.4 STORES VOCABULARY

When the operation of coding is complete, the lists of code numbers, descriptions, size, etc., are published in a document known as the stores vocabulary. In a large organization it is not unusual to find that the vocabulary consists of twenty or thirty volumes covering more than 100,000 items.

Identification-codification

It is now customary to codify all regular stores items for purposes of correct identification, for avoiding duplication or triplication of the same items and for ease in making substitute offers from the stores when necessary or desirable. In the absence systematic classification, rationalised store-keeping is not possible. Mere descriptions of items may lead to confusion. One store keeper may classify an item as sal-ammoniac, whereas a research chemist may indent for it under the name Ammonium Chloride only to be told that the material was not available, whereas in fact he may have ample stocks of the item. Ball-bearing for a particular machine may have a part number ES/MT4/ BB 6413 which may be identical with a ball-bearing with a part number FS/AG2/ SKF 3955, but it may be most difficult to identify them as such with the existing part numbers. Hundreds of such examples can be cited from practical cases in various stores in India and in other countries. There were as many as 111 names describing plain single diameter pin. A system of classification, called British system of classification was evolved for identification of stores on a rational basis.

All modern identification systems are based on Universal Decimal Classification (U.D.C,) system, generally used in Public Libraries for identification of books. For identification of stores likewise to-day we use U.D.C. with certain digits reserved for "family" classification and the balance for "individual" identification. However, stores identification systems are devised *'ad hoc'* for any given organisation and do not have to be universal in application as is the case with books.

The Bureau of Indian Standards has been drawing attention to a number of good systems for identification or classification in their company standardization programmes for the last several years. The digits used are partly 'significant' and partly 'sequential'.

As regards significant digits, each one signifies materials of a particular category or sub-category. Where digits are sequential. they generally cover the same category or sub-category of items in a particular sequence, e.g., size.

One system which is not too difficult to apply has been adopted by the Eastman Kodak Co. in U.S.A. Such a system can be applied from 6 digit code to 10 digit code. Let us take a 9 digit code. In this the first 3 digits only will be reserved for "family" and the next 6 digits for "individual" identification. The family would comprise category and sub-category (or class and sub-class) of stores. Individual identification would comprise kind, type, size and minor variations.

Category and sub-category classification would be of significant type and there could be block reservations for groups of items. For instance 100-199 might be reserved for raw materials; 751-799 for packing materials; 250-274 for hardware items and so on. Again in the raw material group 100-109. may represent steel. 110-119 aluminum, 120-129 plastics and so on.

As regards individual identification, kind and type could be significant, whereas size and minor variation could be sequential. Let us take a 9 digit code and assume its composition to be as follows:

xx	x	x	xx	xx	x
— Class	— Sub- Clas	— Kind (K)	— Type (T)	— Size (S)	— Minor variation (M)

This code could accommodate 100 sizes from 00 to 99. Sizes might be listed in ascending order say from 5 mm onwards as follows:

5mm	00
10 mm or 1 cm 1.5 cm	01
2cm	02
and so on.	03

In the example given we have one digit for kind, two for types, two for sizes and one for minor variation. This composition will not apply to all the categories but each category will have its own composition.

4.5 SIMPLIFICATION OR VARIETY REDUCTION

Standardisation and variety-reduction have definite bearing on purchase costs and inventory holdings. Normally, the more the variety, the more has to be paid, on the whole, for purchases; also more quantities have to be stocked both for current consumption as well as for safety or buffer stocks. Variety reduction is an important tool for cost-reduction. Brisch estimated that in U.K. variety reduction of the order of 40 per cent was possible in a number of organisations which could reduce costs by about 8 per cent. Similar observations have been made by the Indian Standards Institution regarding India.

For a developing country like India, or in case of national emergency, variety-reduction is generally the answer and not diversification, which may however be justified at times from the sales point of view. However, in India under present conditions, we should concentrate on variety reduction.

Organisation has achieved an over all variety reduction of 50 per cent and inventory holding costs by about 10 per cent. Another organisation reduced its variety of hard-ware items by more than 80 per cent. These examples show what can be done when a systematic attack is made on the problem.

Fortunately, there are two good tools available for the purpose of variety reduction-namely analysis according to Frequency Distribution of demand or consumption of stores and/Preferred Numbers.

For frequency analysis it is necessary to analyse the records of consumption of stores. One type of analysis is shown in Fig. 4.1 below. It shows that out of 11 different sizes (or types) used in a group of items, one size has maximum consumption, major consumption being accounted for by three sizes in the centre of the figure.

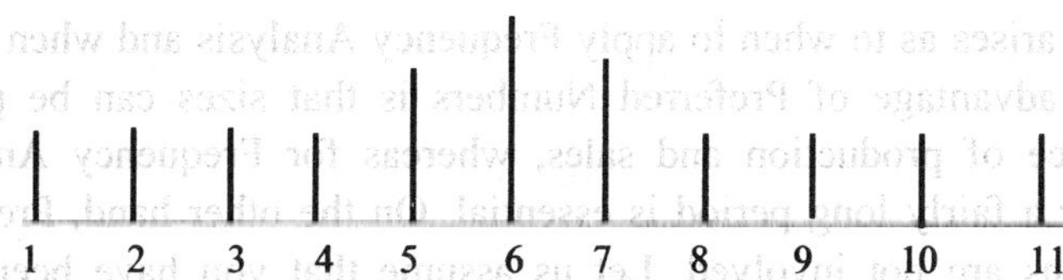

Fig. 4.1

We may in this instance, standardize 5-6 & 7 only and eliminate the other seven sizes. Sometimes it may be possible to standardize one size only, namely size 6.

On the other hand, frequency analysis may not show such a regular pattern as in Fig. 4.1. Let us look at Fig. 4.2 representing a group of 12 items:

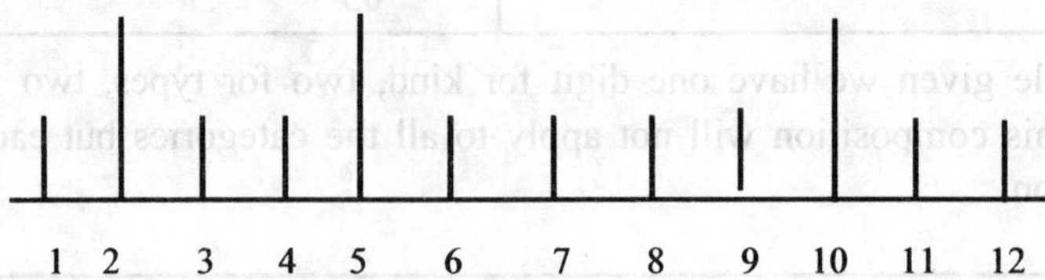

Fig. 4.2

In this instance sizes. 2. 5 and 10 are in most demand. These three sizes may be standardised and the rest eliminated. Alternatively "Preferred Numbers" may be applied for selection of more rational sizes.

"Preferred Numbers" have numbers, dimensions or sizes etc. arranged in Geometric Progression. Those given in the ISI Specifications and which are generally applied are R5. RIO. R20 R40 and R80 series and other derived series. There are tables in which the numbers mentioned serially increase 10 times in 5 steps. 10 steps. 20 steps. 40 steps and 80 steps respectively, the increments being based on $5\sqrt{10}, 10\sqrt{10}, 20\sqrt{10}, 40\sqrt{10}, \text{and} 80\sqrt{10}$.

An example will make this clear. Let us take the case of incandescent electric lamps. The standardised wattages today are as follows:

15 watts

25 watts

40 watts

60 watts

100 watts

150 watts

The increase from 15 watts to 150 watts is effected in 5 steps. This is therefore based on R5 series (Actual R5 series for this item comprise 16,25,40. 63. 100 and 160). In practice they have been standardised for wattages 15.25,40,60, 100 and 150. Choosing of a suitable size near enough to the preferred size according to table is quite permissible from practical considerations).

The question often arises as to when to apply Frequency Analysis and when to apply Preferred Numbers or both. One advantage of Preferred Numbers is that sizes can be pre-determined by manufacturers in advance of production and sales, whereas for Frequency Analysis records. of actual consumption over a fairly long period is essential. On the other hand, Preferred Number be applied where dimensions are not involved. Let us assume that you have been manufacturing a particular textile product in 9 colours and you now want to reduce the variety. Here Frequency Analysis alone can show the most popular colours and you cannot apply Preferred Numbers.

On the other hand Frequency Analysis cannot be used where there is no "consumption" as normally understood. Take stepladders for example. Supposing you want to standardise in 3 sizes-here Preferred Numbers will help as it will be impracticable to have Frequency Analysis of the consumption of various sizes of step-ladders.

With a little experience the analyst will be able to judge for himself whether to apply Frequency Analysis or Preferred Numbers or both to a particular problem.

4.6 STANDARDIZATION

Standardization of stores is the process of reducing the number of varieties stocked to a controlled workable minimum.

In the course of time, in any organization, unless active measures are taken to control variety, the number of items stocked and used will gradually increase. When this has been going on over a long period, if the position is examined critically, it will be found that there are many instances where several items of a very similar nature are purchased and held in stock. To quote a simple example: If the stock of paint were to be investigated, the following information is typical of what would be disclosed:

(i) No specification is in use.

(ii) Paint is being supplied by twelve different manufacturers because of individual preferences by users in different parts of the organisation.

(iii) Paint is purchased in six different sizes of container.

(iv) It is not clear which paints are to be used for external and internal work.

(v) There are ten different shades of green in stock, eight reds, seven blues, and so on.

A proper approach to standardization might result in:

(i) Issue of specifications for five types of paint only to be used, or a decision to buy from only one manufacturer's range of products.

(ii) The number of different sizes of container being reduced.

(iii) Issue of an instruction to the maintenance or other departments concerned, about the type of paint to be applied for various jobs.

(iv) Colour varieties restricted to 50 per cent of the present range.

The result of such a change would be a drastic reduction of the number of items held in stock in the paint classification, cheaper purchase prices, and better control.

Standarlisation of Materials (i) avoids danger of unnecessary, increased and uneconomical purchase, (ii) avoids duplication or multiplicity of stock items, (iii) avoids non-issue of an item already in stock or its substitute due to mistakes in identification.

Normally it will pay to purchase and store items covered by standard specifications. It will ensure right quality as the supplier will be guided by prescribed standards. As generally more than one manufacturer can supply standard items, it will mean better availability, better price and better delivery as a rule in comparison with non-standard items. Finally if an item is to be disposed of as surplus, a standard item is likely to fetch a better price.

At this stage it is advisable to look at various levels of standards which can be classified as follows:

(1) Individual standards.

(2) Company standards.

(3) Industry standards.

(4) National standards.

(5) International standards.

Individual standards are of not much importance in an industrial establishment. Company standards which have been specially adopted by a company for its materials, equipment, supplies and end-products are however, very important. Of course, a large number of company standards will be based on National Standards, that is on specifications laid down by the Bureau of Indian Standards. However, a certain percentage of items need standard specifications to be specially drawn up for the company concerned for various reasons, such as absence of a suitable national standard, special quality requirements not covered by existing specifications, large volume of non-standard requirements and other technical and cost-reduction aspects.

Industry Standards or standards for use by a particular industry are very desirable. They can contribute substantially towards reduction in prices and inventories of materials. They can cover such standards for the industry concerned, for which we do not have any national standards yet. Unfortunately Industry Standards hardly exist in India resulting in a large number of unnecessarily different standards varying from company to company.

The most important level is of course the national level of standardisation-in other words standards adopted for use nationally by the Indian Standards Institution and covered by ISI Specifications. Materials Managers and Purchase Officers would do well to see that as many items as possible are covered by BIS Specifications.

Lastly we come to international specifications issued by the I.S.O. (International Standards Organisation) which is generally commonly adopted by the member countries.

The foreign specifications like the BSI, ASTM, DIN and so on, are not international specifications. They are national specifications of U.K., U.S.A. and West Germany respectively. While importing an item we may be compelled to buy to a foreign specification, but if there is an existing BIS specification we should try to buy according to that specification. What is very wrong to-day is the continuous use of foreign specifications by many organisations where they could easily or with a certain amount of effort adopt BIS specifications or "Company" specifications more suitable for Indian conditions. Such practice leads to purchases at higher prices and in keeping large inventories of items to foreign specifications, with resultant losses in Foreign Exchange.

There will however be instances where almost completely non-standard products may be required by customers. In these cases also, it should be seen to what extent the products can be manufactured from standard stock items.

Non-standard Items as Company Standard Items

There can be certain exceptional circumstances when a non-standard item should be adopted as standard by a company for special reasons, but all such cases must be reviewed very carefully both from technical, as well as financial point of view.

The spares for "A" & "B" category equipments are stocked by the Controller of Stores in depots. Spares for 'C' category equipments are not stocked and are purchased as required and directly handed over to the user departments. The equipments are classified into A, B & C categories based on the revenue from the equipments.

Safety stocks, minimum, maximum, re-order levels, review period, etc., may be established depending on the system of inventory control selected for the various categories of spares.

4.7 CODIFICATION SYSTEM

Codification system used for identification of products achieves following objectives:

- Prevents duplication (i.e., items having the identical design/functional features being grouped together)
- Interchangeability and equivalence.
- Standardisation & Variety reduction
- Efficient Inventory Control

Example given in the Exhibit 4.1 may serve to convey the thoughts on the classification and codification system envisaged for a particular product.

Inventory Control System

It will be worth while to develop a scientific Spare Parts Inventory Control System common to the organisation stores located at different places.

The proposal is briefly discussed in following steps:

Step No. 1: A task-force under the Manager of an expert in the field of spare parts Management may be set up. This task force may have a number of groups, each group attached to a store. The manager of the store can be the head of the team. In a store this group will have representatives from the various departments such as; user dept; Stores, Purchase, Finance, Industrial Engineering, Inspection, Safety and other concerned departments in the organisation.

Step No. 2: All the team members may be given a four week intensive training by the experts in the field on the following areas:

- Codification System.
- Spare Parts Management.
- Computer applications in Inventory Management.
- Spares requirements in company

Step No. 3: Information on the inventory of spare parts in the various stores, consumption, and projected requirements for the sub-sequent 3 years, etc., may be collected. Also information on VED, SDE analyses may be collected. A format similar to the one given In the Exhibit 4.2 may be used to collect the above data from the user department.

Step No. 4: After the above data collection, all the groups may meet at a central place and analyse in details the following aspects:

- Equipment and Spares common to the various stores and their quantities.
- Variety of Spares and their consumption pattern,
- Surplus/non-moving inventories at various stores and the possibilities of their usage by other stores.
- Development of a common Classification and Codification System and the possibilities of establishing a tie-up relationship with the existing Codes in the Various Stores.

Step No. 5: Codify all the inventories using common codification system developed above:

- Prepare a Directory bringing out the Existing Codes Vs. Rationalised Codes and the new Rationalised Codes Vs. the Existing Codes.
- With the aid of a suitable Computer System, carry out the following:

(a) A-B-C analysis based on the consumption.

(b) Carry out a projected A-B-C analysis based on the projected consumption pattern for the subsequent 3 years.

(c) Categorise the inventories to A-B-C classes.

(d) Using the above A-B-C classifications establish the Service Levels for the various categories of spares. Appropriate statistical distribution/O.R. models may be used while deciding the Service Levels.

(e) Establish safety stock, minimum level, maximum level, reorder level, review period, etc., for various categories of spares depending upon the Inventory Control System being selected.

Step No. 6: Train all concerned at the various stores on the new system of Inventory Control and ensure their acceptance.

Step No. 7: Centralised Purchasing Inventory Control System

- A Centralised Purchasing and Inventory control agency may be set up for all the A & B categories of spares. This agency will deal with the purchase of all new equipment and standardisation. Also the import of all spares and capital equipment will be dealt with by this agency. The timely procurement and supply of all A & B category spares to all stores, will be the responsibility of this agency. In cases of emergencies, this agency will arrange to divert the spares from the stores having surplus.
- All stores will furnish the consumption of various spares to the centralised agency in the prescribed format on a weekly basis.

Features of an Efficient Coding System

(1) Possibilities of utilising the non-moving surplus inventories of one store by other store which may be in need of these spares.

(2) It will be possible to maintain optimum inventory levels for A & B classes of items, resulting in huge economy for the company.

(3) Possibilities of transferring stocks between store in cases of emergencies.

(4) Better economics in purchases.

(5) Considerable savings in lead time in the process involved from obtaining import licence to customs clearances.

(6) Last minute purchases of less wanted/unwanted spares to consume the unutilised funds can be dispensed with.

(7) Better classification, variety reduction and standardisation of equipment and spares.

(8) Disposal of all unwanted spares.

Anticipated Difficulties

(1) Improved discipline required in record keeping, stocks accounting .and submission of periodic restores by the local store authorities to the central agency.

(2) Training of all concerned in the new system.

(3) Need Data Entry Systems in stores and a Large Frame Data Processing System with the Centralised Purchasing & Inventory Control agency.

(4) Resistance to changes by the stores Employees.

(5) Other points

EXHIBIT 4.1

PROPOSED CODIFICATION SYSTEM (AN EXAMPLE) — BALL BEARING

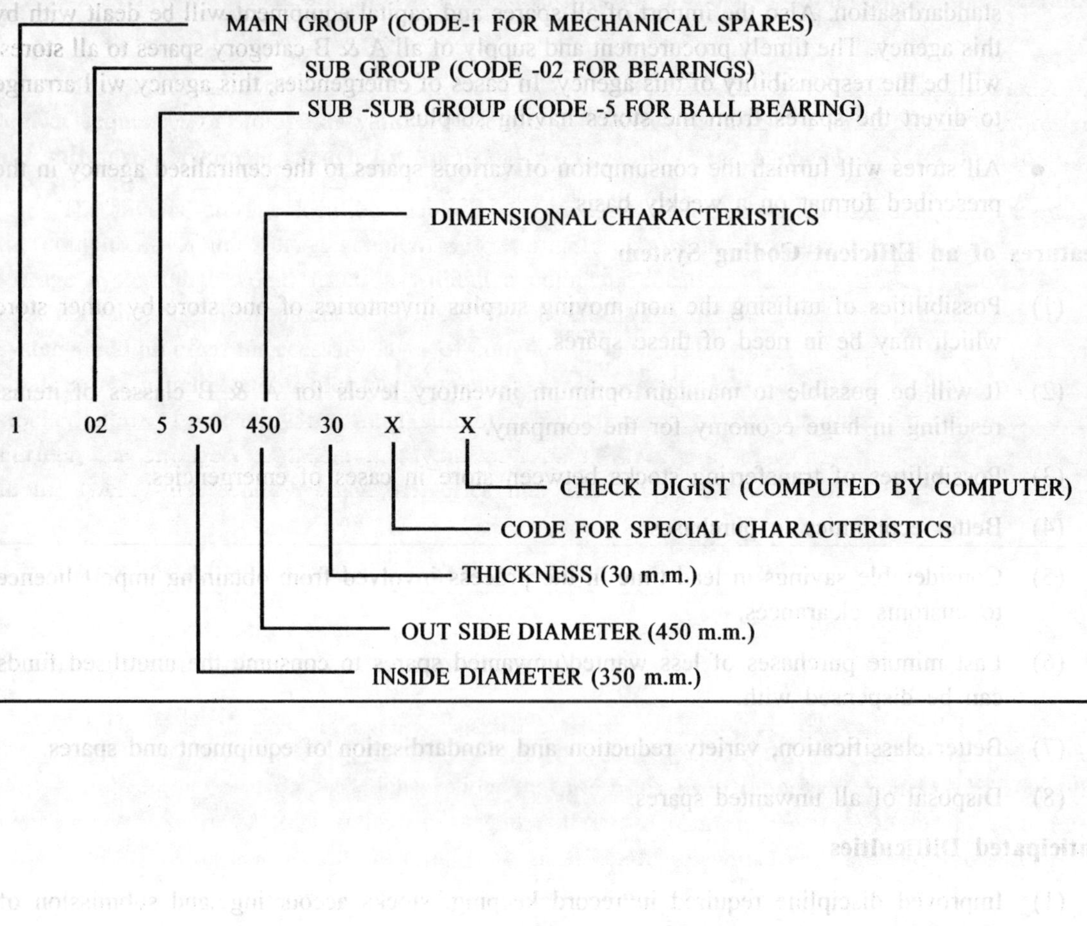

EXHIBIT 4.2

SPARE PARTS REQUIREMENTS ANALYSIS SHEET

Name of the Port.......................................

Equipment Description .... Asset Code No .... Make .... Country of Origin .... Supplier.......... Year of Commissioning .... No. of years in active use.................................Purchase Order No .... Date.......... Cost at Store ₹...................... Present Value............................ Present Condition/ History..

Technical Other Details about the Equiment...

Sl. No.	Description of the Spares	Existing Code	Detailed Specification			Consumption Pattern					Qty. in Stock	Qty. on Order	Expected date of Receipt/ Lead Time	Unit Cost at Store ₹	Classification (Tick the Appropriate Column									Rationalised Code	Classification			Service Level	Policy Decisitons				
			Material	Dimension	Other Characteristics	Past		Projections for Future							if Classified			Your Assessment											Safety Level	Minimum Level	Maximum Level	Re-Order Level	Review Level
						Since Commissioned	Last Year	Current Year	Subsequent Years																								
									Year-1	Year-2					A	B	C	V	E	D	S	D	E		A	B	C						

Explanation

(1) Main Group Classification. (First digit 0 to 9)

(1) Mechanical Spares

(2) Electrical Spares

(3) Spares for Instruments

(4 to 9) To be suitably allocated depending on the situation.

(2) Sub-Group Classification (Second & Third Digits 01 to 99)

All the Mechanical Spares may be suitably sub grouped using these digits up to 99 categories. This will enable in identifying the spares under the families such as Bearings, Gears, Bushes, Belts, etc.

(3) Sub-Sub Group Classification (Fourth Digits o to 9)

Depending upon the sub-groups, the sub-sub group codes may be assigned to identify further the exact type of the item in the main family. In the example given above code 02 stands for the family of bearings and further the code 5 indicate that it is a Ball Bearing.

(4) Code for Dimensional/Design features (5th to 13th Digits)

Depending upon the sub-sub group under consideration, these digits may be intelligently used to denote the design features

(5) Check Digit (Fourteenth Digit)

It may be left to the compute, system to develop this digit.

Note:

(1) The items for which the dimensional details cannot be indicated, the 5th to 13th details may be suitably used to denote the following:

- The equipment to which the spare belongs
- The brief description code for the items
- The location at which the item is used in the main equipments etc.

Example

Gasket used at...... ...place of the engine type fitted in equipment Code No........

(2) The type of Codification System suitable to the situation can be decided only after the survey on the actual situation. The examples given above are for conveying the thoughts on the topic.

4.8 SUMMARY

There are two types of material identification systems, one external for facilitating sales transactions and other internal, designed for use by all departments within the organisation.

Identification of materials by description is cumbersome, lacks precision and not helpful for mechanisation.

A number of good systems for identification and classification of materials are available and companies should select one that satisfies their own requirements.

Significant savings in time, expenses and capital investment are available through variety reduction and standardisation of stores.

Codification is an important tool in identification and classification of stores.

4.9 SELF ASSESSMENT QUESTIONS

(1) Provide objectives of internal and external stores identification systems.

(2) List advantages accruing to an organisation after logical codification of materials used by its different departments.

(3) What is the scope for variety reduction available to indian Industry? How can this be achieved?

(4) Describe characteristics of a typical codification system.

Chapter

5 RECEIVING AND INSPECTION

Objectives

After studying this chapter, you should be able to understand:

- Nature of receiving function.
- Inspection methodology.
- Organisation of receiving stores.
- Formalities in clearing incoming materials.

Structure:

5.1 Introduction

5.2 Inwards Goods Department or Receiving Section

5.3 Inspection Methodology

5.4 Rejection of Goods

5.5 Receipt Section

5.6 Location of Receipt Store

5.7 Organisation

5.8 Functions Responsibilities of Receiving and Store

5.9 Receiving of Materials

5.10 Advanced Systems

5.11 Inspection Concepts

5.12 Clearing of Goods

5.1 INTRODUCTION

Receipt, inspection and storage of materials form the last phase of the purchasing activity. It may sound quite strange but any inefficiency during this last phase can prove detrimental to the overall materials function in quite a large number of organisations.

There are two aspects involved here:

(i) All incoming goods are to be physically counted or measured for accuracy and they have to be inspected for quality; and

(ii) This work has to be done expeditiously and efficiently and the goods must be taken into the store for use without delay.

The main bottleneck usually noticed is the lack of coordination between the inspection staff and the receipt clerks. The inspection staff may be reporting to the quality controller; they may not be part of the receipt section. It is, therefore, necessary that the receiving section is manned by efficient clerks who have not only been thoroughly trained in their work, but also given a clear understanding of the importance of their work with respect to the efficient functioning of the company.

5.2 INWARDS GOODS DEPARTMENT OR RECEIVING SECTION

The receiving section (often also called the inwards goods department) receives all materials coming into the warehouse. This function of receiving and physically handling the materials together with verifying that the deliveries correspond exactly to those specified in the purchase order is usually performed not by the purchase department but by a specialised group. This group is usually independent of the purchase department and quite often is attached to the stores department..

There are four types of incoming consignments:

(i) Receipt from outside suppliers;

(ii) Transfer of goods from other storehouses within the organisation;

(iii) Returns to store from the production or other departments; and

(iv) Scrap or waste or unwanted materials.

Materials from suppliers are normally accepted at the prescribed timings only. Upon receipt of materials, the following documents are checked:

(i) Supplier's delivery note-for correct purchase order reference, part numbers, specification, quantity, etc.

(ii) Packing slip-for method of packing, number and size of packages, etc.

(iii) Quality test certificates.

The material is taken into the receiving stores after this preliminary checking.Then the goods received are checked for quality and quantity. The receipts are entered in a goods receipt register. This register has the following columns:

(i) Name of supplier;

(ii) Item details;

(iii) Quantity;

(iv) Value;

(v) Purchase order reference;

(vi) Date of receipt;

(vii) Time of receipt; and

(viii) Carrier's details (RR No./Lorry No., etc.).

Quantity Checking

The items have invariably to be physically counted. However, where large quantities arc received regularly, only a random sample checking of packages is done.

(a) Per cent Sampling: A certain percentage of the materials received is checked by opening each package.

(b) Random Sampling: In this method, boxes at random are picked up and are checked for quantity.

Apart from quantity checking, there are other types of measurement of items involving:

(a) checking of weight by weighing scales;

(b) checking of length by scale (width being standard);

(c) checking of area by measuring tapes; and

(d) checking by volume (of liquids).

Quality Checking

While quantity checking is a semi-skilled operation, quality checking is a skilled work and calls for specialised training of personnel, proper testing facilities and methods. Goods are inspected for quality to ensure that they comply with the specification. The specification is usually stated in the purchase order and where specifications cannot be described fully, a sample item is given to the receiving section. The quality criteria will vary from item to item. The usual quality checking methods are:

(i) **Visual:** For example, stationery items or grocery items can be checked visually.

(ii) **By Touch:** Cloth material to distinguish, for example, between a rough and smooth surface.

(iii) **By Smell:** Chemicals, oil, (kerosene, coconut oil), powder, etc.

(iv) **By Comparison:** Here the actual supplies are compared with samples.

(v) **By Actual Testing:** Eggs (allowing them to pass through standard size holes); potatoes (distinguishing between small and big ones); bricks (dropping some of them from a height to test their strength), etc.

(vi) **Laboratory Methods:** Chemicals and compounds. Here prescribed tests are carried out by the chemical analyst, in a laboratory-optical, X-ray examination, endurance/life tests, etc.

(vii) **B I S Tests:** On certain items, if there is any doubt on quality, they can be sent to the Bureau of Indian Standards, or test houses for inspection.

(viii) **Use of Inspection Tools:** Like gauges, callipers, dialgauges, etc.

5.3 INSPECTION METHODOLOGY

As mentioned earlier, the inspection procedure is quite laborious and time-consuming when each one of the items is inspected for a certain number of quality traits. Hence statistical methods are resorted to. The common methods are :

(i) **Percentage Samples:** A certain percentage of the item is checked fully for quality and if more than a certain number of items are found defective, the entire lot is rejected.

(ii) **Random Sampling:** In this method; the items are chosen at random and inspected for quality.

(iii) **Sequential Sampling:** In this method. say, every tenth unit is inspected for quality.

Attributes and Variates: Variates refer to anything which is variable. For example, when we buy cloth, its length may be slightly more or less. This "length" is hence a variate. Similarly, the height of a person is a "variate." Attribute refers to the quality criteria, like broken or intact, smooth or rough, good or bad, clean or dirty, etc. What wc do during quality testing is checking for "variates" and "attributes."

Goods Receipt Note: Once the goods arc found to be acceptable by the inspection staff, an inspection report is prepared. Based on the inspection report, the receipt clerk prepares a goods receipt note (GRN). Sometimes, the goods receipt notes are prepared and the inspector signs on the documents for acceptance of the goods. The goods, together with a copy of GRN, are sent to stores for storing the items.

If the goods are rejected, either a discrepancy report or a goods rejection report is prepared and the purchase department is immediately informed to contact the supplier and inform him about the rejection.

The goods receipt note is also often called the goods inwards note (GIN) and has the following columns:

- Date of receipt;
- Consignor;
- Supplier's challan number;
- Purchase order reference;
- Code number;
- Description;
- Quality received undamaged;
- No. of packages;
- Transport;
- RR/Waybill reference;
- Damage/Short Report/Excess;
- Receipt clerk's signature; and
- Inspector's signature.

The GRN is also a certificate to the accounts department for payment and for debiting the stores the value. It is also an advice to the purchase department and to the stores for the receipt of the goods.

5.4 REJECTION OF GOODS

Rejected goods are kept separately in a quarantine stores. The rejected materials may be returned to the supplier for credit, if payment has already been made or for replacement.

A separate register is maintained for rejected goods. This register shows what goods were rejected, where they had been stored and when they were delivered to the supplier. This register is also useful for vendor evaluation.

Legally, it is not necessary to return the rejected goods to the supplier. It is enough if he is informed about it and it is his responsibility to take back the goods.

The receipt section can be centralised. In this case, all stores are received at one place and later on dispatched after inspection to the various stores. The section can also be semi-centralised. In this case, the physical delivery is done to the various. stores by the carrier himself, but all the paperwork is done at one central place. During the delivery, a representative of the receipt section goes to the stores and it is he who receives the materials. He counts the materials and gets them inspected and hands them over to the stores clerk concerned.

A third type of organisation can also exist. In this case, there is a complete decentralisation where each store has its own receipt section.

Samples of various forms used in the receipt section are given in the Appendix.

5.5 RECEIPT SECTION

Receipt and Inspection

The important step in the purchasing cycle is receipt and inspection of the materials ordered. When a supplier ships material. he includes in the shipping container a packing slip which itemizes and describes the contents of the shipment. The receiving clerk uses this packing slip in conjunction with his copy of the purchase order to verify that the correct material has been received.

After a shipment has been inspected for quantity and for general condition of the material, the receiving clerk prepares a receiving report. A typical form is shown in exhibit 5.1 To complete the report. the receiving clerk merely writes the identification and receiving figures in the appropriate spaces included on the form.

EXHIBIT 5.1

ACCOUNT NUMBER	MART	NO	YES	DEPARTMENT	DELIVERTY POINT	REQ. NO.

XYZ Company

MATERIAL RECEIVED RECORD

AREA CODE: 415
321-2300 EXT

PURCHASE ORDER NO. **C**

Please show the above number on all documents and containers

DATE

SHIP TO: RECEIVING DEPARTMENT. STANFORD UNIVERSITY

Arrive at Destination by	Ship vis	F O B: DESTI-NATION / SHIP POINT	ORDER PLEASED WITH (NAME)	TEAMS

ITEM	QUANTIYT	UNIT	DESCRIPTION	QUANTITY RECRD BY SHIPMENT 1	2	3	4

SHIP NO	DATE RECEIVED	PACKING LIST	CARRIER	PACKING BILL NUMBER	DOCK REGISTER NUMBER	NUMBER CARTONS	RECVER BY (DEPARTMENT SIGNATURE)	DATE
1								
2								
3								
4								
5								
6								

Copies of the receiving report are typically distributed as follows:

- Copy I is used by the purchasing department in closing out its working file of the order.
- Copy 2 is used by the accounting department in reviewing the order for payment.
- Copy 3 is sent to the user as notification that the material has arrived or as a delivery copy if immediate delivery is made.
- Copy 4 is retained in the receiving department's operating record file.

Before some shipments can be accepted, technical inspection is necessary. A discussion of these procedures is found in Chapter 4. In some companies. distribution of the receiving report is withheld until the technical inspection report has been prepared. In other companies, distribution of the receiving report precedes distribution of the inspection report. Some companies send an in inspection report to every department so the records of that report will be complete. Other companies provide copies only to purchasing, accounting, and inspection.

The Invoice Audit and Completion of the Order

To ensure that the purchaser makes proper payment for the materials actually received. sound accounting practice dictates that some type of review procedure precede payment to the supplier.

A typical procedure involves a simultaneous review of the purchase order the receiving report and the invoice. By checking the receiving report against the purchase order the purchaser determines whether the quantity and type of material ordered was in fact received. Then by comparing the invoice with the purchase order and receiving report he verifies that the supplier's bill is priced correctly and that it covers the proper quantity of acceptable material. Finally by verifying the arithmetic accuracy of the invoice he determines the correctness of the total invoice figure.

Invoice auditing is technically an accounting function. Theoretically the purchasing departments job is completed when material has been received in the plant and is ready for use.

In the purchase of complex or technical materials a strong case can be made for assigning the auditing task to the buyer who handled the order. This individual is familiar with the materials and their technical nomenclature with prices and contract provisions. and with all ensuing negotiations. Invoices for such orders often are difficult to interpret and evaluate without a detailed knowledge of these things. When purchasing audits the invoice. its records are closed after the audit Closing the order simply entails a consolidation of all document and correspondence relevant to the order: the completed order is then filed in the closed-order file The completed order file thus constitutes a historical record of all activities encompassing the total purchasing cycle.

5.6 LOCATION OF RECEIPT STORE

The receipt Section must have information of material scheduled for arrival so that they can be prepared to receive it and count and inspect it on arrival. Various systems are used, including the use of multiple copies of Purchase Orders to record part shipments and to avoid the writing of receiving reports.

The receipt section, sometimes also called the Receipt Store or the Inward Goods Department, is responsible for the receipts of all materials coming into the company.

The first point to remember with regard to the receipt store is that a large number of outsiders like transport contractors, material handling labourers, supplier representative, etc., come to this place. It will be appreciated that in any storehouse, security is of the highest importance, and as such, there should be a total prohibition of outsiders coming there. In view of this need for security the receipt store should literally be cordoned off from the main stores, though for all practical purposes it may he located in the same building. The receipt store should also be away from the dispatch section. This is to avoid any mix up of incoming and outgoing consignments.

The principal advantages of having a separate receiving stores opposed to merging it with the main stores are:

(i) Outsiders are denied access to the various stores or production shops.

(ii) Possibility of uninspected materials or goods not covered by the G.R.N. (Goods Receipt Note) being taken into stock is reduced.

(iii) There is a double check of all incoming materials.

The location of the receipt store should be such that movement of lorries, etc., is facilitated. These vehicles come to deliver goods and there should be no congestion or problem of parking or turning of the vehicles. Similarly. for goods received by rail, the receipt Stores should be adjacent to the rail siding so that goods can be transferred to it straightaway.

There must also be adequate space to receive the materials, open the packages, and store the materials before taking the goods into stock.

Goods received in the receipt store may be destined for several locations:

(i) They may have to be shifted to the Quarantine Store to await inspection

(ii) Direct transfer to the main stores

(iii) Direct transfer to the production floor instead of going through the store.

(iv) Direct transfer to the consumer department requiring the goods.

(v) Heavy items like steel may have to be stored in the yard.

It is important to pinpoint how double handling can be avoided. For example, to unload steel plates or cement in the receipt store and transfer them later to the yard is double handling. The best method would be to get the transporter to unload steel in the yard and cement, in the consumer's shed. This avoids duplication of handling of steel and cement, the paperwork is done at the Receipt Store office. This is true also of other articles which have to be delivered to places other than the Stores.

5.7 ORGANISATION

The receipt store is usually part of the Stores set-up and is under the Stores-in-Charge or the Controller of Stores. Depending upon its size and complexity. it will have a few clerks and a supervisor can be at a fairly junior level in most cases, but for a very large Receipt Store. there can be senior officers also.

The receipt store can be of three types:

(i) **Centralised:** Where all the goods are received at one place.

(ii) **Semi-centralised:** Here the paperwork can be done at one place and the actual deliveries at the shop door or yards, etc.

(iii) **Decentralised:** In this case there is a separate receipt section attached to each store or group of stores. This might be because of the specialised nature of the article. or because of the distances between production shops.

Incoming materials are usually received from:

(i) outside suppliers.

(ii) other stores by stock transfers.

(iii) suppliers after repairs of jigs, tools, fixtures, etc.

(iv) outside parties, of goods subcontracted.

(v) various departments of scrap salvage and surplus materials.

(vi) customers, who reject materials which are returned to the Finished Goods Stores.

Organisation (Summarized Version)

Goods may be received in a storehouse room outside suppliers, from production shops or from other storehouses within the organization. They may come by hand, by post, by road, rail or air. They must be properly looked after when they arrive. The amount of documentation and checking depends greatly on the nature of the goods, and the management techniques of the business. Of course, it is desirable to avoid the expense of a lot of paperwork if this can be done without undue risk, but the possibility of theft, fraud or mistake is always present.

Similarly, the extent of physical examination, weighing, counting, etc., of goods received should be arranged in the most economical way to avoid unnecessary delay or expense.

In appropriate conditions, stock records may not be kept at all, there may be no orthodox stores accounts, and relations with suppliers may be such that their invoices are paid on sight. In that event, both physical and documentary procedures would be much simplified. For example, neither goods inwards books nor goods received notes are essential if the management chooses to rely on suppliers' advice notes for information about goods received, and the suppliers' invoice alone is acceptable for accounting purposes.

A tight and stringent control is required by management, that stock records and stores accounts are kept, and that documentary evidence of satisfactory receipt is required before suppliers' invoices are paid.

Time of Deliveries

If storehouses are not to be open for business twenty-four hours a day and seven days a week, then it is advisable to see that all suppliers are informed of the days and times during which the facilities are available to accept delivery. This information can be given on the order form.

Dispatch

In a large storehouse there must be a routine for dispatch to the places served, including the following:

(i) A routine system for the time of receipt of issue notes, the selection of what is required and marshalling of the needs of each customer.

(ii) A timed schedule of loading vehicles.

(iii) A detailed transport plan for journeys to users, timing and routeing each vehicle and providing, as far as practicable, for full loads outwards and return loads.

(iv) A regular system of checking to ensure that all items due for dispatch are loaded, and that no unauthorized items are put in the vehicles.

5.8 FUNCTIONS, RESPONSIBILITIES OF RECEIVING AND STORE

Because the purchasing and supply departments are normally responsible for materials until they are ready for use, it is essential that purchasing managers understand the fundamentals of receiving and stores operations. Receiving and stores departments are either placed under the jurisdiction of related activities in a materials management department. Whether a firm adopts the materials management concept extensively or not, receiving and stores are a vital element in its total materials system. Effective coordination with the purchasing, inventory management, and traffic functions is imperative.

Receiving stores function and operations provide both service and control functions. First, they generally organize and control the flow of materials into the production operation. second, the stores organization acts as a custodial and controlling agency. It is responsible for the safety and physical control of a sub-stantial portion of a firm's current assets. And finally for many items the existence of a stores operation permits quantity buying and the attendant savings in price, paperwork, and handling.

Specific Responsibilities

A receiving department is responsible for the receipt, identification, and general inspection of most incoming materials. It also notifies the interested individuals of the arrival and condition of the material.

Subsequently, the stores department is responsible for appropriate physical storage of all production materials, some in-process inventory, and most MRO items. In some firms, stores also handles finished goods storage.

The stores manager must develop a system for classifying, marking, and locating all materials so they are readily accessible and, at the same time, protect them against pilferage, unauthorized usage, and unnecessary damage or deterioration. In a closed system, the department must also control physical issuance of material and provide effective service for the operating units.

Cost Implications

Receiving and stores activities *indirectly* influence product costs in several ways. Inventory carrying costs stemming from deterioration, damage, and pilferage of materials, as well as related indirect labor costs, are controllable to a great extent by these managers. Additionally, an alert stores organization can help reduce costs of obsolescence by developing systems to detect slow-moving and inactive materials. Efficient use of scarce storage space can also reduce costs.

At the same time, a stores operation typically impacts a firm's *direct* labor costs. Strategically located storage facilities that provide prompt service for operating personnel help reduce the unproductive time of these people. Individuals and machines waiting for the delivery of material add nothing to the productive effort of the organization.

5.9 RECEIVING OF MATERIALS

Receiving is essentially a clerical operation. Because many clerical activities are regarded as "routine," however, the importance of the receiving function often is underrated. Most problems or errors in a purchasing transaction should come to light during the receiving operation. If the problem (quantity shortage, damaged materials, incorrect items shipped, and so on) is not detected and corrected during the receiving operation, the cost to correct the mistake later is always higher. For example, if a shortage is not discovered at the time of receipt, any combination of departments can be drawn into the problem later.

The receiving *report,* completed upon receipt of a shipment, is the only document a firm has that details the material it actually received. It also contains important supplier information-delivery timing, shipment damage, reject percentage, split shipments, and so on. This document is used as the basis for invoice payment, for continued purchasing negotiation, and for closing the order. Accuracy is therefore essential. Clearly, poor receiving performance can produce costly consequences. For this reason, receiving should be supervised by a person who is reasonably familiar with the physical characteristics of the material.

Receiving Procedure

A typical receiving procedure consists of four steps:

(1) **Unloading and Checking the Shipment:** The number of containers unloaded from the carrier's vehicle is checked against the carrier's manifest (freight bill) to make certain the full consignment has been delivered. All containers are also inspected for external damage;

any damage found is inspected by the carrier's representative and noted on the receipt which the receiving clerk signs. Failure to follow this procedure before accepting a shipment can relieve the carrier of all liability, except liability for concealed damage not evident until the container is unpacked.

(2) **Unpacking and Inspecting the Material:** A receiving clerk is held responsible for three verifications. First, checks the material received against the seller's packing slip and against a copy of the firm's purchase order to verify that the correct items have been shipped. Second, the quantity of the shipment is verified in the same manner. Finally, the clerk inspects the general condition of the material to determine whether any external damage was incurred during shipment.

(3) **Completion of the Receiving Report:** The paperwork system used varies significantly from firm to firm. In some companies a multipart receiving report form is produced as a by-product when the purchase order is generated. When the receiving clerk has finished the inspection, he/she completes this form by recording the quantities of the items received, indicating those that are still open, and noting any other useful information on the form. In other firms that utilize a computerized purchasing/inventory system, the clerk records the receiving data on the receiving report or a short form, from which a data entry clerk keys the data directly into the computer system. The system then updates the order and inventory records and may also generate a receiving report in either hard copy or electronic form.

Regardless of the system used, four operating groups generally require notification that the material has been received: the requisitioner, the purchasing department, the accounting department, and the inspection department if technical inspection is required.

(4) **Delivery of the Material:** For non-stock materials, the receiving department is usually responsible for delivery-directly or via an internal delivery service. In the case of inventory materials, the practice varies. In some firms the receiving department is responsible for internal deliveries, while in others this function is performed by an internal transportation service. In still others, stores clerks are responsible for picking up their own materials.

Upon delivery of the materials, the recipient customarily signs the receiving report or a delivery receipt, relieving the receiving clerk of further responsibility for the material.

5.10 ADVANCED SYSTEMS

Location Control System

The loss of a stocked item (due to inaccurate recording of its location) can have a devastating effect on customer service, even after pipeline **lead time** has been truncated to an optimal minimum. When a store stocks hundreds or thousands of items in tens of thousands of locations, inadequate location control systems may make finding a lost item as difficult as finding a needle in a haystack.

The fully automated storage-and-retrieval system solution solves almost all such inventory loss problems. Under such a solution, the storage-and-retrieval system control computer directs the storage-and retrieval machine to specify locations and keeps track of location contents. Unfortunately, the completely automated solution is not yet one that is cost-effective for the majority of stores. Therefore, superior store systems must include features to help storekeepers avoid errors in reporting locations and other features designed to help find and correct misplaced items when, despite precautions, items recorded in one location are actually placed in another. Exhibit 5.2 shows a location code-item number combination that takes advantage of the natural store layout, container size, and item number to identify the area in which an item is stocked. The first digit of the **"location code"** consists of the **ABC** activity code. In the example, it is "S" (Super activity code designates items stored in the fastest-moving zone of the store). The second digit identifies the type or size of shelving or storage racks, based on the size of the standard or custom container (or pallet) specified to the item's suppliers. Since the storage location scheme, within each group of shelves or racks of the same size, is an approximate item number sequence, no further location coding is necessary.

In the previous example, the proper storage location of an item is narrowed down to a very small zone, namely the activity zone, and, within the zone, to the shelving or racks that correspond to the container size for that item. In most store populations, the relatively, small number of items stored within a specific, limited area makes it especially easy to scan the area and locate a particular item number or an empty space in which to place a new receipt. Should a receipt be placed relatively far from where its item number would dictate, the area would usually be small enough for a storekeeper easily to locate the item and move it to its logical location. A receipt placed in the wrong sequence but in the right activity zone and container or shelving area would normally soon be found and the mistake would often be automatically corrected while stocking or issuing other items in that area.

EXHIBIT 5.2: STOCK LOCATION CODE

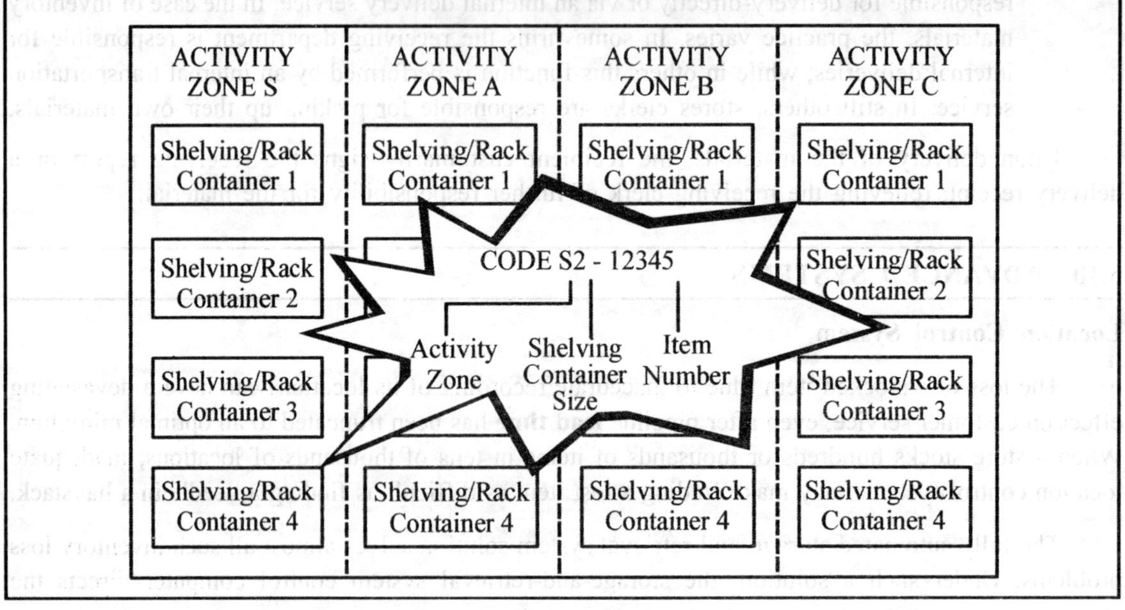

Further, it is impossible to store an item in the wrong container size area since the container would not fit the rack or shelving. Thus, special efforts to make checks to verify location accuracy will no longer be necessary if any store that has achieved superior control via activity zones, container sizes and correspondingly sized shelving and racks. However, during the interim period, before these objectives have been met, it will be desirable to be able periodically and rapidly to verify that a detailed stock location's contents match those recorded in the system.

Exhibit 5.3 is an example of a system generated document for checking that all items recorded as being in a specified location are there, or that the quantity of each item is the same as recorded These stock location checking transactions can be merged with a batch of order-picking documents to maximize storekeeper's efficiency by enabling them to verify locations while picking orders. Interspersing the location check and order-filling transaction makes it easy for the store keeper to process both transaction types while making a single trip to the general locations in which transactions for both types occur.

Since location verification documents are normally simultaneously issued for all items stocked in one storage bay or part of a bay, an entire portion of the store could be checked at once. Thus the check not only verifies the correctness of items that should be in the area but also can detect items stocked in the area that should not be there. When the document is used for location check only (in the space labeled" Customer Number and Name", a mark in either "Location Check" or "Cycle Count" indicates the document type), the storekeeper files in only the "Location Ok?" field. When the document calls for "Cycle Count", the storekeeper would fill in the three fields as shown by the manually entered data in the exhibit. Note that by recording only the number of containers and quantity per container and using the computer to perform the quantity calculation, the potential for the storekeeper to make a multiplication error is eliminated.

EXHIBIT 5.3: LOCATION/COUNT CHECKING

<table>
<tr><td colspan="6">STOCK CHECK</td></tr>
<tr><td>Item No.
12345</td><td>Order No.
None</td><td colspan="2">Customer No. & Name
Location check Cycle count</td><td>Subplant</td><td>Dock</td></tr>
<tr><td>Stock
location
S 23451</td><td>Qty.</td><td colspan="2">Staging Location</td><td colspan="2">Item Description
WIDGET</td></tr>
<tr><td rowspan="2">Single Item
Order</td><td rowspan="2">Location
Ok?
X</td><td colspan="2">StockCount</td><td colspan="2" rowspan="2"></td></tr>
<tr><td>Container
2</td><td>Quantity per
200</td></tr>
<tr><td colspan="6"></td></tr>
</table>

The simplest way for a storekeeper to check the presence of the contents of all of the items recorded in specified locations is to scan the contents in a store bay or part thereof

Inspection and Control of Quality

Materials inspection should be conducted on a regular basis for two compelling reasons. First, it provides a quantitative measurement of suppliers' quality performance, which, among other uses, is essential to the development of an effective supplier evaluation program. Second, it simply represents sound business practice.

The purchasing department's responsibility for material is fulfilled only when acceptable material is in place, ready for production use-not before. For this reason, purchasing management should have at least an advisory voice in the establishment of a firm's inspection system and- the policies which govern its operation. One method of achieving this is to include the purchasing manager in a staff group which has managerial responsibility for interfunctional coordination within the total plant operation.

Inspection of Material

The conduct and administration of an inspection operation are highly specialized activities, quite apart from normal purchasing activities. As a result, the average buyer usually possesses only a meager understanding of the "hows" and "whys" of inspection operations. It is also unfortunate because it limits a buyer's ability to serve as an effective liaison on quality matters between his or her firm and the supplier.

All buyers, however, will find it rewarding to become familiar with the basic characteristics and capabilities of the instruments and techniques used in inspecting the key materials they buy.

5.11 INSPECTION CONCEPTS

To place the topic in proper context from the standpoint of operations, our discussion begins with a concept of the receiving and inspection procedure.

Receiving and Inspection Procedure

When a purchase is consummated, the receiving and inspection departments both receive copies of the order, which specifies the inspection the material is to receive. When a shipment arrives receiving personnel check the material against the supplier's packing slip and against the purchase order to ensure that the firm has received and will be billed only for the material ordered and delivered. The receiving clerk then inspects the material in a nontechnical manner (looking for shipping damage, etc.) to determine its general condition. Finally, a receiving report is prepared on which the results of the investigation are noted. In some cases, no further inspection is required. In the case of more complex materials, a copy of the receiving report is forwarded to the inspection department, advising it that material on a given order has been placed in the "pending inspection" area and is ready for technical inspection.

The inspection department performs the specified technical inspection on a sample or on the entire lot, as appropriate, and prepares an inspection report indicating the results of the inspection. If the material fails to meet specifications, a more detailed report is usually completed describing the reasons for rejection. Rejected material, in some cases, is clearly useless to the buying firm, and the purchasing department immediately arranges with the supplier for its disposition. In other situations, the most desirable course of action is less clear-cut. The purchaser often has three alternative courses of action:

(1) Return the material to the supplier.

(2) Keep some of the more acceptable material and return the rest.

(3) Keep all the material and rework it to the point where it is acceptable.

Economics of Inspection

Whether incoming material requires by inspection beyond general receiving inspection depends in part on the way in which it is described in the purchase order. If the material is identified by brand name or by commercial grade, visual inspection by receiving personnel is usually adequate. Materials that are described by performance characteristics, by detailed specifications, or perhaps by sample, may well require technical inspection.

In the case of an item specified by performance characteristics, inspection is usually accomplished by testing the product under simulated or actual operating conditions. For material requiring tests beyond the capability of the buyer's firm, arrangements are frequently made to have a commercial testing laboratory perform the specified tests before shipment. When this is done, the testing company submits a certificate of test that accompanies the material.

Materials purchased to unique specifications invariably have many features that are subject to inspection. However, some features typically are more critical than others.

Necessity of Inspection

A sizable number of items purchased by industrial firms do require technical inspection. Fundamentally. the decision hinges on the practical economics of each specific situation. Two basic costs are involved: (1) costs of inspection and (2) costs resulting from defective parts entering the production operation and/or reaching the customer. An attempt to minimize the sum of these two costs is the guiding criterion in arriving at the basic inspection decision. The decision is also influenced by another factor which affects both cost elements-the average percentage of defective product normally submitted in the supplier's shipments.

The initial decision involves a choice between 100 percent inspection and no inspection. For purposes of. illustration, assume that a manager is confronted with the following hypothetical situation:

- He buys widgets in lots of 1,000 every week (N).
- The cost of inspecting a widget (C_1) = ₹ 0.20

- If a widget failing to meet specifications enters the production operation, the average added production or sales cost to correct the situation (C_D) = ₹ 10/-
- Records indicate the past shipments of wIdgets have typically contained approximately 3 per cent defective units (p).

A simple calculation indicates that in this case the less costly of the two alternatives is to perform 100 per cent inspection:

Total cost = cost of inspection + cost resulting from defectives accepted.

For 100 per cent inspection,

Total cost = ($N \times C_I$) + cost from defectives accepted

= $(1{,}000 \times 0.20) + 0$

= ₹ 200 per lot

For no inspection,

Total cost = cost of inspection + ($N \times p \times C_D$)

= $(0 + 1{,}000 \times 0.03 \times 10)$

= ₹ 300 per lot

5.12 CLEARING OF GOODS

The procedure for clearance of different types of receipts are described below:

(i) Rail: On receiving the railway receipt, the Clearing Section staff should keep in touch with the railway station or goods shed concerned. If the goods have not arrived a suitable endorsement should be obtained on the railway receipt from the goods clerk. Demurrage charges are payable if goods are not collected within the free time allowed.

If the railway receipt has been misplaced or has not been received the consignment should be cleared under an indemnity bond.

If the consignment is not received within a reasonable time a formal claim should be filled on the claims authority at the destination within the prescribed time limit. Copies of the letter should be sent to the station master at the originating station with a request to trace the consignment, to the consignor, to the insurance company (if insurance is arranged for by the consignee), and to the accounts department of the consignee. If insurance has been arranged for by the consignor, the latter will notify the insurance company on receipt of intimation from the consignee.

If the consignment remains undelivered, even after lapse of three months, the claim may be confirmed and the accounts department may be requested to send the bill to the claims authority.

If the consignment is received in good condition after presenting the formal claim, a suitable intimation should be sent to the various parties mentioned above.

If tampering is suspected or if the package has arrived in a damaged condition, open delivery should be taken in the presence of the railway claims inspector and a report should be prepared regarding the damage or loss. In the report, which should be countersigned by the railway claims inspector, a claim will be made on the railways for the loss involved. Simultaneously, a formal claim should also be made on the insurance company so that in the event of the claim not being admitted by the railways, the amount may be realised from the insurance company. But, if the railways do not accept the claim on account of non-compliance of packing regulations, in all probability the insurance company also may not accept the claim.

(ii) Sea Consignment: When a consignment is sent by sea, the consignee receives the following documents from the consignor:

(a) Bill of Lading

(b) Invoice and Freight Sheet

(c) Packing List and Certificate of Origin

(d) Insurance Premium Bill and Insurance Certificate if insured by the consignor. If insured by the consignee, the Insurance Premium Bill, etc. should be obtained from the Insurance Company.

On receipt of the shipping documents, the clearing agent prepares the Bill of Entry in accordance with the existing Customs rules and correct tariff items as laid down in the Indian Customs Tariff. The conversion of the foreign currency value into rupee equivalent on the bill of entry is kept pending till the rotation number of the vessel concerned is announced by the Customs. This rotation number of the vessel is announced immediately the Collector of Customs accepts the' Import General Manifest (T.G.M;) submitted by the agent of the vessel

On obtaining the Import Rotation Number of vessel concerned, the relevant bill of entry duly filled in with full particulars of marks, weight. details of consignments and the foreign currency converted into rupees at the exchange rate prevailing on the date of filling the bill of entry, together with suppliers' invoice, import licence, etc., is to be filed with the import department of the Customs. Here the clerks compare the details on the bills of entry with the J.G.M., note the bills of entry, and distribute them to the appraisers who check them with the supplier's invoice, the classification of the consignment in accordance with tariff items, the value with its conversion and the correctness of the import licence. (Most of the delays in clearing consigriments occur in the Appraising Department for want of satisfactory explanation from the importers to the queries raised by the appraiser). Once the appraiser is satisfied with the declaration made on the bills of entry, thc same is classified and the necessary physical Examination Order (E.O.) is. issued on the duplicate bill of entry. This is passed for pre-audit scrutiny of the import licence and validity period. A rubber stamp endorses this. The details of the licence are then entered in a register in the statistical section after which the bill if entry is finally released.

On receiving this finalised bill of entry, the duty is paid to the Accounts Department of the Customs, which retains the original for their records and returns three copies of the duty paid bill of entry with their account number and date. The Dock Challan is then prepared according to the scale of charges of the port authorities and is submitted at the Dock Collection Office for payment of landing charges along with the duplicate copy of the duty-paid bill of entry, invoices and packing list.

On realisation of the Port Commissioners' dock charges, the dock challan with its enclosures is submitted at the Shed Office for acceptance and the Examining customs Officer (E.C.O). is contacted to comply with the Examination Order Issued by the scrutinizing appraiser. The E.C.O. checks the consignment with the shipper's invoices signed by the scrutinizing appraiser and if found correct and satisfactory, issues orders for passing the consignment out of Customs Control. Delivery of the consignment is effected by lorry or by rail on the authority of the pass-out of Customs Control Order. The time limit for clearing the goods. without port rent is three working days from the date of landing of the cargo concerned.

If any package has been short-landed a certificate to this effect should be obtained from port authorities and a claim should be filed on the shipping agents with advice to the insurance company.

If a package has landed (as can be found from the manifest) but is not traceable, a "not found" application is to be submitted to the Port Commissioner, who will investigate the whereabouts of the package.

If any package is in a damaged condition. a survey should be arranged with the agents within three days of landing of the goods. If such a survey cannot be arranged. an insurance survey should be conducted before collection of the material from the docks. A claim will then be made on the agent with advice to the insurance company. If, on inspection of the goods at the consignee's godown, any damage or shortage is reported the insurance company should be notified. A survey may or may not be held by the insurance company depending upon the amount involved. It is necessary to preserve the original packing case until advice is received from the insurance company.

If the case is intact and if any shortage is found the matter should be taken up with 'the suppliers, keeping the insurance company informed of the position. Follow-up action should be taken until the claim is accepted by one or the other party.

(iii) Air Consignments: The Customs procedure for handling air consignments is more or less similar to the procedure for handling consignments by sea except that Air Consignment Notes are used in place of the bills of lading.

(iv) Inland Post: There are no special formalities regarding receiving parcels by inland post and normally they arrive in good condition. Liability for damages is accepted by the post office only in the case of insured parcels. If a parcel is not received, the matter should' be referred to the sender so that he may take it up with the post office of origin and with the postmaster-general concerned.

(v) Foreign Post: In major post offices, there is a separate section to deal with foreign post parcels. When foreign parcels are received. the post office will send out intimation memos to the addressee, indicating the number of packages. contents. and the place of origin. On receipt of such intimation memos. the addressee or the clearing agent should call on the Customs officer of the post office, examine the contents with the relative invoice, finalise the Customs formalities and obtain delivery immediately on payment of Customs duty, if any. The post office will if so desired, deliver the package at the address given on the parcel and collect the dues.

(vi) Miscellaneous: In order to ensure .that all incoming consignments have been cleared and received in time, it is advisable to record a summary of the consignments in a register.The register should have the following columns:

(1) Date

(2) Name of consignor

(3) Particulars of R/R or B/L (Number and date)

(4) From

(5) To

(6) Mode of transportation

(7) Contents

(8) Weight

(9) Freight

(10) Prepaid or to pay

(11) R I R received by

(12) Cleared on

(13) Particulars of expenses incurred

  (a) Freight paid

  (b) Transport charges

  (c) Handling charges etc.

  (d) Misc. charges

  (e) Total

(14) Voucher passed (date)

A register may also be maintained for recording all claims. The register should be reviewed once a week or fortnight and follow-up action taken until conclusion.

EXHIBIT 5.4: MATERIAL REJECTION MEMO

XYZ COMPANY

Ref: P. O. No.____________

Your Challan No.____________

TO:

Dear Sirs,

The following material delivered by you vide references noted above have been rejected by us for the reasons given below.

Material ordered:

Amount rejected:

Reasons for rejection:

Please arrange to remove the material from our Receiving Department at your earliest convenience.

Please send us the replacement immediately.

Please issue credit.

Yours faithfully,

For MENONJI AND SONS.

XYZ Co.	MATERIAL REJECTION NOTE		NO. DATE		
NAME AND ADDRESS OF SUPPLIER				CHALLAN NO: &. DT. P.O. NO. AND DATE	
S. NO.	MAT. CODE	DESCRIPTION	QTY SUPPLIED	QTY REJECTED	REASONS FOR REJECTION

<table>
<tr><td>AUTHORISED BY</td><td>INSPECTING OFFICER</td><td>DISTRIBUTION
1. SUPPLIER 4. STORES
2. PUR. DEPT. 5. ACCOUNTS
3. INV. CONTROL 6. OFFICE COPY</td></tr>
</table>

EXHIBIT 5.5: REJECTION DAMAGE/SHORTAGE REPORT

<table>
<tr><td>REJECTION</td><td>DAMAGE / SHORTAGE REPORT</td><td>SERIAL NO.</td></tr>
<tr><td colspan="2">TO: CARRIER</td><td>TO: CONSIGNOR</td></tr>
</table>

ORDER NO. ....

With reference to Messrs. .... Advice Note No. .... dated ....
advising dispatch of the goods detailed below per .... on ....

	☐ the goods have been rejected reason of material not conforming to order specification
Enter X in	☐ the goods have arrived, but the shortages shown below were found on receipt
Appropriate box	☐ the goods have arrived, but the quantities shown below were found damaged on receipt

VOCABULARY NO.	DESCRIPTION	QUANTITY ADVISED	DECREPANCY RESS ORDER REJECTION
....	....	....	....
....	....	....	....
....	....	....	....
....	....	....	....

....

Signature of Storekeeper

Date ....

N.B. Any correspondence about this report should be sent to the following address and should quote the Serial No. shown above:

Purchasing & Stores Department,
X Co. Ltd.,
14 Smith St.,
Manchester.

Rights of Rejection

A purchaser has the right to reject material if it does not conform with the terms of the contract. If an over shipment is received the purchaser can either reject the complete shipment or reject the quantity in excess of the contract. When a purchaser does not wish to accept wrongly delivered material be is required only to notify the supplier of this fact describing specifically the nature of the defect or default. He is not legally bound to return the rejected material. He is however obligated to protect and care for the material in a reasonable manner while it is in his possession. If he neither returns the material nor notifies the supplier of his rejection within a reasonable period of time, he is then obligated to pay for the material.

Process of Rejected Goods

When the goods receiving from the supplier do not conform to order specification then the inspection and stores reject the material assigning reasons of rejection. They can also be rejected being received in damaged state.

Damage/Storage Report

The storekeeper raises a serially numbered damage/shortage report from in any of the following circumstances:

(1) If goods are delivered damaged.

(2) If goods received show a shortage in comparison with the supplier's advice note or packing note.

(3) If goods have not arrived within the allowed time for the method of carriage.

This form is normally raised in four copies, distributed as follows:

Copy No.1 to the carrier.

Copy No.2 to the supplier.

Copy No.3 to the office responsible for clearing invoices.

Copy No.4 for retention in the storehouse.

Every day the storekeeper examines the file of suppliers' advice notes to ensure that claims for non-delivery are submitted within the allowed time for road and rail carriage or postal service, as the case may be. This is important because carriers, including the railways and the Post office will not accept liability for non-delivery, loss, damage or shortage unless they are notified immediately in writing of the circumstance and a detailed claim in writing is made within a few days.

As a general rule in cases of non-delivery, damage, shortage or excess delivery, the storekeeper's duties cease with the preparation of the damage shortage report. Further correspondence with the carrier or suppliers is normally dealt with by the invoice section after this stage. the storekeeper, however, retains the package in which the goods are recevied, so that it is available for subsequent inspection if required. In due course, the invoice section will give the storekeeper disposal instructions for the damaged goods.

A specimen of a rejection and damage/shortage report is illustrated in Exhibits 5.4 and 5.5.

5.13 SUMMARY

Receiving materials against purchase orders is an important function in storeskeeping. Efficient receiving permits use of materials after their arrival in the shortest interval. Different methods and levels are to be applied for inspection of materials before their acceptance.

Receiving stores has to be organised in such a way that materials awaiting acceptance are easily located and retrieved.

It is the responsibility of the receiving department to advise purchase, accounts and user departments about acceptance and/or rejection of materials received. It has to take care of rejected material until their disposal is arranged by purchase department.

Specific formalities have to be followed in clearing materials arriving by sea, rail, air, road, post office, etc.

5.14 SELF ASSESSMENT QUESTION

(1) Why is receiving considered as an important function in storeskeeping.

(2) Describe inspection methodology as it is applied to different categories of materials.

(3) How should receiving stores be organised?

(4) What documents Receiving Stores needs to prepare in its day to day operations?

6 Chapter
STORAGE AND PRESERVATION

Objectives

After studying this chapter, you should be able to understand:

- Objectives of storage and preservation
- Importance of stores manual and its contents.
- Factors leading to damage to materials in stock.
- Preventive measures to contain damage to materials in stock.

Structure:

6.1 STORAGE AND PRESERVATION

The term "storage" is a comprehensive one referring to the keeping of goods safely and in good condition. Some people, however, would like to draw a distinction between "storage" and "preservation".

Storage refers to the physical act of storing or housing particular materials. These might be screws, large machinery, equipment or parts, liquids like petroleum, dangerous substances like sulphuric acid, or a gas like oxygen. Each material has its own storage requirements and knowledge is necessary as to how and where they are to be stored, their handling and issue and so on.

Preservation, on the other hand, includes the protection of the material from mechanical damage (which can happen through overloading, damage from neighbouring materials with sharp projections, etc.), from damage by inadequate or faulty packaging, from too high or too low a level of humidity, heat or cold. or from damage by pests like white ants, etc. Again materials require different types of protection according to their nature.

The sole objective of preservation being to keep goods free from damage.

To start with, it is desirable for all Stores staff to have a fairly good general knowledge of the principal materials stocked their sources, their uses, the process of manufacture, their characteristics and technical terms relating to them, methods of measurement, common defects in such materials, and finally a first-rate understanding of what should be done with respect to their storage and preservation. In several' companies where the Stores are small, the storekeeper may also have the responsibility of receiving and inspecting the materials. A store-keeper is assumed to have such knowledge and is usually penalised if anything goes wrong.

6.2 STORES MANUALS

Need for the Procedures

(1) Manuals of Instruction

To operate any storehouse, some discipline and routine is inevitable and oral instructions have obvious limitations and a certain amount of written guidance is a necessity. The bigger the organization, the more important and numerous written procedures are likely to be and, at some stage, it becomes desirable to revise, extend, standardize and arrange all the existing instructions to produce one comprehensive document, called a stores manual. The document is usually printed and issued in the form of a book. It is also common practice for all stores forms to be reviewed, redesigned and standardized, and for specimen forms to be produced either as a part of the manual or as an appendix.

(2) Advantages and Disadvantages of a Manual

The principal advantages and disadvantages of a stores manual are listed below. As a general rule, the need for a manual increases with the size and complexity of the organization involved, and the advantages are therefore more marked in a large concern.

(a) Advantages

(I) Provides in readily accessible form a complete record of all standing instructions.

(II) Facilitates the maximum standardization of procedures and paper work. This is of major importance, because the standards adopted are those considered to be most satisfactory and economical for the organization concerned. There is also an incidental saving on the cost of printing forms, which may be considerable.

(III) By reason of standardization, staff can be trained more quickly and efficiently, they become accustomed to a common procedure and are therefore more easily interchangeable. It is also a simple matter to define the duties of each member of the staff, and this assists supervision.

(IV) If all storehouses are operating on the same methods, their efficiencies can more easily be compared.

(V) If the contents of the manual are agreed in principle with other departments concerned, e.g., production, finance and audit, their procedures can also be, designed to fit in with the provisions of the stores manual. This ensures that a satisfactory service is provided and that the arrangements for internal check are adequate.

(b) Disadvantages

(I) A detailed manual tends to limit local initiative unless proper arrangements are made to consider new ideas and to keep up to date.

(II) Where there are a number of out-stations, it may be that complete standardization of procedures is not entirely beneficial to all the units. It is difficult for local staff to appreciate the advantage to the organization as a whole when, in the interests of standardization, they are required to change some of their methods for new procedures which are more expensive or even less efficient in the particular circumstances. This can usually be overcome by arranging 'dispensations' to units where such a situation arises, allowing them to depart from the manual instructions within limits in the interests of local efficiency.

Preparation of the Manual

The following paragraphs outline a typical procedure for preparing and distributing a stores manual of instructions.

Stores Directive

If there is not already a written directive with the full authority of the management covering stores policy and organization, a suitable document is prepared and issued as the first step, stating clearly the responsibility and authority of the stores department on such matters as:

General policy on stock investment.

Control of storehouses and stockyards.

Authority for provisioning and stock control.

Responsibility for stock checking and review of obsolete and redundant stock.

Custody of stock records and stores accounts.

Authorization of issues.

Centralization of storage where considered desirable.

Limitation of stockholding points.

Standardization of procedures and forms.

Staff gradings and complements.

The directive therefore defines the limits within which the stores procedures operate, and conveys authority to the stores department to act within these limits. It may be regarded as the stores 'charter' and is indispensable if policy is to be effectively enforced.

Previous Instructions

All existing written instructions and forms are collected and carefully examined. Those which are out of date or have been superseded are eliminated. The remainder are sorted into groups according to their subject matter, e.g., stock checking, issue procedure, provisioning, etc.

Existing Practices and Systems

Visits are made to all stockholding points to check that current practices and systems are in accordance with present instructions and, where this is not so, to note the differences and the reasons for them. At the same time a record is made of all procedures, forms, books and other documents already in operation on matters not covered by the instructions currently in force.

6.3 CONTENT OF THE MANUAL

At this stage, in the light of the content of the stores directive and the material accumulated relevant to the present position, the scope of the manual is decided and chapter headings listed in logical order. As far as is practicable, these chapters are self-contained and arranged in such a way that they can be issued as separate documents for the use of individual members of the staff whose duties do not require them to have a complete copy of the whole book. For instance a unit storekeeper does not necessarily need information on the detailed procedure to be observed in the stock-control section or in the stores accounts. A specimen list of chapter headings is given below:

Chapter

(1) General Instructions

(2) Procedure at Unit Stores

(3) Procedure at General Stores

(4) Stock Recording

(5) Stores Accounting

(6) Stock Control by Quantity

(7) Stock Control by Value

(8) Stock Checking
(9) Standard Parts
(10) General Stock
(11) Capital Stock
(12) Fixed Assets Withdrawn from Use
(13) Obsolete and Redundant Items
(14) Reclaimed Material
(15) Scrap
(16) Packages
(17) Stationery Stock
(18) Canteen Stock

Appendix

(I) Stores Vocabulary – Classification and Section Headings
(II) Target Stock Levels
(III) Summary of Duties of Stores Personnel
(IV) Schedule of Returns
(V) Periods of Retention of Documents
(VI) Flow Charts
(VII) Specimen Forms

When the Chapter headings have been decided, the next step is to list under each chapter the individual items of procedure to be described and the standard forms appropriate to these procedures;

Standard Forms

When the first draft is complete, specimen standard forms are prepared. This work is best done or at least co-ordinated by one person to ensure consistency. Some points in this connexion are:

(i) All forms have a number, e.g., PS. 203.

(ii) As far as practicable, the following information appears in the same relative position on every form:

Form number

Serial number

Date of origin

Vocabulary number

Destination

Signature box.

(iii) The number of different sizes of paper used for forms is kept to a minimum, and the stationery buyer is consulted about the most economical sizes and grades of paper.

(iv) Care is taken to see that the thickness and spacing of lines is satisfactory.

(v) The number of copies to be prepared is restricted to what is absolutely essential.

(vi) The British Standard BS.1808, on the specification size and layout of commercial forms, is worth studying.

(vii) The use of coloured paper to distinguish between forms of different types or copies of the same form is considered.

(viii) It is often helpful to show specimen entries on the forms.

The following is a list of specimen forms accompanying a manual.

Form No.	**Description**
PS.200	Unit stock record
PS.201	Log sheet
PS.202	Goods received note
PS.203	Damage/shortage report
PS.204	Rejection report
PS.205	Demand on central stores
PS.206	Transfer form
PS.207	Advice note
PS.208	Issue note
PS.20	Issue order
PS.210	Adjustment voucher
PS.211	Central stores stock record
PS.212	Return to store note
PS.213	Package slip
PS.215	Stock check list
PS.216	Stock discrepancy report
PS.217	Standard price list
PS.218	Price change notification
PS.219	Classification control account
PS.220	Stock review card
PS.221	Purchase requisition
PS.222	Authority for addition to general stock
PS.223	Unit storekeeper's monthly report

PS.224	Central Storekeeper's monthly report
PS.225	Return of stocks and consumption
PS.226	Summary of stock-checking adjustments
PS.227	Analysis of stock of steel
PS.228	Obsolete and redundant review report
PS.229	Stores vocabulary originating sheets

Flow Charts

Flow charts (which are often included in manuals) are diagrams showing the route travelled by a particular form and its copies, and the operations performed en route. This briefly illustrates the major points of procedure and is useful in several ways:

(i) At the time when a manual is being compiled, the preparation of charts quickly shows up any flaws in the procedure as drafted.

(ii) Charts show the source and destination of documents at a glance and give a much clearer picture than can be obtained by reading the text of the manual itself.

(iii) Flow charts are useful for the purposes of instruction and, when fixed on the wall above a desk, provide a ready means of reference.

Refer Exhibit 6.1 for a specimen.

Duty Sheets

A stores manual will say that certain duties are to be done at stated times by specified persons. The details are fully described in the body of the document but it is often convenient to summarize such duties and list them on a separate 'duty sheet' as an appendix, e.g.: Duty Sheet for Stock Control Officer

Duty	**Manual Paragraph Reference**
Fix maximum stocks for unit stores	102
Examine return-to-store notes and give disposal instructions	183
Sign issue orders	194
Authorize issues on loan	197
Review outstanding loan issues	199
Notify unit storekeepers of stock and consumption monthly	216
Examine value of outstanding orders monthly	263
Approve purchase requisitions raised by unit storekeepers	315
Make test checks on the accuracy of stock-record posting	346
Approve central store provision demands	410
Approve sales of material to contractors	427

EXHIBIT 6.1

Specimen Flow Chart

Form PS. 212
Return to Store Note

User Department	Storehouse	Stock Control Section	Stores Accounts
1. Raise PS.212 in 3 copies (para.277)			
2. Return material with No.1 and 2 copies to storehouse →	→		
	4. Receive material and No.1 and 2 copies		
3. Retain No. 3 copy			
	5. Action No.1 and 2 copies (paras. 278-80)		
	6. Refer No.1 Copy to stock control section if necessary, to obtain instructions →	→	
		7. Receive No.1 copy	
		8. Insert Instructions tions for dealing with material on No. 1 copy and return No.1 copy to storehouse (para .280)	
	←	←	←
	9. Receive No. 1 copy		
	10. Deal with material as instructed		
	11. Post No. 1 Copy to stock record (para. 282)		
	12. Pass No. 1 copy to stores-accounts section →	→	→ 15. Receive No. copy
	13. Return No. 2 copy to originator as receipt		16. Analayse to cost code and classification. Post from summary to classification control account (para. 586)
← 14 Receive No. 2 copy and file	←		17. File No.1 copy

Returns and Reports

The manual gives full details, including forms, for all regular returns or reports to be prepared by stores staff either internally within the stores department or externally to other departments or to general management.

There is a summary in the manual listing all such reports and returns, showing who is responsible for preparing them, where they are to be sent and the dates at which they are to be submitted. The manual does not deal with returns and reports of a temporary or non-repetitive nature.

Consultation with Users and Other Departments

When the first draft manual is complete, with specimen forms, flow charts and lists of returns and reports, several copies are made. These are circulated to the heads of user departments (production, maintenance, toolroom, etc.) and other interested departments such as finance and audit. Individual consultations with each of these departments are then arranged to discuss any suggestions they have concerning the effect of the manual provisions on their own responsibilities and procedure, and ultimately to obtain general agreement.

6.4 PUBLICATION AND DISTRIBUTION

After receipt and consideration of all representations from other departments and out-stations, the final draft of the stores manual is prepared and printed.

Technical advice is sought on the most suitable paper and print, and in view of the use for which the document is intended, a strong and serviceable binder is provided. As a general rule it is desirable to issue the book in loose-leaf form to allow for the insertion of additions or amendments from time to time.

Copies of the manual are issued to those concerned by title and not by name, Full copies of the text are supplied only where necessary, but all supervisors whose duties are substantially affected at least have a copy of the sections appropriate to their work. Receipts are obtained for all copies issued, and a permanent record is kept showing the original distribution.

Authority

The manual is issued with the authority of the board of directors or general manager, or equivalent.

6.5 IMPLEMENTATION OF THE MANUAL

Instructional Courses

The issue of a manual implies that all the recipients will read it. So that it shall be fully understood, it will be found helpful to arrange a short course of lectures or demonstrations by qualified officers.

Programme

To ensure that the provisions of the manual are observed as soon as possible, especially where major procedural changes are involved, a programme for its implementation by stages ought to be agreed, showing the dates by which each major section of procedure will be in force in each storehouse or section of the office.

Amendments and Additions

Manuals should not be amended unless it is unavoidable, but in practice some amendments and additions are necessary from time to time to keep pace with changing conditions.

6.6 PRESERVATION OF MATERIALS

Different materials by their natura and due to weather conditions are subject to certain types of damages. These likely damages and types of protection that srores needs to provide to contain damages are shown in Table 6.1 below.

TABLE 6.1: STORAGE AND PRESERVATION OF MATERIALS

Material	Likely damage	Effects of weather	Methods of Storage	Type of Protection
(1) Bricks- - facings	chipping on face, and corners, breakage, effects of mud slashes	Saturation from rain, possible frost damage, exessively dry from solar radiation	in neat stack max height 1.8 m on even platform	top and half-way down the sides covered by water proof sheeting well secured, also sheet ground and sides if in muddly conditions
- Commons	chipping on face and corners, breakage, effects of mud slashes	saturation from rain, possible, frost damage, excessively dry from solar radiation	in neat stacks max height 1.8 m on even platform	not absolutely necessary
(2) Blocks - clinker	breakage	saturation from rain, possible frost damage excessively dry from solar radiation	in neat stacks max height 1.8 m on even platform	top and half way down the sides covered by water proof sheeting, well secured
- concreate	breakage	very little but varies with density	in neat stacks max height 1.8 m on even platform	top and half-way down the sides covered by water proof sheeting, well secured
- clay hollow blocks	breakage	saturation by rain possible frost damage	in neat stacks max height 1.8 m on even platfrom	top and half-way down the sides covered by water proof sheeting, well secured

(3) Cement - bagged	broken bags causing spillage	cement hardening in damp atmosphere	in stacks max height 2 m on even platfrom off ground, ensure oldest bags used first	placed in a closed shed with large doors for easy access, allow for ventilation to maintain a dry atmosphere.
- bulk	spillage	cement hardening and forming lumps in damp atmosphere	in silo	adequate protection afforded by the silo
(4) Plaster - bagged	broken bags causing spillage	plaster hardening and forming lumps in damp atmosphere	in stacks max height 2 m on even platfrom off the ground, use oldest plaster bags before commencing latest delivery	preferably within the buliding, alternatively completely covered over with well secured water proofed sheeting.
(5) Plasterboard	fracture of sheets, corners damaged	saturation by rain brings disintegration	in stacks laid horizonatally max height 2 m on continuous even platfrom	fully coverred with well secured water proof sheeting, preferably taken into building as soon as possible.
(6) Timber - joints	twisting warping, bowing	saturation by rain	in neat stacks laid horizonatally on an even platfrom	water-proof sheet/ cover leaving ends uncovered
- roof trusses	twisting, warping, bowing	saturation by rain	in neat stacks laid horizonatally on an even platfrom but stacks not to exceed 12 in number	warer-proof sheet/ cover leaving ends uncovered, but allow for adequale ventillation
- flooring boards	twisting, warping, bowing	saturation by rain	in neat stacks laid horizontally on an even platform off the ground using spacing slabs	water-proof sheet/ cover leaving ends uncovered, but allow for adequate ventillation
- chipboard	fracture, damage at corners	saturation by rain brings about disintegration	in most stacks laid horizontally on an even platform off the ground using spacing slabs	preferably within the building; if external fully covered with waterproof sheet
- joinery	fracture, twisting warping, bowing	saturation by rain	in well constructed racks off the ground laid horizontally	top and sides covered with waterproof sheeting, ends left open for ventilation and access, ensure timber is primed

- fabricated units	fracture, twisting, warping, bowing	saturation by rain	stacked verticallly against a strong support on runners	fully covered with water-sheeting, well secured, but allowing some ventilation.
- doors and door sets	face markings, winding	saturation by rain	door-sets stacked vertically as above, doors vertically or horizontally if on an even base; classify in sizes and types	in an enclosed shed having a dry atmosphere and handling room. Must be lockable.
(7) Metal - copper tubes	buckles	only over a long period of time	In racks giving adequate lateral support	In a shed with full security
- cast iron pipe	fracture	rusting over a long period of time	in racks, for large diameters. Use wedges or shaped timbers to prevent rolling	no protection required required if stored in a in a compound
- Sheet metals	bent and misshapen, scratching finish	very little effect	in stacks laid horizontally on an even platform off the ground	protective membrance between sheets
- fabricated	breakages to fittings and buckling	very little effect	vertically against a strong support on a platform or runners	galvanised and aluminium units to be kept clean of ashes as these will corrode.
- ironmongery	breakage of fittings, loss by theft	rusting of small steel parts	in bins or sheves classified in sets or types	located in a full security shed for maximum protection.
(8) Sundries - sanitary	breakage of fittings, chipping and cracking	little or no effect in the short term	separately on an even base	preferably placed at point of use within building.
- plastic goods	breakage, buckling, crushing	some plastics affected by solar radiation	in racks with adequate lateral support	protection from pilfering.
- Screws and nails	loss by pilferage	rusting	in strong boxes or bins according to size	in a central location location with security
- kitchen fittings	twisting warping, facial marking	saturation by rain	in stacks max 2 units high on an even base	in a shed with adequate access, or direct to point of use in the building.
- precast concreet floor beams	breakage and cracking	no effect (water can lie in thc hollows within the beams)	stacked horizontally off the ground with timber space	little required
- sand gravel	none	saturated with rain frozen in frost,	on hard flat base with some form of	covered to prevent excess water content

		contaminated with soil, etc.	enclosure to prevent spreading	and give protection from frost.
- lime, sand, mortar	none	saturated with rain, frozen in frost contaminated with soil, etc., also solar radiation	on hard flat base with some form of enclosure to prevent spreading	covered to prevent excess water content and give protection from frost and excessive drying.
- steel/re-inforecement	bent out of shape	slight rusting	on hard flat base on timber runners	none required.
- scaffolding	buckling	rusting to steel tubes and fittings	in racks according to length or in contained stackes on runners	fitting well greased before use.
(9) Acid	Corrosion	Non-applicable effect of heat and light	Store in a separate godown well ventilated and cool floor; should be lined with acid proof material; not enough hard to damage jars and carboys; cock sealed with molten wax or plaster of paris or with quicklime and lineseed oil	Keep away from paper, wood, etc. Goggles and Rubber gum-boots and gloves be used by staff. Retail issues should be discouraged. Soda ash is used in order to prevent any leakage/damage from the jar.
(10) Acetylene	Leakage	Nil. 'Avoid heat fire.	The gas, dissolved in accetone (solvent) under a pressure of 15-21 kg. cm^2 is contained in cylinders	Cylinder padded with coir cover unload over condemned pneumatic tyre or mattress.
(11) Brushes	Brittle of bristle	Loosing of glue due to damp and heat	Avoid moisture and insects. Keep in original cartons. Spray wiht insecticide.	Very dry heat makes the bristle brittle Darkness helps the growth of moths. Should not be stocked for more than six months.
(12) Carbide	Discharge of gas	Moist, damp weather discharges gas	Storage of carbide above 12.7 kg. requires licence and stocking is governed by Carbide of Calcium Rules.	Water or moisture coming in contact with carbide gives off acetylene gas which is highly inflammable. All fires or artificial light shall be kept away from carbide.

(13) Bamboos	Splitting and damage by borers	Splitting	Submerge in water. Should be immersed in 50% solution of creosote or mustard oil, mix them for about 25 minutes under a temp. of 85^{0}C. This should be followed in a similar cold Mixture.	An insect called borer causes decay to bamboos. I. S. 1902 deals with preservation of bamboos. Should be immersed in 50% solution of creosote and mustard oil.
(14) Casting	Breakage, chipping off	Nil. It is seasonal which is good	Cast iron castings improve by ageing in atmospheric, temperature. Steel castings may remain in open, with a coat of paint. Non-ferr-ouscastings should be kept inside the shed as these items can be stolen.	Ensure that these do not rust
(15) Battery Cells	Discharge of cell and copper sulphate	Deterioration	In cartons in orginal packing	Dry cells have limited life. Stock should be controlled accordingly.
(16) Cloth	Damaged by insects like silver fish wooly bear, cloth moth	Fungus due to dampness	Moisture and water are harmful. Store woolen goods in steel almirahs 1.5 m wide. Felt should be wrapped with paper	Rats and white ants are destructive agents. Wooly bear, moth, silver fish are barmful for wool. Insecticides should be sprayed. To be kept in air-tight boxes or cup-boards or racks. Exposure to hot air and steam and drying berfore repacking
(17) Coal	Damage by fire size is reduced	Size is reduced and dried up	Should be piled in rows of stacks perferably not over, 3m. high and 30 m. wide at the base, each pile being preferably not in ex-cess of 1,50, 000 kg. clear space of 3m is to be maintained between piles.	Should not be stacked against wooden posts nor come in touch with hot or warm pipes or flues. Shunting railway engines should not throw sparks. In case of fire, water, is not used will only raise steam and heat.

(18) Electrical cable and wire	Breakage and spoilage of insulation	Spoilage of insulation	Keep away from oil and acid	Drum should be kept on edge. Cable end should be sealed with solder or pitch
(19) Electrodes	Spoilage	Damp	Dry heat and humid atmosphere to be avoided. Should be kept in original containers in cool dry place prefera-bly in aircounditioned godown.	Rough handling may loosen the flux coating.
(20) Firebricks	Chipping	Saturation from rain	Store inside a shed	Absorption of water will cause disintegration.
(21) Glass sheet and plantes	Breakage	Breakage	Should not be stacked horizontally nor one upon the other. These should be kept up-right, slightly slanting.	Sunlight has bad effect on glass.
(22) Leather goods	Deterioration	Fungus grows if kept damp; cracking due to dryness.	Wet salted hides should be kept in cool room. Dry salted hides should not be stored in wet condition. Tanned hides and finished leather should be kept in dry room.	Turnover regularly and wipe with clean cloth, slightly moist with oil. Apply french chalk powder on chamois leather.
(23) Machined parts	Damage	Corrosion Rusting	Castings with machined faces may be kept outside but the machined faces, particularly threaded portion and holes should be protected properly with grease, plugged where neces-sary. Journals should be packed with wooden slates, over a coat of paint (white lead).	Protect from rain water coming in contact with machined surface.
(24) Oil	Evaporation; absorption moisture	Mixing of dust and water	Oil is stored in bulk in tanks either underground or over ground.	Dust and dirt should be avoided. Watch against leaks. If stored for a long

			Oil is received in tank wagons and arrangement for decanting by gravity or by Pumping should be Provided. Oil is stored in retail, in drums marked with grade and kind of oil. The drums are piled up horizonatally. For retail issues from drums, hand operated force pump may be used.	time, viscosity changes, therefore rapid turnover should be aimed at. Vegetable oils deteriorated by action of air light, moisture causes rancidity and hydrolysis. Should not be stocked for more than 12 months.
(25) Oxygen	Leakage	Expansion due to heat	Oxygen in gaseous state is supplied in steel cylinders, fitted with cap over the end which house the valve. (The pressure of filling is 125 kg/ CM^2). The floor of oxygen godown should be padded with earth or sand or ashes to prevent damage to cylinder. Oxygen may be supplied through pipe as liquid also.	Proper fitting of caps should be ensured to prevent leakage. Crease, oil and any combusitable material should not be kept nearby. All cyclin-deers should have coir cover to act as cushion. Violent handling must be avoided. Oxygen Cylinders are returned to supplier when empty. These should be issued on the principle of FIFO.
(26) Paper	Damage, brittle, getting redish	Damage	Sensitised paper keep in dark	Must be issued before expiry of life.
(27) Pctrol	Evaporation Absorbs mixing of impurities	Nil	Storage of Petrol above 25 liters requires licence. Store according to Petroleum Rules.	Separate godown as per petroleum Rules with the approval of Inspector of Explosives. Precautions against fire.
(28) Pipes	Damage and Bending	Corrsion (pitting) and Rust	Ends may be plugged, and threads protected vertical standing in conical form prevents	Coat of reclaimed oil or any anti-corrosive material, but on steel pipes. Racks hooks, with turnedup

			accumulation of rain water, when kept outside.	end, to prevent from rolling off.
(29) Rubber goods	Cracking and chusing of shape, crasing, stickyness and brittleness.		Separate godown with low room temperature (16^0– $20\ ^0C$) fairly high humidity and complete darkness during periods of very low atmosphere humidity, i.e., during dry summer, special care should be taken to maintain high humidity.	Do not keep stock for more than 6 months. Sunlight has adverse effect. Keep away from grease or oil. Apply french chalk. powder periodically.
			Tyres should always stand on end. Tubes should be wrapped in greased paper, dusted with french chalk.	
(30) Paint, Varnish and Enamel	Solidification	Evaporation, absorption of moisture	Dry paint not affected by climatic effects. Stiff paint contains 15% to 20% oil. If kept for more than 9 months, then top surface forms incrustration. Ready mixed paint settling takes place after 3 month. The drums should be inverted to prevent settling enamel. Improves by storage up to 2 years but after that it has a tendency to oxidise and thicken. Varnish - long storage assists in settling of impurities.	Guard against moisture and rain Should not be kept in stock for more than 12 months. Varnish contains spirit and is inflammable
(31) Tools	Damage	Rusting and Corrosion	Cutting surface protected by coating with grease or spraying with plastic or dipping in paraffin solution (glass coat) for files greasing by	

			mineral jelly, reduced with mineral oil to suitable consistency, may be used and then wrapped with paper.	
(32) Timber - Components - (Tools handles)	Change of shape, borer and white ant	Saturation or cracking, change of shape	Impregnation by oil, by submerging in an oil bath heated by steam.	Coltar is preventive for white ants. (white ants can be exterminated by cowans process which involves inoculation of white ants with virus)
(33) Wooden sleepers	End Splitting	Saturation by rain spliting by heat and dryness	Adopt unit piling method sleepers stacked such that end-splitting is avoided by putting clamps (steward clamp)	Apply creosote oil or solegram.

NATURE OF VARIOUS TYPES OF GOODS:

IMPLICATIONS FOR STORAGE AND HANDLING METHOD

Chief physical shape, etc.	Characteristics other data	Examples	Primary containers	Some support/ holding and storage methods
(a) Rectiliner (solids)	Rigid	Concrete blocks	Self	Flat pallet, load board on self-stack
	Semi-rigid	Cheeses	Protective wrappings, cartons etc.	Post pallets with shrink wrap
(b) Cylicders (solids)	Rigid	Drums	Self	Self-stack, flat or special pallets.
	Semi-rigid	Tyres	Self plus wrappings	Special rack or special pallets.
	Very flexible	Rubber buckets	Self	Post pallets, nested, special racks/bins
(c) Spherical (solids)	Rigid	Ball bearings	Greased wrapping and cartons	Unit containers, tote pans
	Semi-rigid	Plastic floats	crates	Box pallets
	Very flexible	Rubber balls	Nets, bags, Sacks	Box pallets
(d)Irregular	Rigid	Roller bearing (complete)	Greascd/cartoned	Box pallets, tote pans.

	Semi-rigid Very flexible	Rubber mouldings Rubber gloves	Cases, Cartons,etc. Boxed, dusted with french chalk.	Box pallets, tote pans. Post pallets if boxed
(e) Long lengths (solids)	Rigid	Steel joists, etc.	Nil	Tree racks, bar racks, bar pallets, etc.
	Semi-rigid	Wire bars	Banded, and/or Banded on to battens	Honeycomb racks, etc.
	Vary flexible	Cable	Single lengths (as "wirebars") long leangth on drums	Special pallets
(f) Sheets	Flat-rigid	Steel sheets	Banded	Load boards, vertical/borizontal racks
	Semi-rigid	Corrugated perforated	Banded on back boards,	Vertical storage-on racks Load boards, etc.
	(Fragile)	Glass, etc.	Special lined crates	Vertical storage-on edge
	Very flexible	Foam rubber, plastic	crated	Post pallets, load boards, etc.
(g) Irregular sollids (soft)	Non-rigid	Cloth	Rope or cloth	Post pallets, self-stack bales
	Non-rigid	Contents may be hardware of software	Sacks or bags	Flat or post pallets
	Non-rigid	Carpets	Roped or bound	Cradle racks to protect pile from pressure points.
(h) Granules powders	Screen, angle of repose, specific gravity	Sand Flour, etc. Other goods	Loose in bulk Sacked or in containers Sacks, kegs, drums,	Bulldoze, skips, etc. Bulk sacks As appropriate to type of primary container, etc.
(i) Lumps	Screen, angle of repose, specific gravity	Coal	Loose in bulk, or sacks in small lots	Concrete bunds, etc.
(j) Liquids	Coefficient of expansion; viscosity; boiling and freezing points; vapour pressures; specific gravity, etc.	Oil Chemicals	Drums, bulk containers	Drum and pallet racks, tank farms, etc.
(k) Gases.	Speciffic gravity; freezing; liquification and flash points	Propane etc.	Cylinders. bulk containers, etc.	Special pallet racks, tanks farms etc.

6.7 DETERIORATION OF MATERIALS IN STORAGE

Most materials deteriorate over a period of time. Broadly, for the purpose of this subject, materials are divided into two categories:

(i) **Organic substance** in their natural state and items fabricated from these, like cotton, silk, wool, leather, rubber, timber, foodstuffs and other agricultural produce etc. These are susceptible to damage by biological agents like insects and micro-organisms. Some of these are also damaged by non-biological agents also. For example, rubber is sensitive to heat, light and dryness. Similarly, cotton can lose its strength by exposure to the sunlight.

(ii) **Processed materials** and goods manufactured there from like metal stores, electrical and signaling equipment, optical instruments, chemical stores, drugs etc. These may deteriorate through non-biological phenomena like rusting, corrosion etc. Of course, some of these are also attacked by biological agents. Bacteria can sometimes play a part in the corrosion of metals.

India is a tropical country and we have a large amount of rain and consequently a high degree of moisture and humidity. Moisture plays a very big role in the damage to materials and the greater the moisture content in the air, the greater the risk of damage to materials. Except in a few cases, e.g., rubber, dry conditions for storage are essential.

Similarly, insects and micro-organisms pose a major threat primarily because they reproduce at an astronomical rate and in less than no time, can spread havoc in the Stores.

In many cases, one will find that both biological factors (insects, fungus, bacteria, rats etc.) and non-biological factors (moisture, heat, light, chemicals, gases etc.) may jointly cause damage.

Today, unlike in the past, a warehouse is likely to contain a very wide variety of items which are very sensitive and which will lose their chemical or physical properties if not preserved properly. It will be appreciated, that it is an obligation on the part of the Stores personnel to preserve the materials in factory fresh condition and this responsibility can be fulfilled only if the Stores personel have a clear idea of how the various materials under their custody have to be preserved.

Insects: Insects probably offer the greatest challenge to the Storekeeper. While 25 years is generally recognised as the span of a human generation, for insects, it is 4 to 8 in one year. The number of progeny from one insect also can be in hundreds. Another peculiarity is that a new generation adapts to the environment and presents immune qualities. For example, DDT killed mosquito once very easily, but it is difficult to control them by DDT now as the later generations have developed immunity to DDT.

Insects are small in size and can easily hide in cracks and crevices. Most of them have wings and this enables them to search far and wide for food and escape from their enemies. They can also feed on a wide variety of substances, liquid or solid.

Pest Control: The starting point of control is Stores hygiene which will include immaculate cleanliness, segregation of infested materials, prompt removal of sweepings and packaging' material specially items like hay which can carry a lot of living organisms) thorough and periodical inspection, proper ventilation, illumination, etc.

6.8 STORES HYGIENE

(a) Cleanliness: of store rooms acts as a deterrent to insects and other pests who thrive in accumulated debris and cracks in floors and walls. Dust and dirt should be removed regularly and the larger cracks should be filled with pitch or cement. White-washing of walls and swabbing of floors with phenyle at suitable intervals also help to keep down insects.

(b) Ventilation: Air must he allowed to circulate freely throughout the storage area; the only exception is in respect of rubber articles where ventilation has to be restricted to a slow natural circulation of air. Free aeration helps in keeping the stored materials and the storerooms dry and prevents accumulation of heat within the stacks, bundles and stores. Thus it helps to reduce the chances of spontaneous combustion of materials.

(c) Segregation of Infested Stores: Stores damaged by biological agencies should be segregated immediately the damage is noticed and given suitable treatment.

(d) Disinfestations of Godowns: Storerooms in which materials infested by micro-organisms have been kept should be periodically disinfested as shown below, especially before the storerooms are utilised for stacking un infested items:

(i) The rooms should be emptied of all infested material and cleaned thoroughly.

(ii) The walls should be white-washed.

(iii) The floor should be washed with phenyle or creosote liquid.

If the storeroom contained stores infested by insects, the following measures should be adopted:

(a) The room should be emptied of all infested material and cleaned thoroughly.

(b) The room should be fumigated with insecticide (smoke forming) and kept for 2 hours, or

If the walls have not been freshly white-washed, or 15 days after the fresh white-washing of walls, DDT (5% solution or 10% "dispersion) should be sprayed on the floor and on the walls upto a height of about 3 meters. Two liters of solution or dispersion will suffice for spraying an area of 100 square metres. The dunnage should also be similarly sprayed with DDT. The spraying should be repeated at intervals of six weeks.

Dunnage and top Cover: The term "dunnage" is applied to any material or structure placed between the ground and material or storage equipment with the following objectives:

(1) Providing a firm and stable base for stacking;

(2) Preventing moisture from the ground from passing up into the materials resulting in rot, corrosion and/or direct damage to stores;

(3) Preventing "white ants" and other insects from crawling from the ground into the stack on their gnawing rampage;

(4) Allowing circulation of air underneath the stack to get rid of accumulated dirt which may harbour harmful insects or other organisms.

Dunnage should be at least 45 cm high for outside stacks built on the ground and 30 cm high for stacks on pucca floors and may be of several types

(1) Pillar or pier type, made from cement concrete blocks, brick in cement, unserviceable drums filled with sand or dry earth to increase their bearing capacity. Stores are kept on platforms resting on the dunnage pillars. The platforms should be perforated or otherwise so made as to allow maximum possible ventilation from below. The use of trestles on pucca floors is satisfactory.

(2) Logs, ballies or sleepers suitably spaced out horizontally and crosses with thinner pieces of wood similarly spaced out on them. Pillar type of dunnage is always to be preferred as it allows maximum ventilation and facilitates cleaning beneath the stack. This type of dunnage can be satisfactorily rendered anti-termite as detailed below:

A metallic sheet (about 24 gauge) is fitted at or near the top of every pillar. The edges of the sheet project about 8 cm from the slides of the pillar and should be separated by 5-8 cm from the lower surface of the stack. This forms an efficient, termite barrier.

Temporary pillar 23cm x 23 cm may also be made from bricks 5 or 6 layers high without mortar. Such Dunnage may be rendered appreciably anti-termite by dipping the bricks of the middle 2 or 3 layers in 20:80 mixture of Creosote Oil and Used Engine Oil before the bricks are incorporated in Dunnage.

In cases where the Dunnage is made from timber or other susceptible materials it should he treated i.e. stores should be soaked for 6-12 hours in 50:50 mixture of Creosote Oil and used Engine oil/waste oil. Otherwise the Dunnage itself might be eaten away by termites.

Stacks should be suitably sheltered from rain. Leaky roofs of godowns should be promptly repaired and tarpaulin covers spread over. Outdoor stacks should not be torn.

Stores should be examined periodically so that deterioration, if any, may be detected promptly at the early stage and dealt with suitably. To facilitate this inspection, stacks should be small and away from one another and from the walls.

Older stocks must be issued out first to minimise deterioration in storage.

A good system of keeping away insects is to provide nets to doors and windows to prevent insects from entering from outside.

The most popular method of insect control is through the use of insecticides. A large variety of chemicals are today available in the market which can control insects. However, care has to be taken to ensure that they are relevant to the kind of insects one is seeking to destroy and secondly that the chemical used does not affect the materials stored. For example, it should not contaminate foodstuffs or produce stains on sensitive items. Thirdly, the operators applying or handling the chemicals should not be harmed. This would apply to pet animals and plants also.

These chemicals are used in various forms like gas, liquids, powder, and smoke or as repellants.

Termites: (White ants) these live in colonies and are of various types:

(i) Those who live in the soil. They build a mound of soft soil around them and the King and Queen may often be 1/2 to 2 metre below the surface. (The workers are sterile. The Queen can lay upto 10,000 eggs yearly).

(ii) Those who live in dry wood without any contact with the soil.

Termites are wingless and have a powerful biting and chewing type of jaws. They attack a vast range of materials - tlimber, bamboo, cotton, woolen or jute textiles, leather, paper, foodgrain, etc. They attack houses and wooden pillars and since they operate usually from inside, one may not even notice their presence. They can be detected sometimes by the earthen tunnels which they construct on the way to the Store or sometimes on the walls of the Store.

To preserve structural timber and other susceptible items, use suitable preservatives. (See under Timber and bamboo).

If the site of the building is termite infested, proper treatment is vital. An effective treatment is 50:50 Creosote/oil raked in liberally into the top 10 cms of layer on the ground. Waste engine oil is ideal and inexpensive. Anti-termite metal shields can be provided to foundation.

A good method to prevent termites is to have a 30 cms clearance between the ground and bottom of the rack and 15 cms clearance from walls.

Provide an anti-termite Dunnage and preferably, treat the Dunnage with creosote.

Rats: Apart from eating grains and other foodstuffs, they cause holes in bags leading to spillage while handling and transportation. They also contaminate foodstuffs by their excrement and also act as disease carriers.

Textiles, paper, office records and even timber are attacked by rats. They are usually active at night.

Methods of preventing rats are by using rat poisons, having rat traps, fumigation, rearing cats and by rat proofing the storehouse by ensuring that doors fit well, the floor is concrete not wood, that there are no crevices or holes in the walls, windows, etc., and keeping a constant watch over rat holes. A good poison bait is barium carbonate, zinc phosphate or oxide mixed in wheat flour and formed into pellets by kneading with water.

Marine Borers: The most destructive marine borer is Teredo or the Ship Worm which attacks any wood that touches sea water, boats, jetty piles, etc. In several instances Teredos have consumed the piling under very expensive docks and brought them down in as little as two or three months. Some teredos are microscopic in size; others are as large as large snakes, upto 30-35 cms in diameter and 5 meters long. With a rocking motion the head of this creature (which belongs to the snail family) tunnels through the hardest woods and has also been known to bore through concrete; these tunnels are unusually lined with a white calcareious deposit which helps to identify the pest.

Methods used lo combat these animals including sheathing of the timber with copper, zinc or Muntz metal sheet, or impregnation with preservatives such as creosote or arsenic or copper naphthenate. Tarring and painting of the timber gives some transitory protection.

6.9 FUNGUS & ROOT

Fungi and bacteria are micro-organisms which are invisible to the naked eye and are very low in the evolutionary scale in the slat kingdom and do not posses the green pigment (chlorophy) which: is commonly associated with the higher plants. They are so small in size that a special unit of measurement which is 1/1000 of a millimeter is used to express their size. They occur practically everywhere in the soils, in water and even in the air. It has been estimated that one small spoonful of fertile soil can contain over 2000 millions of these micro-organisms; in other words there are as many of these organisms in that small quantity of soil as there human beings in the whole world. They grow and multiply rapidly when favorable conditions exist, namely presence of acceptable food, materials, adequate moisture, suitable temperature (70° to 95^0F) and availability of oxygen. Their growth is phenomenal and their presence on materials is recognised by a mouldy or musty smell, dampness to the touch, discoloration of the material often accompanied by a velvety growth of fungus on the surface of the material and loss in its strength and weight. When such micro-biological damage occurs in textiles, cordage etc. the store is said to be affected by "Rot and mildew"; in timber it is known as "decay".

Preservation Procedures as a Separate subclause

In the 1994 revision of ISO 9001, preservation has been added as a separate subclause in clause 4.15. This requires the supplier to apply appropriate methods for the preservation and segregation of the product when it is under the supplier's control. While preservation is mentioned in the standard along with packaging, implying the application of preservation measures during packaging, this requirement also applies before and during earlier stages.

Once the material is received by the supplier, preservation during storage and processing should be ensured to prolong the life of product, by inhibiting the adverse effect of natural elements. The type of preservation measure will depend upon the nature of the product and its susceptibility to deterioration or degradation. In hardware it may imply the application of anti-corrosive coatings, in rubber parts the use of talc, and for food products certain chemical preservatives may be used to inhibit the deterioration process.

Segregation is another requirement of this subclause, Segregation in this context differs from the segregation of nonconforming products discussed in chapter 17. Here segregation is meant to prevent possible product mixing, exposure to adverse conditions, or cross-contamination. For somc industries, products can be identified only be their containers. Therefore special precautions need to be taken to segregate the products when they are not in their respective containers. Some of the materials for which proper segregation measures would be required are:

- Toxic materials;
- Explosive and flammable materials;
- Various chemicals in the drug industry;
- Materials for the production of processed food products.

Segregation is not limited to products. Containers and tools also need to be segregated in certain situations. For instance, small particles of other material left in containers or on tools may contaminate food or drink which may therefore violate health and safety regulations. In all situations where there is a risk of undesirable product mixing, suitable segregation measures should be adopted.

6.10 SUMMARY

Storage and preservation are important functions in stores management. Detailed instructions for stores personnel are required to achieve objectives of storage and preservation. These are consolidated in the stores manual. This manual has to be carefully prepared by stores management, circulated to all managers for their comments and acceptance and released with senior management approval. Training, discussions and demonstrations have to be arranged for smooth implementation of the manual.

Materials stored, by their very nature and due to weather conditions, are subject to different types of damages. Hence, all items stocked are studied by stores management from their preservation point of view and measures arranged for protection of materials from likely damages.

Stores hygiene has to be maintained and chemical coating, sprays or fumigation are arranged to keep storage area free from contamination from any source.

6.11 SELF ASSESSMENT QUESTIONS

(1) What is the role of stores manuals in stores management?

(2) List steps undertaken by firms to ensure smooth implementation of stores manuals by all employees.

(3) What factors are responsible to cause damage to the materials held in stores? How can such damage be minimised or avoided?

(4) Damage to materials can be avoided by proper segregation of materials in the stores. Explain.

7 Chapter

MATERIAL HANDLING

Objectives

After studying this chapter, you should be able to understand:

- Need for material handling.
- Material handling Procedures.
- Care to be exercised in maintaining equipment.
- Pallets, containers and other material handling equipment.

Structure:

7.1 NEED FOR MATERIAL HANDLING

Material handling has rightly assumed great importance of late. A scientific approach to the over all problem can reduce handling costs and time, damages and breakages, ensure timely flow of materials and cutdown overall processing time and idle time and so on. In India, it will be increasingly necessary to mechanise materials handling without which our productivity will be much lower and wastage greater.

A questionnaire is given below for preliminary analysis of materials handling problems. It is based on a questionnaire, issued a few years ago by the Technical Co-operation Mission of the United States Government in New Delhi.

(1) Are you moving materials an excessive distance?

(2) Are you handling items 2/3 times (or more often) when once should suffice?

(3) Do you have 10/20 men doing a job which one man could do with proper mechanical equipment?

(4) Do you have congestion of materials in storage and/or production areas?

(5) Do you have production delays because of lack of feed-in or take-away machines?

(6) Do you handle items individually, in place of batches?

(7) Do you use such aids as pallets, bins, skids to expedite handling and assist in materials control?

(8) Is your flow of product continuous and uniform or not so on account of bottle necks in handling of materials?

(9) Can you work indefinitely at a maximum production rate?

(10) Do you have too many persons hunting for stock items?

(11) Are your Central stores, Sub-stores, plant stores, finished good stores. store yards, and warehouses suitably located?

(12) Are the Stores so designed and constructed so as to permit maximum utilization of space and facilitate mechanical handling of materials in storage?

(13) Do items become lost often?

(14) Do you have excessive stock damage and waste?

(15) What materials handling equipment do you have? Is the equipment standardised?

(16) Do any workers lift excessive weight? beyond these limits?

Women	-	5O	Ibs.	or	25	kg.
Men	-	100	Ibs.	or	50	kg.

(17) What is the accident rate in materials handling?

Answers to these questions indicate need to review and improve your material handling system.

To begin with, it is desirable to make the following analyses to determine the most effective methods of materials handling.

(1) What items have to be moved and why? How frequently have they to be moved? It needs examination of stores items and raw materials, works-in-progress and stock of finished goods.

(2) Where to move the items? Process sheets, flow-diagrams and flow-chart analysis will give good indications.

(3) How to move the items? This will require analysis of operations and time and motion study. It will also need careful determination of the equipment to be used for the movements in the interests of overall efficiency. Equipment characteristics will have to be studied and the advantages and disadvantages of alternative handling equipment will have to be weighed carefully.

Material handling today has become highly specialised. It will be worth while to take advice of specialists in this field for plant layout, stores layout and for the handling problems of all materials including raw materials and stores, work-in-progress and finished goods.

Rules for Handling

Manufacturing companies deal with various types of materials. These could be raw materials and semiprocessed articles for further processing. purchased components and assemblies for integration. and other materials used in the manufacturing process. It is necessary to ensure that the quality of all these goods is not affected by improper handling. poor storage conditions. inadequate packaging and faulty delivery procedures.

Proper handling requires careful planning effective control and documented procedures from the time the materials enter the factory until the finished product reaches the customer and is put into use. When the customer has specified his or her needs in regard to packaging and delivery. these should be incorporated in quality plans and work instructions. Even if no such specifications are provided. the company should develop its own procedures and specifications to comply with this important requirement of the quality system.

Handling

Handling procedures have to be carefully formulated in order to prevent product damage or degradation of quality. The following criteria should be taken into consideration:

Weight and size of the article or material.

Availability of suitable features for attaching hooks or lifting devices.

The need for special containers for movement between workstations.

Avoidance of excessive vibration and sudden changes of temperature for certain types of materials.

Special precautions for handling fragile materials.

Prevention of stains scratches and chipping of paint during assembly and storage.

Ensuring that the product does not get mixed up with other products of untested or differing quality. It is important that product identification is not obliterated during handling and that it is easily visible for quick identification.

Personal cleanliness of workers handling sensitive materials like drugs and delicate items such as electrical and optical components.

Companies using hazardous materials should have comprehensive procedures for the protection of the personnel involved.

Regular maintenance of handling equipment.

CHECKLIST FOR HANDLING, STORAGE, PACKAGING, PRESERVATION AND DELIVERY ISO 9001, CLAUSE 4.15
Do the procedures for handling and storing input materials, work in progress and finished goods awaiting dispatch, ensure protection against damage or deterioration?
Are proper containers used to protect the product from environmental hazards and mechanical damage?
Are environmental conditions appropriate to the material being stored, in order to prevent degradation in storage?
Is there a system for segregating different types of materials to prevent product-mixing and cross-contamination, where such risks exist?
Do the procedures have instructions on materials with a restricted shelf-life?
Are there procedures for the preservation of material inhibiting the adverse effect of natural environments?
Are packaging and delivery requirements examined during contract review?
Is packaging and label marking adequate for the identification and segregation of products during storage?
Are required documents for installation, operation and maintenance included in the package of the finished goods?

7.2 TRAINING IN MATERIAL HANDLING

For obtaining the best service from any machine and to minimize damage to equipment, buildings and materials, the drivers and others concerned with the operation of any mechanical-handling facilities must be both efficient and careful. Therefore they should be adequately trained and instructed in their duties and in the need for safety precautions at all times. Equipment is expensive, and time taken to instruct operators properly will be well repaid in improved performance. In this connexion, it is worthy of note that instructional handbooks are often available, e.g. the *Operator's Safety Code* for industrial power trucks published by the Industrial Truck Manufacturers' Association.

Proper training is essential for anybody who uses any handling equipment, whether hand-operated or power driven.

First of all, the machine itself has to be considered. There are international standards for the stability of fork trucks and all reputable manufacturers abide by these standards or exceed them. Appropriate safety features are provided on the machine such as overhead guards, leg guards and load guards to protect the operator. In most instances the truck has two separate braking systems - electrical and mechanical. Nevertheless, these machines are potentially dangerous. Serious or fatal accidents can easily happen if the driver is not expert at his job.

It is Not Wise to be Casual about Training: Operators should not be taught the business simply by learning how to do it from a workmate on the same job. A proper training instructor should be available. This person should of course have practical experience and be able to operate the truck himself. But also he should have training skills and theoretical as well as practical knowledge.

Before training, potential operators should be selected by a preliminary test. What is required is manual skill. This cannot be assessed by an interview, however long, and can only be judged by a practical test. It takes less than an hour to give someone elementary instruction and demonstration in how to use the controls and how to transport an empty pallet. Then he can be given a ten-minute test on his own to see how much he has learned. From the number of errors he makes, his suitability can be determined. Unless his performance is above average, It is best not to choose him for further training.

When suitable people have been thus selected, they should have a carefully designed training course covering at least these main points:

(i) Knowledge of safe loads and operating methods.

(ii) Manual dexterity and co-ordination.

(iii) Readiness to recognize and correct mistakes.

(iv) Remembering the proper sequence for every operation.

(v) Ability to judge the height and position of forks and the relation between the steering lock and the movement of the other parts of the machine, particularly the forks, the top, and the back end.

(vi) Accuracy, especially in picking up a load squarely.

(vii) Understanding the theory of handling the truck and its safe operating limits.

At the conclusion of this training course, he should have a practical and a theoretical test. If successful, it is a good idea to give him a certificate showing the date of test and what kind of trucks he is qualified to operate. In the course of time it may be desirable for qualified operators to be tested again at intervals of say three or four years.

On a wider scale, these improvements in economy and efficiency could evidently be magnified if standardization could be arranged on a national or even an international basis, and efforts are currently being made to achieve this end. There has already been progress in regularizing to some extent the sizes of bales of raw materials, oil drums, railway containers, etc., and particular attention is now being paid to unit loads of all kinds, especially palletized loads.

Care of MHE

To avoid accidents, **care must be exercised** in the use and treatment of lifting machines and gear of all kinds and details of statutory requirements. The following points give some general indication of the precautions necessary:

(i) Every lifting machine should be marked with an individual identification number and the safe working load. Machines should be tested before being put into service, and at regular intervals thereafter.

(ii) Cranes with movable jibs must be provided with an automatic load-radius indicator clearly visible to the driver and, in some cases, have to be fitted with warning bells which ring when the load is exceeded.

(iii) where the use of a goods lift is prohibited for carrying persons, there must be a notice on the lift to that effect.

(iv) Controls, hand wheels, etc., on lifting equipment are to be provided with name plates indicating their function.

(v) Chain and rope slings, hooks, shackles, etc., must be stamped or labelled with an identification number and the safe working load. All are required to be inspected and tested at specified intervals and, for some tackle, regular annealing is essential. Items which fail on test are to be scrapped.

(vi) Registers of all lifting tackle should be kept and entered up with particulars of inspections and tests.

(vii) When not in use, portable and transportable lifting appliances should be kept in a weatherproof store under the control of an appropriate storekeeper. Suitable facilities are required for hanging all items of tackle and the location for each article should labelled. Issues for use must be made only by the storekeeper.

Safety Precautions

In common with all other industrial operations, safety is a very important matter in storekeeping. This is obvious for even the simplest manual tasks - there is a right way and a wrong way of lifting a heavy weight if strain is to be avoided. Where machines of any kind are employed, the safety factor becomes more important still because the risks of personal injury are greater. There are of course official regulations on the subject which must be met, and the use of British or International Standards will ensure that the stores equipment itself is fit for the job and designed with safety in mind. The modem approach is to apply the science of ergonomics - that is to design the general working environment and the machinery so that the operators may work in the safest and most efficient way. Personal protective equipment such as gloves, goggles, breathing masks, safety helmets, special boots, etc., should be used where appropriate.

Safety of Materials Handling Equipment

Some general safety rules in regard to use of mechanised material handling equipment are as follows:

(i) When a driver leaves the vehicle the hand brakes should be applied. Equipment must not be left unattended while the motor is running.

(ii) Vehicles should not be reversed until the operator has checked to see if the way is clear. Another person must act as a guide if this is not possible.

(iii) The vehicle must be switched off when refueling or lubricating.

(iv) Loads when being shifted must be securely fastened. A red flag must be used on any load that extends beyond the sides, front or rear of a vehicle.

(v) When a truck is being loaded or unloaded by a crane all occupants must dismount from the truck and stand clear.

Some general rules regarding specific equipment are given below:

(i) Cranes:

(a) Truck cranes must be properly blocked and be on firm footing before lifting a heavy load with a low boom. Employees must stand clear of the crane's swing and keep out from under suspended loads.

(b) Riding on crane blocks or crane loads should be strictly prohibited.

(c) Operators should not leave the crane cabs without disengaging the clutch and applying all safety locks. Cranes with long booms must be secured against high winds.

(d) Crane booms and booms on other motorized equipment must not be operated closer than ten feet from live high voltage overhead electrical wires.

(ii) Forklift Trucks:

(a) Periodic check of brakes. steering apparatus, horn, lift mechanism, controls, guards and tyres are necessary.

(b) Pushing a lift truck in order to start it should be prohibited.

(c) Trucks must be parked in such a way that they do not interfere with the passage of other vehicles or persons. Never park within six feet of rail wagons.

(d) The driver's hands should not be wet or greasy.

(e) Driving over objects lying on the floor or roadway should be avoided. Driving over scrap wood, piping or other such materials will cause damage to the truck and may topple the load off the forks.

(f) Drivers should travel at a safe speed, slowing down when making turns.

(g) Watch for persons who may rush out in front of the truck, and for others approaching vehicles.

(h) When driving without a load, keep forks about six inch above ground.

(i) Avoid sudden stops and starts. This may cause skidding or toppling of the load.

(j) Do not overload the truck beyond the rated capacity.

(k) Never carry a load so high that the front cannot be seen. If necessary, operate the truck in reverse.

(l) Carrying loose materials on forks should be avoided. Use pallets wherever possible.

(m) Never allow anyone to stand under elevated loads.

(n) The load should be picked up under the centre of its weight to avoid tipping the truck over or shifting the load.

(o) The load should be tilted against the backrest before moving the truck.

(p) Make sure to return the tilt to vertical before lowering or picking up the load.

(q) Lower the load slowly. A sudden stop will cause the machine to tilt forward, tipping it over.

(r) Warn other employees to stand clear when stacking or removing materials.

7.3 PALLTEISATION AND CONTAINERISATION

Container specitications:

Length = 1/3 or 1/4 Trailer Length

Width = Trailer width

Two Access Sides

Lightweight

Collapsible for Backhaul

Weatherproof

Secure

For example, open sided, roofless trucks and trailer, widely use in Japan and Germany, enable shippers to take advantage of the power of large shipping containers by opening access to loads from all the vehicle's sides Exhibit 7.1 spells out some of the critical "land container" specifications for the new large containers, which will increase the percentage of time the trucks and trailers will spend in transit, thus improving their overall utilization, lowering the size of the truck fleet required, and speeding products to market. The new container sizes will be fractious of the over all trailer length and will be the same width as the trailer. For maximum flexibility, the new containers will have access doors on both side.

Today's trailer and truck cargo bodies are often made of aluminum to minimize their weight. (Excess weight adds fuel cost and cuts load capacity new containers must also minimize weight.) Further to make back-hauling of containers most practical, they must be easily collapsible. The new enclosed containers will also protect contents from the weather and will be designed to provide protection against theft while in transit. The open trailers, Custom manufactured for handling new "land container" will have built-in hydraulic or electric clamp for locking the containers on the trailer and highly efficient beds of conveyance balls that will make pushing containers on to and off of the trailer an easy one man task. The ball system permits loading and unloading from the sides of the vehicle as easily as from the rear. Dividers between containers, on the floor of the trailer, will help guide them effortless into position.

EXHIBIT 7.1: TRAILER SPECIFICATION

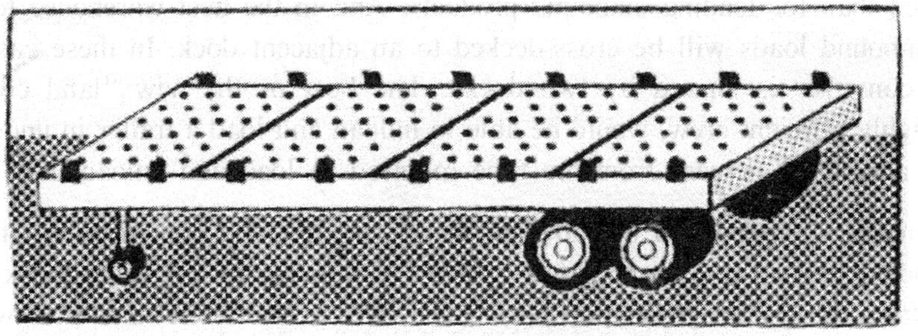

Side Loading/Back Loading
Easy Load ball Conveyor Trailer Bed
Hydraulic Container Clamps

The advantages of new "land containers" and its trucks and trailers are enhanced when teamed with new corresponding docks designed to accommodate them.

Exhibit 7.2 is an example of one such dock design. In this exhibit, ball conveyors in the docks, on each side of the trailers, enable a four container trailer to be unloaded and loaded in a few minutes. One-man conveyance design will make it easy to push each container off of or on to the trailer. These docks are designed to facilitate either inbound or outbound loads.

EXHIBIT 7.2: CONTAINER DOCK SPECIFICATIONS

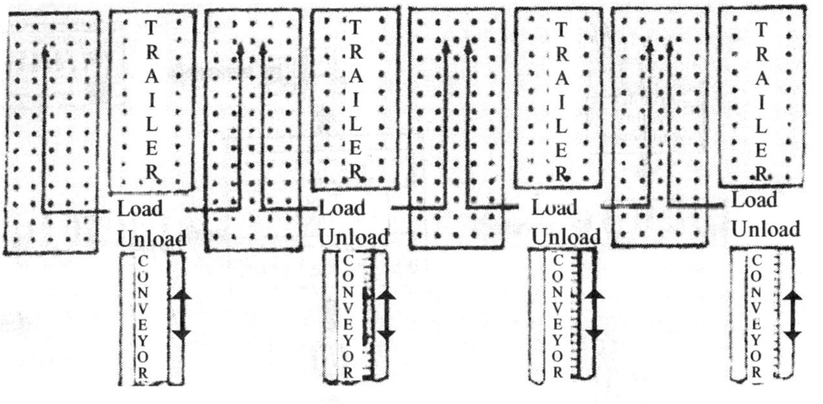

Easy Move Ball-Bed Container Staging Conveyors
Two-Way Inbound - Outbound Conveyors
Cross-Cock Facilitation

Infact, the most efficient use of a facility will be purposeful turn around of inbound vehicles with out bound loads. For this reason the design includes conveyance facilities on both sides of the trailers. In this example, each dock, on average, has only one and one-half conveyors. In fact, in many factory and warehouse facilities, two per dock would be necessary. In the factory, inbound materials and components are much denser than outbound product, so less unloading conveyor space is required than for loading outbound products. And in the best warehouse facilities, a high percentage of inbound loads will be cross-decked to an adjacent dock. In these cases the inbound and outbound conveyor is shared by two docks. The best of the new "land container" docks manned by a highly efficient crew, would be able to unload and load a trailer in under five minutes, a reduction of almost 90 percent from the time required to load and unload unit load packages.

Small containers, loaded and unloaded into and out of "land containers" at the back of the trailer, are handled by one or two conveyor systems that move receipts into stock and shipments from stock or from the end of production lines. (The most cost-effective facilities will utilize two-way conveyors to minimize capital requirements.) The distance from conveyor end into the most remote corner of the new "land container" is a mere fraction of the distance from the conveyor to the front end of a closed trailer. This reduces the time spent in loading and unloading to approximately the same fraction.

The savings from "land containers" and their correspondingly designed trailers and dock facilities extend out into the network of supplier and customer factories and through the distribution channels. As Exhibi 7.3 indicates, the large semi truck and trailer rig that leaves the product factory with three "land containers" would be used when its deliveries and backhauls are not short, local trips. However, it delivers its three containers to a regional cross-dock facility, where its containers are transferred almost directly to much smaller trucks for short delivery hauls.

EXHIBIT 7.3 : COTAINER DISTRIBCTION NETWORKS.

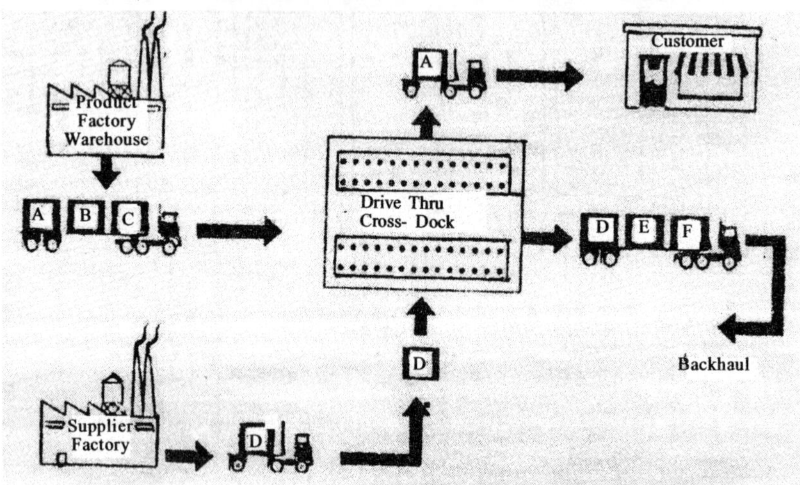

7.4 TYPES OF MATERIAL HANDLING EQUIPMENT

Equipment Eight general types of equipment are commonly used in storing materials:

(1) Pallets and skids

(2) Open and closed shelving

(3) Cabinets (with or without counters)

(4) Bins

(5) Stacking boxes

(6) Special storage racks

(7) Gravity feed racks

(8) Outdoor platforms and racks

Figures 7.1 and 7.2 illustrate several storage installations using some of the common types of storage and materials handling equipment.

(For more details refer chapter-3 Materials Handling Equipment)

Fig. 7.1: A Two-level Storeroom Using a Combination of Metal Shelving, Bins, and Cabinets. Materials Handling Equipment Shown Consists of Roller Conveyors Joined by a Belt Conveyor.' (Courtesy of Lyon Metal Products Inc.)

Most industrial storerooms used to be equipped with wooden shelving and storage facilities. Wooden facilities still offer several advantages. Wood is softer than metal and provides safer storage for delicate items which might be dropped or scuffed in the bin. Wooden facilities can also be built to special configurations and can generally be installed quickly and inexpensively.

Automated Warehousing: For some firms, the automated warehouse is now a reality. A combination of the random-access storage concept, highly sophisticated storage/retrieval machines, and a computerized control system has produced today's automated storage/retrieval system (AS/RS).

Fig. 7.2: Wooden Pallets Being Used to Provide Efficient Storage for Heavy, Unwieldy Industrial Valves. The Materials-Handling Equipment is a Gasoline-Powered Fork-Lift Type of Stacking Truck. (Courtesy of the Clark Equipment Company.)

The storage facility frequently is a 10-25 meter high-rise structure, constructed of open steel columns. Typically it is configured into storage, cubicles of different sizes, and utilizes various types of installation. (see figure 7.3)

Fig. 7.3: Automated Warehouse Installations, Using Computer-Operated, Captive-Rail Storage/Retrieval Machines. (a) Palletized Installation. (Note the Storage Operation Progress.) The Materials-Handling Vehicles in the Foreground are Computer-Controlled "Robocarrier" Vehicles. They are Precision Battery-Powered Vehicles that "Track" a Network of Guide Path Wires Embedded in the Floor. (Courtesy of Eaton-Ken way.) (b) Containerized Installation. (Note the Container Rretrieval Operation in Progress.) (Courtesy of the Storage Technology Corporation.)

When men and machines are in motion between times when they are actually performing work, unnecessary cost is being added to the process. In such cases, stores operations are rich in opportunities for improvements. For example, empty and partially loaded trucks, tractors and trailers are far too often in motion less than full time. Many companies and industries have made the mistake of designing and using specialized vehicles and containers that are extremely cost-effective in out bound trips but always return empty.

Exhibit 7.4 depicts examples of two-way transport in the warehouse. In the forklift example, any time a trip is made into the warehouse to retrieve an item for issue, a receipt transaction requiring stocking in the same area is carried into the storeroom and stocked. Next, the forklift travels to the nearby item to be issued, retrieves it, and delivers it into the packing and shipping process. Although this example portrays forklift trucks, the objective of making all transport two-way loads is equally applicable to fully and semi-automated storage and retrieval machines and storekeepers pushing carts. In the bi-directional conveyance example docks are multipurpose, used for both shipping and receiving. Conveyors into and out of the stockroom support the dual function.

EXHHIBIT 7.4: TWO- WAY TRANSPORT

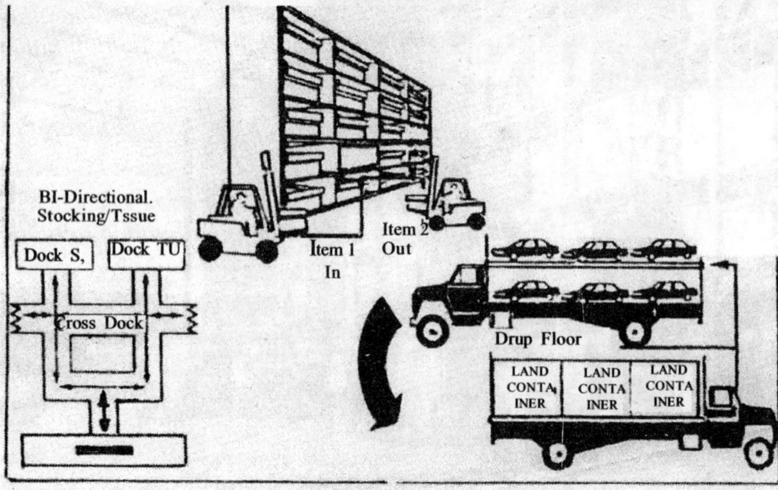

docks and conveyors connecting all docks thereby supporting cross-dock transfer of receipt to outbound truck In the third example, trailers designed to transport automobiles from factory to customer would best be intermodal. And, by virtue of a hydrautic lift upper deck that can be lowered, they can accept new standard" land containers" for the backhaul. Although such a design may be less efficient for out bound loads than existing rigs, its overall utilization will be much higher.

In warehouses, people, lift trucks, high-rise retrieval equipment and conveyors travel much farther than necessary and often make virtually return trip empty. One of the reasons that automation has seldom proved more cost-effective than manual alternatives is the inclination of many stores and warehouse designers to make lavish use of equipment without making more than minimal effort to ensure that automation designs minimize required investment by avoiding wasted travel time and motion, Even though automated equipment eliminated labour cost, it entails higher depreciation. Therefore, reducing the amount of required wasted time and motion of automated equipment is every bit as important as minimizing wasted labour. Further, a far greater percentage of high-cost stores equipment sits idle more than it works. Tractors, trailers and entire stores sit idle more than one-half of the 68 hour week. Keeping all stores equipment and facilities in virtually perpetual motion, fully loaded, is one of the exciting potentials for lowering stores costs and required investment.

Time and Motion Study of man power and equipment, using video recoding to capture and analyse operations, is a vital ingredient of stores design methodology. Understanding nonproductive time is the cornerstone of inventing ways to minimise waste. In the stores, the techniques that yield high levels of productivity include separate substores for different package sizes and activity frequency zones within those facilities.

7.5 SUMMARY

A scientific approach to material handling is required to reduce costs, handling time, damages, breakages and delays.

To achieve objectives of material handling store management needs to formulate procedures and rules of material handling for use by stores personnel.

For efficient and incident free material handling, employees have to be provided with adequate training at the start and at regular intervals thereafter. Storeskeeper has to assign required time and resources to maintain material handling equipment with due care.

In addition to traditional bins, shelves, racks, fork lifts, stores management must review new containers, palletized equipment and automated integrated material handling systems and implement one that suits their organisational needs.

Time and motion study is very effective in reducing material handling turn around time and ensuring full utilisation of both stores labour and equipment.

7.6 SELF ASSESSMENT QUESTIONS

(1) In what manner does efficient material management benefit an organisation?

(2) Enumerate steps for training material handling personnel.

(3) What are the requirements for handling, storing and packing materials as issued by the international organisation for standards under ISO 9000?

(4) Describe the role of automation in material handling systems.

8 Chapter

ISSUE OF MATERIALS FROM STORES

Objectives

After studying this chapter, you should be able to understand:

- Manual and automated material picking systems.
- Various steps in issue of materials.
- Methods adopted to issue tools, capital items, materials for processing by subcontractors.

Structure:

8.1 ISSUE OF MATERIAL FROM STORE

The service level by the stores is always under a scanner having high expectancy of efficiency by the consuming departments.

The service given by the stores department to other departments becomes effective at the point where a storekeeper makes issues of goods continuously and users will naturally judge the efficiency of the stores organization by the standard of service provided to them.

8.2 AUTHORIZATION OF ISSUES

Stores in stock represent money, and should not be misappropriated, wasted or improperly used. For this reason, issues cannot be made indiscriminately and, before goods can be withdrawn from a store house, there must be some authority for the transaction. This may be in the form of a signed document, a verbal instruction or a routine arrangement. The normal method is to use an issue note signed in the appropriate box by an authorized person. Storekeepers should have full details of the names, designations and specimen signatures of all persons empowered to approve issue notes. In some circumstances it is desirable to restrict the authority of different levels of management within certain financial limits; for example foremen may be permitted to sign for goods upto a value of ₹ 1000, shop superintendents upto ₹ 10,000, the signature of the works manager being required above that figure. In a similar way, authority may be restricted for certain types of materials to officers in specific departments, e.g., only the chief electrical engineer or the foreman electrician being in a position to demand cable or electrical fittings, and the garage foreman being the sole authority for motor vehicle spares.

8.3 ISSUE OF MATERIAL FROM STORES

Issue of materials from stores to the production, maintenance and other departments:

(A) Materials should be issued by the Store Keeper on receipt of properly authorised document usually called a Material Requisition Note.

MATERIAL REQUISITION NOTE

Production Order No. .... **Note Sr. No.** ....

Job No. :.. **Date** ....

Description	Code No.	Unit	Quantity Issued	Cost		Balance after entry in bin Card
				Rate ₹	Amount ₹	

Authorised by:	Issued by:	Received by:	Bin Card No.	Stores Ledger No.	Cost Office Ref. Priced by:

(B) This form is an authorisation to the Store Keeper to issue the materials and it is usually signed by Foreman. On issue of the materials, the Store Keeper has to enter in the *Issue'* column of the Bin Card. It is priced by the Cost Accounting Department according to one of the agreed methods for pricing of issues and posted in the *Issue'* column of the Stores Ledger account by debiting the concerned job, process or overhead control account as per the particulars furnished in the Stores Requisition Note; Number of copies prepared will be dependent on the requirement of the organization. But minimum 4 copies are required as follows:

(1) Stores Department;

(2) Cost Accounting Department;

(3) Material Control Department; and

(4) Office Copy retained by the consuming department.

Normally, only one item of material is requisitioned in one form. This facilitates easy issue of materials and also the postings where cost accounts are mechanised.

(C) For excess materials required in a particular job or process than the quantity mentioned in the production order or bill of material, they are issued by the Store Keeper under special authorisation by the Manager.

Materials Returned From Production, Maintenance and Other Departments to Stores Department

(A) Excess materials from production, maintenance and other departments are returned to Stores Department together with a Material Return Note. This note is an authorisation to return the excess materials to the Store Keeper.

MATERIAL RETURN NOTE

Production Order No. **Mrn No. :**

Job No. **Date**

Department :

ORIGINAL M.R. NO.

Description	Code No.	Unit	Quantity Returned	Cost		Balance after entry in Bin Card
				Rate ₹	Amount ₹	

Authorised by:	Returned by:	Received by:	Bin Card No.	Stores Ledger No.	Cost Office: Priced by:

(B) The form is also similar to the Stores Requisition Note. The quantity returned is to be entered in the 'Receipt' column of Bin Card preferably with red ink as to be distinct from the receipt of new material. The value also may be entered in Red Ink in the Stores Ledger. Then the information regarding the materials returned may be obtained easily for the purpose of managerial information.

(C) In the Material Return Note, original Material Requisition No. under which the material was drawn is to be given and this facilitates the credit to be given to the same job/process No. at the rate at which it was originally debited.

(D) Different colours for the form may be used for returning the scrap and spoiled materials or this may be termed as Scrap Return Note.

Transfer of Materials From One Job to Another Job

The transfer of material from one job to another should be strictly prohibited unless the procedure is adequately recorded on the Material Transfer Note. This should indicate all necessary data for debiting and crediting the concerned jobs or processes affected. One copy of this note should be sent to Cost Accounting Department for debiting and crediting the jobs and processes involved. No entry is required in Bin Card and Stores Ledger.

MATERIAL TRANSFER NOTE

Mtn N.	**Date :**
From:	**To:**
Department :	**Department :**
Job/Process No. :	**Job/Process No. :**
Order No. :	**Order No. :**

Description	Code No.	Unit	Quantity Returned	Cost		Balance after entry in Bin Card
				Rate ₹ ₹	Amount	

8.4 ORDER PICKING

Order Picking Systems (Advanced Authorized System): One of the most important measures of the quality of an order picking system is how much work is required or better yet how much work can be avoided by using superior systems output and input features. When ideal electronic data interchange systems are in place, most of the initial data required to produce order picking (or schedule filling) documents can be provided by the **"black-box"**. For example, shipment schedule dates and quantities should come from the customer dealer electronic order (schedule) entry system, and such information as customer name and address, and item price, weight and cubic volume should come from master file data.

Store systems must support the new, improved store order filling operations with products that meet operational needs, in order to achieve the best results. For example, system outputs should not temporarily need to be manually filed, awaiting action, only to be retrieved when a storekeeper is ready for them. Such avoidable manual review of order picking documents or computer screens and human analysis and decision making is wasteful, because it should be performed by the computer system. The above criteria lead to the selection of the following basic system performance specification.

(1) Pick documentation should be output to the store, **just-in-time**, when an order picker or order picking team is ready for another batch. The output sequence of picking batches should be computercontrolled.

(2) Systems should be able to output both wave picking batches (for picking several orders simultaneously) and single orders. Batch picking should be the norm, and individual order picking the exception. Individual order picking is usually used to respond rapidly to

emergency orders or to prepare pick-up orders brought to the store by the person who will take them to the customer.

(3) Picking documentation should be geared to outputting the next batch required, just-in-time, in anyone of several order picking zones when a storekeeper completes picking a prior batch. The store management objective is to have multiple individuals or teams simultaneously working on the customer order batch, in several store zones.

(4) Picking documents should be computer-sequenced by stock locations with various store zones, thus minimising the storekeeper's order-picking travel distance. This requirement is as applicable to highly automated storage and retrieval systems as to manual order picking.

(5) Picking documentation should never be issued for order items that are out of stock, according to the system inventory balance. Physical stock checks used to verify availability prior to picking are not only unnecessary but also costly. Thus, if frequency of out-of-stock conditions is expected to persist well into the future, the system should be designed to dispose off order line items automatically either for back order or for cancellation, with notification to the customer to place a new order for shipment on the date of the next scheduled availability.

(6) Surprise shortages due to inaccurate computer inventory balances will perhaps never be completely eliminated. Order-picking systems should therefore include an exception transaction to identity order items that are out of stock, regardless of what the system inventory balance shows. The disposition of the shortage (back order, cancel or even hold the entire order until shortages are cleared) should be automatic.

(7) Every item picked for every customer order must flow smoothly, without delay, from order picking, to order sorting, to order packing, to truck staging (or directly on to the truck) and through the customer receiving process. Accordingly, the order document should (See Exhibit 8.1 for an illustration of such a document's contents) travel through the entire process with the picked items.

EXHIBIT 8.1: ORDER PICKING IDENTIFIER

PICK IDENTIFICATION				
Item No.	Order No.	Customer No. & Name	I Sub-plant	I Dock
Stock Location	Quantity,	Staging Location	Item Description	
Single Item Order				

(8) Bar coding the identification document, Exhibit 8.1, is essential to eliminate ensuing key entry if reporting progress of the order item through the order-picking and shipping process is an important business need. Further, when storekeepers take a hand carried bar code scanner on trips around their zones, they can use it to read the identification document either to answer inquiries or to input transaction progress or status.

(9) The computer should use master file data such as item weight and cubic volume data to calculate shipment weight and volume. For truckload shipments, the master file data should be used to preplan full truckload's content's.

(10) Identification documents, Exhibit 8.1, should contain data for controlling shipment staging locations, floor space and cubic volumes. Those data are used to route orders to specific truckload staging areas (or conveyors) or directly to the preplanned truck dock for Immediate loading. Computer power should be used to minimize warehouse space required, maximize truck capacity utilization and minimize travel time and distance between store, staging and loading docks.

(11) The system should accommodate electronic kanban, converting electronic kanban receipt transactions into order-picking kanbans. The kanbans should include some receiving location data such as warehouse/store receiving and storage zones.

(12) Orders for single items must not require the store to sort the single item orders by order number, following order picking or to merge them with other items on the order, because there are no other items. Exhibit 8.1, should have a flag that can be used to route single items directly from order picking to packing or shipping.

(13) Multiple-item orders often foster a desire to check systematically and report the completion of each step in the picking, packing and staging (truck loading) process. Doing so ensures that all items on every order have been merged, packed and staged or loaded and that none have been lost or delayed. The best managed stores would consider the progress reporting an unnecessary, wasteful step. Indeed, they would use a single completion transaction transmittal for each lot of orders for which picking and packing are completed to update the status of every order in a lot.

Many order-picking systems are designed to accommodate big delays between the time picking documents are computer generated and the time the orders are actually picked. This was necessary in the past, because systems operated on daily batches and released all order-filling documentation for one day's orders at the same time. Modem systems can process several smaller batches several times a day and can even process individual orders one at a time. Today it is no longer necessary to process daily batches. Store systems should generate smaller order-picking batches immediately prior to when the storekeepers are ready to begin picking the next batch. This will dramatically slash the time between a batch release and picking completion.

Order Picking Systems (Manual)

The process of choosing the right materials from the storage bins in accordance with the indent is called order picking. This also involves making necessary entries in the bin cards. It has to be done speedily and accurately because a lot of productive time of operators can be wasted' if they have to wait unduly to obtain the materials indented.

A significant factor in efficient order picking is the proper layout of the stores, with sufficient aisle spaces, and most important, appropriate and sufficient space for collecting the goods for final issue from the stores and collection by production personnel.

For a large store it is always better to have specially trained pickers for specific departments. They are usually familiar with the materials and will pick the right item.

In a small store, there must be one or two persons who, it should be ensured, are fully trained and arc thoroughly familiar with all the items in stock.

A simple procedure that may be followed is that:

(a) The indent is received by the stores clerk who looks up the stock card and ensures availability of the material. If the indent is otherwise correct, the issue is authorised and the location code entered against the item.

(b) The entry is made in the stock card.

(c) Indents are numbered serially and filed datewise.

(d) The clerk gives the indent to the order picker who takes the materials from the bins and simultaneously enters each bin card.

(e) The materials are handed over to the dispatch clerk who counts them and issues them to the indentor's representative, taking the latter's signature.

Fast moving items should preferably be placed nearest to the dispatching area. And should also be placed at the most convenient heights. The medium moving ones are arranged behind them, and the slow moving last of all. It is not always required to arrange all the items in terms of code numbers.

Mechanical aids for order picking are important for improved speed. Mobile trolleys are the most popular.

Quite often, materials have to be weighed or measured from a bulk storage. Some may be liquids which require particular care in decanting or filling into drums or carbuoys. Special equipment or devices for cutting sawing weighing or measuring will be required. These will obviously vary from material to material.

In some cases, it might be necessary to cut or slice material as per indentor's requirements. Examples are 20 metres of cloth from a big roll, or steel bars cut to small lengths. Special facilities are required for these.

The process of issue of stores consists of a very large number of distinct elements. These should all be integrated into one interlocking efficient system.

8.5 PROCEDURES FOR ISSUE

The procedure for issue of materials from the store will vary with the type of the material consumed. Some of the important types are discussed below:

(i) Small Tools: Tools may be hand tools like hammers screwdrivers, pliers, and wrenches or tools used in machines such as dies, drills, milling cutters or portable electric or pneumatic tools.

Some organisations have a policy of keeping a tight control over the issue of tools. Where this is done. production floor operators who know only too well that the absence of the right tool at the critical time can seriously hamper production have a tendency to hoard their own private reserve stock

For optimum utilisation of productive time some organisations have open access Stores for small tools where the operator can pick up what he wants by merely signing a slip for it. This can lead to wastage, because the operator would tend to obtain the tools on the slightest pretext. Secondly, this may provide an opportunity for pilferage.

Many store are having a tool room which is efficient is adequately stocked and is able to effect issues without delay. One method of control usually observed is to recover the old tool before the issue of a new one. Some organisations maintain detailed tool performance records. The importance of such a system is purely relative and depends upon the company and the nature of its production.

(ii) Special Tools: These are jigs and fixtures used in production. Jigs are tools which hold materials and guide the operator so that materials will be formed, cut or machined to the correct dimensions. Fixtures are pieces of equipment specially designed for holding materials or parts which are undergoing machining or other processes and are usually designed to fit particular machine tools. Jigs are associated with specific drawings job.

The number of tools of each kind to be stocked has a direct relationship between the cost of the tools and the demand for it. Many large companies who have a high demand for tools may have their own specialised tool room.

Where the requirement is for a single job the tool is issued and then returned to the store after use. The system followed can be simple like the issue of a file from a filing cabinet or a book from a library. A small card is placed in the bin from where the tool is removed showing the name of the person' to whom it is issued. The card can also be placed in a specific tray or drawer.

Where special tools, jigs and fixtures are custom manufactured. it may happen that the tools will become the property of the client. In such cases they have to be separately retained and issued only against a special request. The usual procedure is to have a customer code inscribed on the tools and keep all the tools in one place along with a list

(iii) Raw Material: In a manufacturing unit indents for materials are raised by the production control department and sent to the Store in advance so that materials can be delivered on time to commence production operations. Deliveries can take place on the shop floor by Stores personnel or can be collected from the Store by production floor operators.

(iv) Components for Assembly: In mass production units like a scooter factory there is a complete list of components for one unit of production. If 80 sets are required, instead of wasting time on writing details for these items. one indent is made for 80 sets. This can be a daily issue over a standing indent.

(v) General Stores: Items like cotton waste, kerosene, oil, etc., are issued every day to various departments in small quantities and as such the posting of the related requisitions may involve a good deal of time. There are three ways by which the posting work can be reduced.

(a) A daily or weekly quota may be fixed for each department and free issue within the limited quota may be made. The indents for the quantity issued may be authorized by head of the stores or some other competent person. (The fixing of quota, controls consumption).

(b) Respective departments may be asked to draw their requirements once a week instead of once a day.

(c) Print a group indent und a master indent of the items involved. The various departments will draw their daily requirements only on the group indent. At the end of the day. the total quantity on the various group indents will be added and transferred to the master indent.

The above method of posting from the master indent can be done even once a week if there are no other difficulties.

8.6 ISSUE TO SUBCONTRACTORS

Many items like finished goods, jigs, tools patterns (like a mould or a design pattern in textiles) may have to be sent to subcontractors for further processing. For example, an item might have to be chromium plated though a subcontractor after it has been manufactured or a casting might be required to be machined by outside machineshop.

Such issues have to be arranged with care. Firstly, a duly authorised indent is necessary and secondly, the issues should be made only to an authorised representative of the subcontractor. Proper accounts of all such issues should be kept contractor-wise, showing full details of items issued and dates of issue and of return.

Need for Subcontractors

Subcontracting is the work of obtaining the prime manufacturer's requirements, mostly of fabricating parts and components, from outside sources in order to manufacture a certain product in the prime manufacturer's plant. Subcontracting is being practiced to a much greater degree nowadays compared to the past, mainly for the reason that it effects cost reduction. A large firm may like to concentrate on its efforts on producing major items and leave several minor ones to small manufacturers whose overheads are likely to be low and who will, thus, be able to supply the material at competitive rates.

In any engineering industry, subcontracting is a common feature. A large number of components are generally off-loaded to smaller manufacturers. For an engineering industry these items normally include castings, forgings, machined and fabricated components made out of steel, non-ferrous metals, rubber, etc. Since each of these forms a separate type of industry, the small-scale sector usually has a number of people specializing in one or two of these categories of business. These small units, in turn, rely on the big companies for their subcontracting work.

Vendor Development

The various steps involved in vendor development can be summarised as follows:

(a) Identification of suitable vendors, considering their capacity, quality and financial standing.

(b) Development of vendors to suit the nature of work to be done at the right delivery, price and quality.

(c) Optimisation of the number of vendors, based on the volume of work.

(d) Maintenance of continuous business relationships with vendors.

(e) Appraisal of vendor performance with regard to quality, quantity, price and delivery.

(f) Deletion of bad vendors and addition of new vendors.

The type of component, required may be a simple turned part, or a complicated sintered component, or a sophisticated fabricated assembly. The buyer, therefore, must be very careful in selecting the supplier. He has to ensure that the supplier is capable of working as per the specific drawings supplied. The supplier may also be required to work to close tolerances for machining required. In some instances, this may involve only part machining, because it may be sometimes more economical for the buyer to let a subcontractor do only part of the machining on a component. This, however, greatly depends on the buyer having the necessary equipments of a CNC machine, for the remaining machining which will be required to be done.

The subcontractor may be expected to work from issued material and also existing tooling. Or else, the raw material, and the tooling are to be supplied by the subcontractor.

Records

Records of all raw materials sent to the subcontractor and obtained back from him are important factor in subcontracting.

Another important feature of subcontract work is that the subcontract buyer is responsible, prior to his company's annual or six-monthly stock-taking, to obtain from his subcontractor stock figures of the material that is held at a given date. This should consist of finished parts that may be awaiting dispatch also work-in-progress and raw materials including castings, etc. This can be obtained by writing a letter to the buyer requesting for this information. Such a letter should be accompanied with prepared stock-taking forms with the necessary headings, giving, part number or size description and quantity. The buyer should indicate in his letter the date by which the supplier should furnish the required information.

On receiving back the forms from his suppliers the buyer should check from his records the stock quantities supplied by the subcontractors against outstanding balances on his records. On doing the needful the buyer should pass on the forms to his accounts department.

Tools

It is often advantageous to supply the subcontractor with tools, for it could be that due to a bottleneck in the buyer's plant. the production of a component was subcontracted only as a temporary measure and that at a later stage it could be produced at the buyer's plant itself. Provision of tools to the subcontractor would avoid unnecessary duplication of tools thus reducing costs. It will also allow the subcontractor to commence production at once without wasting time on procuring necessary tools and equipment.

Where special tools are involved, it is usually taken into account when quotations are received, which will cover a component price and a part of tooling cost. Once the buyer has agreed to pay the cost of the tools, the tools are held by the sub contractor for the sole purpose of producing the components required by the buyer. The supplier is therefore, responsible for maintaining the tools in good condition.

8.7 LOAN OF MATERIAL AND MISCELLANEOUS ISSUES

Loan of Material

As a general rule, the issue of articles on loan from storehouses should not be encouraged, but it is sometimes unavoidable. For example, in the maintenance department, a number of comparatively expensive tools or pieces of equipment are required for short periods of use at frequent intervals. Such items are ammeters, surveyors' chains levels, electric handlamps, tap and die sets, special tools, and so on. These may not be on stores charge, but are controlled by the storekeeper and kept in the storehouse when not in use. It is necessary to keep stock records for the equipment concerned and also to maintain a register showing all loans made in date order. Workmen sign the register for everything issued to them and sign again when items are returned to the store. The storekeeper inspects the register at regular inquiries, about anything which has been out on loan for a protracted period, and reports to the appropriate supervisor any case where he is not satisfied. As an alternative to signing the loan register workmen are sometimes provided with metal or plastic discs (known usually as 'tallies'). These discs bear the man's name and/or works number and are handed over in exchange for loaned equipment.

Issues to Employees on Repayment

Sales to employees from stock are often encountered in respect of tools, protective clothing, firewood, etc. Storekeepers concerned with these sales are instructed in writing as to the articles permitted and the persons to whom they may be sold. Payment is made either in cash or by deduction from wages, but storekeepers should not normally be allowed to accept or handle cash. Lists of sales are kept showing the date of the transaction, the employee's name and number, and the vocabulary number, description and quantity of goods sold. The purchaser signs for his items, and the original list is sent to the cashier to collect the money or to the wages officer to arrange deduction from wages, as the case may be. Another copy is used for posting the stock records and subsequently passed to the accounts section. A third copy is retained by the storekeeper.

Allocated Issues

In accordance with manufacturing schedules, some materials may be received on a programmed-delivery basis and kept for use only on the production line for which they have been purchased. This is done to make sure that there will be no interruption of production and the storekeeper will check that issues are not made elsewhere. For example, 20 mm diameter bright-steel bar to a given specification may be allocated to the production component 'XYZ'. If the maintenance department wishes to have some of this material to repair a machine, it cannot be issued unless the maintenance manager can obtain special authority from some senior official, such as the works manager.

Another type of allocation is that certain items are reserved for specific jobs or purposes to avoid the unnecessary use of material which is expensive or in very short supply. For instance, good quality deep-drawing steel sheet, although usable for many standard stamping and pressing jobs, may be restricted issue only to special jobs where deep-drawing quality is essential.

Capital Issues

Where the replacement of capital goods is a normal day-to-day feature, or where a capital development or reconstruction programme is in operation, special attention is usually given to the control and recording of the issues of capital material from storehouses. Instructions are given about the authorization of such issues, and stock records (including bin card if any) are marked to show that the items concerned are reserved for a particular capital project. The storekeeper checks that, when issue documents are presented to him, the capital-project number quoted thereon for cost-allocation purposes corresponds with the project number which appears in his own records, and in some cases it is thought necessary to employ a special form of issue note.

Finished Products Sent to Customers

The storekeeper is informed of the issues to be made by means of a sales advice note, issue order or similar document from 'the sales department giving details of the items, the consignee's name and address, and any special requirements about packing, labeling or method of transport. Thereupon the storekeeper selects packs and dispatches the goods in accordance with these instructions, and documents the transaction by preparing an advice note, and a packing note.

Items for Repair and Sales of Scrap

When articles are sent out for repair or reconditioning, e.g., an electric motor to be rewound, when scrap is dispatched to a customer, or when goods are returned to suppliers because of excess deliveries or rejections, the procedure followed is similar to that for finished products sent to customers.

Free Issues to Suppliers Contractors

In some industries and in Government departments, materials, parts, tools, fixtures, patterns, etc., are supplied to contractors in connexion with products which are being manufactured by them. Issues of this kind are recorded in such a way that the total amount issued to any given supplier may easily be ascertained, and a record kept of the number of free issues which have been returned by the supplier incorporated in finished products or otherwise. In this way the balance of free issues in the hands of any contractor for any particular order at any given time can be established.

Issues to Production

In mass-production factories, with the co-operation of the production control department or some other technical planning office, production materials are issued in quantities and at times to correspond with the manufacturing programme. The goods concerned are usually collected into a marshalling area in the first place. Thereafter they may be dealt with in several different ways:

(i) Collected from the storehouse by the production department.

(ii) Delivered by the storehouse staff to the point on the production lines at which the process of manufacture is to commence.

(iii) Transferred into 'open-access' stores within the production shops. Open-access stores are storage areas on the shop floor which are not enclosed and are fitted with bins or racks containing materials which are taken and used by production personnel without documentation.

The documentation for scheduled issues is usually prepared by the production control or some such similar department, and the storekeeper's authority for issue is conveyed to him by his copy of the schedule.

8.8 SUMMARY

Materials are to be issued for production and other purposes after authorization by specified officers. Material Requisition note, Material Return Note and Material Transfer Note are important documents used control material issues.

Order picking is undertaken by Stores Manager using manual or automated systems as per the size and requirements of the organisation.

Stores has to issue materials for production as well as for further processing by subcontractors. In addition to raw materials stores also issues tools, repair components, capital items, etc.

8.9 SELF ASSESSMENT QUESTIONS

(1) What are the three documents used during material issues activity? Draw a specimen of any one.

(2) What are the main features of automated material picking system?

(3) Enumerate steps in manual order picking.

9

Chapter

SCRAP AND SURPLUS MATERIALS DISPOSAL

Objectives

After studying this chapter, you should be able to understand:

- Importance of scrap and surplus materials disposal.
- Factors that generate surplus materials.
- Means to control surplus materials.
- Methods to obtain maximum returns from surplus materials.

Structure:

9.1 Surplus Materials Disposal

9.2 Three Concepts for Disposal

9.3 Idle Equipment

9.4 Transferring Equipment

9.5 Sales Strategies and Tactics

9.6 Donation

9.7 Disposal as Parts and Scrap Metal

9.8 Scrap and Waste Materials

9.9 Scrap Considerations

9.10 Disposing of Surplus Profitably

9.11 Use Within Firm

9.12 Return to Suppliers

9.13 Selling to Other Firms

9.14 Selling to Deaters and Brokers

9.15 Selling to Employees

9.16 Donations to Educational Institutions

9.17 Contractual Considerations

9.18 Steps Taken by Bureau of Public Enterprise (B.P.E)

9.19 Importance to Stores Management

9.20 Summary

9.21 Self Assessment Question

9.1 SURPLUS MATERIALS DISPOSAL

Industrial surplus materials are those in excess of the reasonable operational requirements of the concern. Generally those materials which have not moved for more than 3 years and not required in near future are treated as surplus materials in an organisation. Surplus is of two kinds— whether it may be materials (raw materials, stores and spares, etc.) or equipment and it may arise out of the following circumstances:

(1) Curtailment in the production programme.

(2) Purchase of huge quantities than required.

(3) Purchase of wrong specification of materials.

(4) Obsolete items due to change in methods or production processes — whether it may be manual or mechanical.

(5) Obsolete items due to change in design or specifications of materials,

(6) After the completion of the project,

(7) Goods damaged.

(8) Undetected errors in Bin cards.

(9) Materials stored in the wrong location and consequently lost sight of.

(10) Spares not usable because of obsolete equipment.

(11) Surplus, obsolete and damaged equipment.

(12) Surplus spares owing to the related equipment itself having been declared surplus.

Guidelines for Declaring Surplus Equipment/Stores and Spares

In case of the companies which are multi-unit organisations, a list of surplus equipment/stores and spares should be sent to Head Office. The list of surplus stores/spares should be prepared under the groups concerned and should indicate part number, code number, description, quantity declared surplus and value. In respect of the equipment declared surplus, the following data may be furnished:

(a) Name of the equipment;

(b) Date of commissioning;

(c) Hours worked;

(d) Cost of purchase;

(e) Present book value;

(f) Present condition;

(g) Cost of spares held in stock.

In turn the corporate office should find out the requirement from other units and declare as such in respect of those items which are not required by other units as well. There will be no reserve price for the surplus equipment under disposal. However, the book value may be considered as reserve price in respect of surplus stores and spares. There may be some items like cables with copper content in which case the market value may be higher than the book value because of the trend of higher prices. In such cases reserve price may be fixed suitably higher than the book value. Adequate care should be taken for proper up-keep of surplus equipment and stores and spares etc, and in maintaining them in good working condition till actual disposal. All the surplus items should be segregated and kept in separate stores under lock and key arrangement. Provision for estimated loss, on account of difference between book value, and estimated realisable value may also be made in the accounts in order to meet the requirement of audit.

Scrap

Scrap consists of the residue or pieces cut out of raw materials during the manufacturing operation. It includes the following:

(1) Worn out materials.

(2) Spoiled raw materials. These cannot be rectified further.

(3) Defective and worn out parts.

(4) Rejected components.

(5) Non-returnable containers.

(6) Packing cases.

These scrap items possess some commercial value. These may be reclaimed and used in other industries as raw materials. If the residue does not possess any value, it is a waste and thrown out. If finished goods do not meet acceptable standard and cannot be rectified further, they can be sold as seconds and scrap.

Technical standards should be laid down for control of scrap. For example, scrap should be within the limits of 5% of input of raw materials. If actual scrap exceeds 5% reason should be investigated. The reason may be due to defective designing, wrong quality of material, wrong inspection, negligence of workman, sudden machine breakdowns, defective tools and improper instruction by foreman, etc. Corrective action should be taken by the responsible person depending on the review of above mentioned reasons.

Disposal of Surplus and Scrap

Before the action is taken for disposal of surplus items (whether it may be materials or equipment) one more attempt should be made to ensure that these are not really required by the company or any branch of the company. If it is usable for some other purpose after necessary modification, must be used to avoid the loss on sale of surplus items.

Surplus items and scrap can be disposed of in the following ways:

(1) Circulation within the concern for the possible use within the company with or without modification or among the sister concerns. If it is a government undertaking, a list of all surplus items and scrap should be sent to all the government undertakings with a request that their required items may be taken at book values. This will avoid the loss on disposal, if any.

(2) Surplus items may be returned to the supplier at the original purchase prices or at negotiated prices.

(3) Direct sale to another firm.

(4) Sale to dealers, brokers, middlemen or scrap contractors, etc.

(5) Direct sale to scrap consumers like foundries.

(6) Inviting offers for purchase from the various firms at quarterly intervals. Contracts should be entered into with highest offerors.

(7) Disposal on Annual Contract basis.

(8) Sale to employees.

(9) Donation to educational institutions, charitable institutions hospitals, etc.

(10) Sale by public auction.

The firms should publish Disposal tender notices in all leading news papers and also in the newspapers of the locality and Indian Trade Journal. There should be enough time gaps between the date of publication and the last date for receipt of tenders. Matcrials management department should finalise the recommendations of the tenders preferably within 30 days from the date of opening of tenders. The decision should be taken with due regard to the market prices also. Items for disposal will be offered for sale in lots and strictly on "as is where is" basis.

Alternatively, the action may be taken for the disposal of surplus equipment/stores & spares by means of conducting auction. In this case also the firm should publish in the major newspapers both in English and regional language giving the details of auction programme and particulars of the items available for disposal. Alternatively auctioneers may also be appointed for conducting the auctions on behalf of the firms. In such cases, the commission charged by the auctioneers will have to be paid to them. Normal auction procedure is to be followed and 10% to 25% of the bid value should be collected immediately on the spot from the highest bidders. Local sales tax as applicable will have to be paid by the bidder in addition to the bid amount. The successful bidder shall arrange his own transport and labour for loading and transportation of the equipment and materials auctioned to him. Lifting of the materials should not be permitted on weekly holidays and beyond normal working hours. The transit insurance should be paid by the bidder only.

Obsolescent: An item is said to be obsolescent when it is going out of use, but is not yet completely for instance a transport firm that has been running lorries of model A decides that in future all replacement vehicles are to be B, from a different manufacturer. From the data when this is announced, most of the spare parts in stock for model A become obsolescent. This does not mean they are immediately worthless, because they can be used for repairing the vehicles to which they belong as long as these models are in service. On the other hand, the number of model A lorries will decline as time goes on, and they will all eventually be disposed of. It is extremely unlikely that the spares in stock will be used to the very last item and there is the expectation that some of them will exist when all the model A lorries are withdrawn. Therefore, there is a likelihood of loss by virtue of the fact that these remaining spares will have to be sold at only scrap value.

Obsolete: An item regarded as obsolete when it is no longer usable by the enterprise concerned, because of a change in operational practice or production methods. In the example quoted above when all the model A lorries have disappeared the model A spares will no longer be obsolescent, but obsolete.

Obsolescence is one of the largest dangers to which inventories are subjected and should receive first consideration where quantity purchases are contemplated. For example, if the shelf life of an item is 100 days, it would be unwise to buy in excess of a 100-day supply for the sake of price reduction. Also, if the particular item is susceptible to obsolescence due to design changes or other factors, it would be unwise to stock beyond normal lead time plus safety factor. In every purchase decision, thought must always be given to the possibilities of design changes or other factors which would make the material obsolete.

How obsolete and surplus stock arise: Such stocks arise from various factors like:

(i) A change in the design of the manufactured equipment.

(ii) Change in the method of manufacture.

(iii) Unforeseen reduction in the volume of production.

(iv) Change of the product itself, i.e., where it has been decided to do away with the manufacture of the particular product or make drastic changes in its shape, size or qualities such that it becomes quite different from the old products.

(v) In the case of spare parts of existing equipment when it has been decided to phase out or sell the old equipment and buy a new model.

(vi) Regular collection of scrap, sorting of scrap and disposal of scrap.

(vii) Periodic scrutiny for obsolescence and excess or surplus material; prompt decision in declaring material as obsolete or surplus.

Essentials for Scrap Disposal

(a) Examination of the amount of scrap accumulating during quarter/year

Is it too low?	*Why too low?* Stealing? Careless collection?
Is it too high?	*Why too high?* Wrong size/shape/specification of material? Wastage in production/processing handling etc.

In either case further investigation is needed for applying corrective measures.

(b) Regular collection/separation of scrap/processing of scrap.

(c) Salvage of scrap for re-use **(sales)** examine if a discarded **(equipment)** part/equipment can be mended for re-use rather than buying a new one or can it be kept as a stand-by (safety-stock for insurance).

(d) When scrap cannot be sold at all/arrange for removal, even on payment.

(e) When scrap is unavoidably excessive, examine if a bye-product can be manufactured from it.

(f) Find the best policy and method for sale of scrap which has to be sold, including tendering, auction, negotiation (consider sale to actual users).

Summarising disposal of scrap should be considered on the following lines:

Salvage Process	for re-use stand-by-use sale	mend before buying use for bye-product manufacture.	get better price for scrap by better policy/ method of disposal	get removed by paying

Essentials for Surplus Disposal

(a) Examine once again possibility of use of a surplus item by change in design/specification or if you can use it for a special end-product or an end-product to an older design for using up the surplus; or for a different purpose/end-use other than the one for which it was originally procured;

(b) Ask sister deptts./organisations if they have actual need for it; but give them a deadline for answer, after which take prompt action for disposal.

(c) Consider sale to an actual user/users; consider "barter" with other manufacturers in your line of manufacture;

(d) Consider sending back/re-sale to original supplier;

(e) Consider sale to others/consider best method and policy of sale in each case.

For sale use *Deadlines* for sale

(a) at good/reasonable price

after that sell

(b) at any price

after that sell

(c) at scrap value

after that

(d) give it away free,

(e) have it removed by paying someone to do so.

Organisational Aspect of Wastage Control

Overall responsibility should be that of the Materials Manager. He should take advice of:

(a) Materials Planning & Programming Committee.

(b) Production Experts/Industrial Engineers/Design and Standards Engineers/SQC & Inspection/ and other Technical experts.

One particular officer in the Materials-Management Department should be personally responsible for wastage control at operating level:

(a) For preventive measures and performance against norms of utilisation to minimise quantity.

(b) For scrap and surplus disposal/salvage and re-use to obtain maximum return from available surplus.

Various Options for Scrap and Surplus Material Disposal

Every company will sooner or later have idle machinery that is worn or obsolete, materials it can't use and scrap. These unwanted things represent irritating problems as far as production and engineering are concerned. Too often articles are disposed of casually, and most residual value is lost.

One function of materials manager is capability of contributing to the company profit picture. This contribution will come from an organized program for the recovery of capital from idle machinery and obsolete and scrap materials. The theme of the programme could be **"don't throw it away-sell it."**

The purchasing and store agent has traditionally been the person responsible for the disposal of surplus. Large multiplant companies have a specific person from the main office to control and complete the program. Large volumes can generate sizable sums of money Expertise in methods of disposal will return many times the cost.

9.2 THREE CONCEPTS FOR DISPOSAL

(1) Reorganising Secondary Value: Used materials are totally useless because they are not in the right location or transportation charges exceed the cost of new material. For example, an old roll-type metal corrugated machine cannot produce competitively against a modem roll-forming machine in the United Sates, but when moved to a less developed country, the production is excellent and the machine is profitable. Obsolescence was only a reality at its original location.

Even items that are only broken pieces have value. The secondary materials business is quite large, especially in scrap metals, which contributes about 40 percent of the total consumption of copper, 30 percent of aluminum and 20 percent of zinc. Many used or scrap materials have ready buyers and established markets.

(2) Timings: The time-necessary to achieve the best use is obtained only by planning ahead before the materials must be moved. Time must be allowed for engineering and production to examine the possibilities for re-use in other applications in the plant. More time is needed to advertise and find an outside user.

(3) Finding a New User: Unneeded materials will be worth very little until some one is found who can use them. Some secondary values are obvious, and for these, a user is usually not hard to find. For example, a machine tool may be worn out too much for exacting tool-and-die work, but it can do a good job as a maintenance tool on rough work.

Salvaging some of your company's past investment is very satisfactory work, as the rupees returned are visible and measurable. With the three concepts in mind and with a sales person's philosophy and approach, a program for the salvage operation can be organized.

9.3 IDLE EQUIPMENT

There are a number of ways to use idle equipment. The following factors for of establishing policy and priority are listed in descending order of importance.

(1) Reuse in same plant on a different job or at a different location.

(2) Save in the plant for a future project.

(3) Transfer to another plant.

(4) Sell to outside company or donate to non profit organization.

Steps 1 and 2 must be based on facts, not hope; otherwise, every corner will become storage space for possible future projects.

Stripping of idle equipment must not be allowed until the salvage program manager approves such action. Otherwise, such stripping may reduce the value of equipment to scrap metal. The loss in sales value will always be more than the value of the parts. The condition of the equipment is a key factor in the secondary value and is of primary concern to a potential new user.

9.4 TRANSFERRING EQUIPMENT

In a multiplant organisation, many opportunities exist to use the value of assets. Office furniture needs replacing for reasons other than being worn out. A small amount of reconditioning can make furniture from main offices into very good mill-type furniture.

Periodically a catalog should be made of equipment suitable for use and circulated to person responsible for specifying equipment. Many factors, such as need for space, cost of carrying, taxes, etc., are the basis for how long an item should be listed.

Selling to an Outside Source

Reuse or transfer are uses that will return the most value. However, this is not always practical or possible. The arrangement for a sale to an affiliated company or one partially owned is an alternative almost as valuable. This is especially true if the affiliated company is in foreign country. Sizable amounts of used equipment dealer's sales are made to foreign countries, particularly those in the early stage of industrialization.

Selling directly to a user will normally provide the best price, because the new user can assess the value with the cost of new item. The problem is to find a new user who wants it at the time you want to sell.

9.5 SALES STRATEGIES: AND TACTICS

(1) **"As is" Condition:** "As is" means all parts as advertised or inspected and in condition reported. There is no warranty other than warranty of title.

(2) **Inspection by Buyers:** When the value justifies the expense, a personal inspection by the buyer can prevent many misunderstandings.

(3) **Packing and Shipping:** While the equipment is normally sold F. 0. B. Plant site, who will load and the type of carrier will affect the cost of packing and shipping. Who pays for these costs must be settled in negotiations.

(4) **Sale in Price:** Sale on a "where is." basis is occasionally useful or necessary. Surplus equipment may be installed, on the plant site, and its removal should be made a part of the contract conditions to protect your company.

(5) **Specifications:** Avoid the use of word "complete", "all parts and accessories", or similar wording when describing the used equipment, or you will be committed for items you do not have. Make description as detailed as possible. The use of a serial number is particularly useful.

(6) **Terms on Sale to Dealers:** The terms can be payment in full with order, or atleast full payment before shipment. Acceptance of a check constitutes an agreement to sale. On sales to user: the terms can be negotiated. For terms other then cash, the credit rating and cost of money must be considered.

(7) **Price:** The real price is found only after the equipment is advertised and put up for sale. The price will be as high as the seller can push it and as low as the buyer can squeeze it. The used equipment business is one of the last where "horse trading" is perfectly acceptable.

9.6 DONATIONS

Donations to non profit organisations are frequently made by many industrial firms. There is social-assistance value in providing equipment no longer suitable in industry as training aids for schools. There is good will and of course, tax deduction. Donations are sensitive and precedent setting. Company procedures and policies should be carefully designated and followed.

9.7 DISPOSAL AS PARTS AND SCRAP METAL

When selling or donating equipment is not possible, there is still potential value. Items of machinery have motors, controls, tooling, and parts and accessories that are relatively, inexpensive to remove and reuse. The balance is sold as scrap metal.

9.8 SCRAP AND WASTE MATERIALS

Scrap metals and other waste products can be valuable income producing by -products of any company system. The amount of time and effort expended must be balanced against the amount of revenue expected. The secondary materials industry is well organized and is prepared to buy many scrap materials if plants are organized for collection.

Reclamation. Many items are sent to the company reclamation department to be reconditioned. Companies in the metals industry having remelting operations for large volumes of their principal scrap metals.

Cost studies are absolutely necessary to prevent wasted effort. It is obviously false economy to use Rs.50/-per hour labour to repair of Rs.20/- valve. The plant costs to rebuild old equipment may easily exceed the cost of new or good used equipment.

9.9 SCRAP CONSIDERATIONS

To obtain the highest net return, stores management should review the following considerations:

(1) When possible, is scrap segregated at points of origin? Maximum value is given to scrap when prepared according to recognized grades or standards. Scrap boxes should be used for segregation at points of origin.

(2) Is too much time spent on scrap preparation? Are storage or preparation facilities adequate and located for lowest cost handling? Are there safeguards in the company against pilfering or incorrect weighing?

(3) Is competition among scrap buyers being encouraged?

(4) Has the cost of transportation been investigated?

Co-ordination of Store Management and Purchasing Departments

The materials cycle is not complete until all materials are disposed of in the most productive manner. Consequently, surplus disposal is the basic function of the stores management department. In a large firm, Head of Salvage and Reclamation (S&R) department traditionally reports to plant manager.

There are many reasons for assigning this responsibility to purchasing. Usually, no department in the firm is as well qualified as the purchasing department to perform this task. The professional and managerial skill required for a successful disposal operation are the identical skills found in a competent purchasing department.

The purchasing department routinely buys a large variety of raw materials, component parts and equipment. It has knowledge of who makes these materials, what other firms use them, how they are used in its own firm and how much they cost. This is the precise, knowledge needed to sell surpluses of these materials successfully. Also, relatively large number of buyer in the metal industries regularly buys some form of scrap or other surplus material for their own manufacturing purposes. Daily contact with representatives from industry, and the reading of purchasing and trade journals, keeps purchasing personnel informed of surplus price trends in many markets. Also, buyers frequently sell a significant portion of their firm's surpluses back to the supplier from whom they were purchased.

9.10 DISPOSING OF SURPLUS PROFITABLY

When material is declared surplus, the stores management, purchasing or S & R department, as appropriate, is informed. Following this action, disposal is made by one of seven methods:

(1) Use within the firm

(2) Return to the supplier

(3) Direct sale to another firm

(4) Sale to a dealer or broker

(5) Sale to employees

(6) Donations to educational institutions

(7) Some combination of the preceding method

9.11 USE WITHIN FIRM

Use within the firm is always most profitable form of surplus disposal. This type of disposal realizes 100 percent of the original cost, where as returns to suppliers typically yield 80 to 90 percent of original cost, and sales to dealers and brokers only 10 to 40 percent.

9.12 RETURN TO SUPPLIERS

If the surplus material cannot be used within the firm, the return-to-supplier method of disposal is generally the next best method. Suppliers typically allow the return of both new and used surpluses as a courtesy to good accounts. Saleable materials returned from inventory are traditionally accepted at original cost, less a nominal restocking change. Since all firms do not progress technically at the same rate, suppliers can frequently resell even obsolete inventory items at full price.

9.13 SELLING TO OTHER FIRMS

Some companies sell surplus materials and equipment directly to other firms. Sales of equipment to other firms depend primarily upon the condition of the equipment, the economics of price, and the availability of similar equipment from other sources. Equipment sales made directly to a user typically result in a better price than sales made to dealers or brokers.

9.14 SELLING TO DEALERS AND BROKERS

Surplus dealers and brokers constitute an excellent outlet for surplus materials. When a firm advertises surplus materials for sale, dealers often respond. Transactions with dealers are usually "where is, as is," and most of the time they are for cash. Surplus machine tool dealers, for example, operate in two ways: by auction, which usually involves selling a plant's entire equipment inventory, or by purchase of small lots. For auctions the dealer receives a commission and seldom does more to the equipment than show it to bidders. For small lot transactions, however, he pays the owners cash, then he often reconditions or rebuilds machine tools before he sells them. Normally, it is not profitable for the original owner to recondition equipment before selling it.

9.15 SELLING TO EMPLOYEES

Many firms make it a practice to sell both the products they manufacture and their surpluses to their employees. It the surpluses are the result of over stocking or obsolescence and the materials are in new or good condition, or if they are odds and ends of scrap desired by do-it yourself employees, this can be satisfactory method of disposal. On the other hand, if the surpluses are not in fully satisfactory condition, such sales, regardless of their attractive prices, can be resentment on the part of employee toward their employers. Used automobiles can be especially dangerous item of equipment to sell to employees.

9.16 DONATIONS TO EDUCATIONAL INSTITUTIONS

At the present time, colleges and schools acutely need machine tools and other types of industrial materials for instructional use. Because the applicable tax laws and regulations are complicated, before making large gifts potential donors should consult their tax advisers to determine exactly what benefits are available.

9.17 CONTRACTUAL CONSIDERATIONS

Generally speaking, the following contractual considerations apply to the three major categories of materials that are sold as surplus.

Scrap Metals, depending on existing economic conditions, are best disposed of by either a short-or long-term contract made with local scrap dealer. The dealer getting the contract should be selected after an investigation of at least three dealers. Because of the breadth of scrap market activities, materials department should generally experience little difficulty in interesting three or more capable dealers who will compete vigorously for the business. Also, the highly competitive nature of the scrap business usually keeps the variation in bid prices within a narrow range. Local dealers have an operating and transportation advantage over more distant competitors; also, they can provide more frequent pickups and more personalized contract service. Published market prices are available for many varieties of scrap, and these prices are frequently used as the bases for long - term contract prices. Bid prices are normally used for short-term contract prices.

Surplus Stock that cannot be returned to the supplier is best disposed of by Sale to jobbers or second-hand dealers. Such sales are most frequently made on a competitive bid basis, and competition for these materials is usually keen.

Surplus Equipment is usually best disposed of by competitive bids from dealers. However, on occasion negotiation is used. Intense competition is traditionally developed after a firm acquires a select group of dealers who are interested in bidding for its surplus equipment on a continuing basis. Fixed prices to dealers are satisfactory when a selling firm is sure of the equipment fair selling price. Auction is frequently used as quick and convenient method of disposing of large quantities of equipment. Occasionally, advertisements in trade journals or trade papers prove effective in selling this category of surplus.

9.18 STEPS TAKEN BY BUREAU OF PUBLIC ENTERPRISE (B.P.E)

Depth Studies: High level expert committees of officials and non-official members are continuing to examine in depth the materials management systems and level of inventories in selected public enterprises. Such studies have since been completed in respect of many units. The implementation of the recommendations of these committees is progressed by the B.P.E.

Inventory Analysis: Yearly report on inventory management received from public sector enterprises are examined in greater detail and units are advised of the necessary steps they ought to take for making further improvement.

Norms for Inventory Holdings: B.P.E. has advised all public enterprises to fix suitable norms for holdings as ceilings for different categories of inventories. The units have accordingly fixed the norms and it has been the constant endeavour of the managements to reduce their inventory levels to those norms. However, the Reserve Bank of India, in July '74 appointed a committee, headed by Shree P.L. Tendon, to frame guidelines for follow-up of Bank Credit. This committee in their report, besides making other recommendations had also suggested certain norms for inventory holding. Public Enterprises were already working within the norms suggested by this committee in the case of fertilizers, pharmaceuticals, paper and cement. In the case of light engineering industries, however, the present levels are slightly higher than the norms suggested. Continuing efforts are being made to reduce the level.

Surplus and Non Moving: BPE has advised the units to review the surplus and nonmoving items, and take immediate action for quick disposal of high value items after categorizing them as XYZ on the basis of value. Chief executives have also been advised that once it is decided that certain materials are not required the same should be disposed of at the best value obtainable and the offers need not necessarily be compared with the book value.

Computerization of Inventory Control: A committee has been constituted to examine the use of computer in PSEs where computers are already installed with a view to ensure their fullest utilization and also to see if inventory management application can be increased.

9.19 IMPORTANCE TO STORES MANAGEMENT

(1) Public enterprises are giving due importance to stores and inventory management and are adopting the latest techniques for making further improvements. As a result there has been good achievement in Hindustan Machine Tools, Electronic Corporation of India, Neyveli Lignite Corporation, F. C. 1. Hindustan Photo Films, I. O. C., O.N.G.C., C.I.L , BHEL. In other units also materials and store management is receiving due attention.

(2) Work in progress is high in mining organizations like Hindustan Copper Ltd, and National Mineral Development Corp. The units are taking suitable steps to reduce the levels.

(3) Finished goods in certain units like RE. C. Ranchi, Biecco Lawrie Ltd. Hindustan Steel Ltd are rather high. Managements of these units are seized of the problem and are taking suitable steps for expediting dispatches so that finished goods do not remain in their stores for long.

9.20 SUMMARY

Industrial surplus materials are those in excess of the reasonable operational requirements. They include slow moving and obsolete materials, scrap, defectives and rejected materials, as well as equipment and its spares.

Management needs to establish a system for their identification, segregation, disposal in a scientific manner.

Surplus materials and equipment can be reused within company with modification or sold to scrap dealers, other firms in the industry or donated to eligible educational or medical institutes. Public enterprises have their own system for disposal of surplus materials.

Sale of surplus materials is the responsibility of purchase department which has maximum knowledge of markets for these items.

9.21 SELF ASSESSMENT QUESTION

(1) Each organisation has to handle the function of disposal of surplus and scrap materials. Why?

(2) Who should manage the scale of scrap, sales manager or purchase manager? Why?

(3) Suggest measures to minimize the quantum of surplus materials and equipment.

(4) Describe strategies for obtaining maximum returns from surplus materials.

(5) How is disposal of surplus equipment handled?

10 Chapter

SAFETY AND SECURITY

Objectives

After studying this chapter, you should be able to understand:

- Safety requirements under factories Act, 1948
- Stores accidents – causes and preventive measures.
- Safe operation of material handling equipment.
- Measures for fire prevention.
- Firefighting equipment used in stores.
- Prevention of thefts and pilferage by outsiders and employees.

Structure:

10.1 FACTORIES ACT 1948

(i) Safety Provisions: According to the Act of 1934, a factory manager could afford *to* wait till an Inspector of Factories gave instructions as to what ought to be done *to* ensure the safety of workers. The Act of 1948 has placed the responsibility for safety matters on the shoulders of the owner or the manager of a factory. He must comply with all the safety provisions without waiting for the inspector's instructions.

Secondly, the Act places legal responsibility on the management for the maintenance and use of safety guards. It is its duty to supervise the use of these guards by the workers.

The specific provisions for safety require that in every factory, all dangerous parts of all machines, such as the moving parts of prime movers, flywheels, electric generators, motors, rotary converters, etc., shall be securely fenced by safety guards of substantial construction which shall be kept in position while the parts of machines are in motion.

(ii) Dangerous Fumes: Adequate provision shall be made in a factory where dangerous fumes are present in any chamber, tank, pipe, etc., for egress of such fumes.

(iii) Explosive Gases, Dust, Fume: If, in any factory, the manufacturing process raises dust, gas, fume or vapour which is likely to explode on ignition, all measures shall be taken to prevent any such explosion by -

(a) Providing an effective enclosure of the plant or machinery used in the process,

or

(b) The removal or prevention of accumulation of such dust, gas or fumes.

(iv) Safety of Factory Buildings and Machinery: If it appears to the Inspector that any building or part of factory is in such a condition that if it is dangerous to human life or safety, he may serve on the manager of the factory an order in writing specifying the measures that should be adopted and the specific date by which they should be carried out to ensure the safety of the building or factory. He may also serve an order to the manager, prohibiting its use until proper repairs or alternations have been carried out.

The term "safety" envisages the safety of the materials in stores, facilities used, including materials handling equipment, and the safety of the personnel working in Stores.

10.2 ACCIDENTS

Accidents can cause damage to materials, machines or facilities and injury or death to workers. The worst case one can visualise is a fire where the entire premises can be completely destroyed. It is necessary, therefore, that all precautions are taken to avoid accidents.

Causes of Accidents in Stores

(i) Materials Falling From Racks: It arises mostly from carelessness by not keeping the materials in a balanced and safe manner on the racks. It can also arise from inadequacy of space in the racks. It can also because safety precautions *on* the, rack itself are inadequate, e.g., there may be no guard on the sides of the rack to prevent goods from falling off.

(ii) Wires, Unwanted, Ropes, Steel Rods or Empty Cartons Kept Carelessly on Gangways: can cause people to trip over them. It usually happens in a storehouse when people are carrying materials. There cannot be too much emphasis laid on good housekeeping; it is of prime importance. Things should not lie around loose anywhere and this rule is to be enforced. Receptacles should be provided at various places to hold paper wrappings, empty cartons, or string used to tie materials.

(iii) Injury Arising from Lifting Very Heavy Loads, or Normal Loads Unscientifically: It is very necessary to provide the right type of mechanical aids to stores personnel lor handling materials. Firstly, productivity will be low if material handling is done wholly by human hands. Secondly, accidents may arise when lifting heavy loads causing injury to the worker and damaging the material. This type of accident takes place usually when placing loads on a high rack or when taking them down. A typical case is of a person attempting to climb a ladder with a load on his head.

10.3 SAFETY OF MATERIALS HANDLING EQUIPMENT

Quite often the material handling equipment used is not adequate. The operator should know how to use it correctly and supervisors should ensure that they use it correctly. There is a correct method of performing even the simplest of manual tasks. This holds good even for lifting a heavy weight, A wrong way can cause strain on one's body resulting in. muscle tear or a sprain. Stores personnel needs to be protected from –

(i) **Collisions With Bins:** This usually happens where aisle spaces arc not adequate or the racks arc not securely bolted, or the bins jut out from the racks und so on. Such accidents usually happen when picking orders or placing fresh receipts in the bins.

(ii) **Falling While Climbing to Reach the Upper Shelves:** Such accidents arise from having improper ladders or when the men are not trained to climb ladders whilst carrying heavy weights. It also happens when the worker displays overconfidence, merely balancing the material on his head.

(iii) **Injury to Hands Arising From the Lifting or Handling of Materials Without Wearing Protective Gloves:** In many cases protective gloves are prescribed for handling materials which are likely to injure one's hands, like sharp-edged steel plates or chemicals. People avoid wearing gloves for two main reasons: the palm sweats when one wears gloves and this leads to discomfort: the second is, of course sheer laziness.

(vii) **Slipping on Oil, Grease or Even Water Spillages:** Oil, water or grease will spill in spite of the best precautions and care. It should be a standing rule that no sooner the spillage occurs than it should be wiped clean and surfacc maintained dry.

(viii) **Injury Caused by Nails left on Empty Cases and Battens of Boxes:** This is one of the common causes of injury in all stores. Boxes, when opened, should immediately be kept in the place meant for them and nails, steel bands, etc., should be removed to prevent injury to workers who might handle them.

(ix) **Injury From Corrosive Acids:** Warning labels indicating the nature of the material and with a 'Danger' sign should be affixed to all containers holding such materials.

(x) **Dropping Goods on one's Feet Without Protective Boots:** Where heavy materials are handled it is usual to provide protective boots.

Most of such accidents are caused by not taking reasonable precautions, by carelessness and indiscipline, especially in the matter of observance of standing instructions. Accidents also arise from substandard facilities like poor lighting, wobbly ladders or racks, badly laid out bins, etc. Good supervision in the matter of observance of safety rules cannot be overstressed. Management should educate, encourage and advise workers to change their attitudes of mind and give the highest priority for good housekeeping.

The science of Ergonomics, be used in the designing of the general working environment, layout and machinery so that the operators may work in the safest and most efficient manner - plus equipment like headgear, goggles, gloves and special boots should be provided where required.

10.4 THEFT AND PILFERAGE

Instances of theft and pilferages are obvious in stores where even the environment is congenial to its manifestation. Precaution against theft involves the creation of an environment which is not congenial by ensuring are that areas are under constant watch.

The following are some of the measures adopted to prevent theft or fraud by outsiders:

(i) The compound of the factory should be protected by a brick wall or suitable fencing, leaving a reasonably safe intervening space between buildings and the wall or fencing.

(ii) A sufficient number of watchmen should guard the stores, factory shops and gates. Security clocks for monitoring frequency of visits by security staff to strategic locations may be used with advantage.

(iii) Windows of stores must be closed and doors should be locked after working hours. Special locks may be used where necessary.

(iv) Keys of all the store should be left with the head of stores department.

(v) Visit by outsiders to Stores and factory shops should be regulated and minimized.

(vi) Expensive and attractive articles like micrometers, ball bearings, etc., should be stored in steel cupboards.

(vii) Valuable materials used in the shop should be locked up after working hours.

(viii) Loading of scrap trucks should be supervised by security staff. The Stores representative attending the delivery may be changed at intervals.

(ix) As far as possible lorries leaving the factory must pass through a single exit so that proper scrutiny of the materials can be made. If lorries pass through several gates such scrutiny is difficult.

(x) Ensure that full drums not taken out as empties.

(xi) Property should be insured against burglary.

Pilferage by Employees: The following precautionary measures may be taken to prevent stealing by factory employees:

(i) It should be a strict rule that no one other than Stores staff are allowed in stores. This is particularly necessary in respect of stores where expensive materials like tools, instruments, bearings, etc., are stored.

(ii) The keys of the storerooms and of cupboards should be accessible only to authorized persons.

(iii) When leaving the factory, employees may be searched at the gates, if suspected of theft.

(iv) As far as possible, employees should not be allowed to bring any personal property into the factory. This must be left at the gate and if this is not possible, bags, tiffin-boxes, etc., may be searched.

(v) Expensive articles may be stamped with distinguishing marks.

(vi) Tools on loan should be periodically verified with loan records. Capital items must be periodically checked with capital or plant inventory.

(vii) A watch should be kept on consumption of materials used in the shop.

(viii) Items like torch cells, bulbs, etc., should be issued against the return of old ones. The latter should always be destroyed.

(ix) Unauthorized visits to the factory after working hours should not be allowed.

(x) Stocks of articles which can be easily pilfered and sold such as carbide tips, ball bearings, brass components, etc., should be locked in steel cupboards and certified by responsible officials at frequent intervals.

(xi) Scrapped tools should be locked up so that they cannot be stolen or returned and new ones taken out in their place.

(xii) Technical books should be distinguished by stamping the company's name with a rubber stamp on some pages.

(xiii) A materials gate pass should be introduced for taking out materials. These should be signed only by a few persons duly authorized for the purpose.

(xiv) Outgoing vehicles may be checked.

(xv) Adequate publicity should be given to any punishment awarded to employees for pilferage.

Malpractices by Stores Staff: The following measures may be taken against malpractices:

(i) All incoming materials must be first received in the receiving section. These should not go directly to the stores. The receiving section and the stores, therefore, act as a double check on each other.

(ii) Materials coming in by truck, particularly expensive raw materials should be weighed for both gross and tare weight, preferably on weighing scales within the factory premises.

(iii) The registration numbers of the incoming and outgoing vehicles must be recorded at the gate. A copy of the record should go to Accounts so as to tally with the vehic1e numbers mentioned on Goods Inward Notes and thus ensure that deliveries purported to have been effected by lorries have been really received.

(iv) A separate set of records of the stock should be maintained by Accounts and Stock Control. The balances in each must be tallied up at least once a year.

(v) Surprise check of the stocks should made by officials delegated for the job.

(vi) A system of continuous stocktaking or stock verification by accounts staff or internal auditors must be instituted. If major discrepancies are found, written explanation should be obtained from the stores staff. Frequency of checks should be increased.

(vii) Scrutinize excessive quantities shown as issued to the shop.

(viii) Keep a watch on consumption of materials, and compare periodically the expenses or cost of jobs of identical nature.

(ix) Vouchers relating to demurrage, transport and. labour charges must be carefully scrutinized and occasionally verified from the railways, transport companies, etc.

10.5 MANDATORY REGULATIONS

Storekeepers should be thoroughly familiar with the statutory requirements, rules, by-laws and other official regulations effecting the storage, safety, etc., of the stores premises. Typical examples are the petroleum regulations.

Storage of Petroleum Products: The storage of petroleum products requires special licences to be obtained from the Chief Controller of Explosives. Such storage is governed by the Petroleum Act, 1934 and the Petroleum Rules, 1978 made there under. Some of the relevant provisions of the Petroleum Rules are given below:

Petroleum products are divided into three categories:

(i) Dangerous petroleum (Class 'A') or highly inflammable gaseous or liquid products whose flash point is below 24.5°C. These are petrol, naphtha, aviation gasoline and LPG.

(ii) Non-dangerous petroleum (Class 'B') or products whose flash point is between 24.5°C and 665°C. These are HSD, kerosene and ATF.

(iii) Heavy petroleum (Class 'C') or products whose flash point is 66°C and above. Examples are furniture oil, LDO and LSHS.

Beside, there is a fourth category called excluded petroleum products. These are bitumen and lubes.

Special Precautions Against Accident

(1) No person shall commit or attempt to commit any act which may tend to cause a fire or explosion in or about any place where petroleum is refined stored or handled, or any vehicle, carriage or vessel in which petroleum is transported.

(2) Every person storing petroleum and every person in charge of or engaged in the storage, handling or transport of petroleum shall at all times (a) comply with the provisions of these rules and the conditions of any license relating thereto; (b) observe all precautions for the prevention of accident by fire or explosion.

10.6 FIRE PRECAUTIONS

The extent of fire risk depends upon the construction of the buildings and the nature of the stock held. The question of building construction is examined in another chapter, and we are therefore not concerned with that aspect here. In the first place, the local authority and the insurance company will no doubt have some interest in the fire risk standard acceptable, and their views or regulations will have to be taken into account. Thereafter it is most desirable to have the advice and guidance of the local chief fire officer. In many storehouses and stockyards, the risk of fire is negligible, but in others it may be severe. the usual precautions, where the fire risk is substantial, are listed as follows:

(i) Smoking on the premises is forbidden and notices posted to this effect.

(ii) Appropriate fire-prevention equipment is provided: extinguishers, ladders, axes, fire buckets, hoses, and so on. In major establishments it is not unusual to find a fire engine or trailer pump and, where the fire risk is high, an automatic overhead sprinkler system may be installed. All such equipment is regularly inspected and maintained.

(iii) Instructions on the drill to be observed in case of fire are posted up on the notice board.

(iv) Works and stores personnel are trained in firefighting duties and practices held at intervals.

(v) The procedure for calling the fire brigade in case of need is thoroughly publicized.

(vi) Specially inflammable stores are segregated in a separate building or in separate stacks.

Statutory and Other Regulations

Storekeepers should be aware of statutory requirements, by-laws or other official regulations affecting the safety of storehouse premises or their contents, e.g. explosives regulations, petroleum regulations.

Inspection by Supervisors

At regular intervals a senior supervisor, such as the stores manager or chief storekeeper, should inspect storehouse and stockyard premises and equipment to satisfy himself that they are in good order and that physical conditions are up to the required standard.

Stores personnel should also be trained in fire fighting and specific responsibilities given to specific people so that there is no confusion when a fire occurs.

Precautions Against Fire Hazards

The Factories Act, 1948 makes various provisions for fire precautions under Sections 36 to 40 of the Act.

Fire is caused usually by an accident. While safety measures are necessary, prevention of accidents is extremely desirable. There should not be any complacency that fire insurance is a coverage against fire losses.

The usually common causes of fire are:

(i) Electrical short circuits.

(ii) Sparks from shunting engines which may ignite an inflammable article.

(iii) Smoking by staff or clients inside the godown.

(iv) Auto-combustion.

Provision of fire extinguishers at vantage points is necessary to prevent spreading of fire. Fire extinguishers may be portable, stationary or mobile.

Chemical extinguishers are of three types:

(a) Soda acid type for general use.

(b) Foam type for use over oil.

(c) Carbon-tetra-chloride type for use in electric short circuit.

Each store should be provided with a fire alarm, water hydrant, water, portable water pump, and sand. Pattern shop or timer depot may be provided with an automatic sprinkler system.

First-Aid Appliances: First-aid boxes, equipped with the prescribed contents, which will readily accessible during all working hours, shall be provided and maintained in every factory. The number of such boxes shall not be less than one for every one hundred and fifty workers.

Fire Prevention

This can be achieved by good housekeeping. For example there should be no oil or grease spills. Cotton waste or rags soaked with oil should be kept in closed containers so that oxygen availability is less and fire cannot take place.

There should be in-built safety, i.e., safety should be considered at the design stage and a suitable layout established.

Some common causes of fires in warehouses are electrical therefore, loose temporary wiring connection should not exist. In case flammable material is stored, wires should run in conduits, and flame-proof wiring switches, etc., are to be used. Excessive electrical load should be prevented as it will cause short circuit. Grounding connections should be checked.

Smoking: Smoking should be allowed only in designated areas. Contents of ashtrays should be cleaned in a metal container. Flammable materials like Kerosene or Petrol should not be used as cleaning agent on the floors walls, doors or any other equipment as it may cause fire. Chemicals should be stored in designated areas. Properties of chemicals should be known. Cleaning materials like phenol, acids should be stored in designated areas only.

Malicious Burning/Arson: Check for any unauthorized entry and for suspicious happenings around.

Fire Protection: Adequate fire fighting equipment should be provided. For every 1000 sft floor area one extinguisher should be provided in such a way that no person has to cover a distance of more than 75 ft to pick up the extinguisher or $C0_2$ extinguisher. For material fire provide soda acid extinguisher. For flammable liquids, foam type extinguisher is advisable. However, if dry chemical powder extinguishers can be provided it would be the best since this extinguisher is suitable for all above types of fires.

Early detection of fire is very important. First three minutes of the fire are most important and equipment like extinguishers is useful if the fire can be extinguished within 3 mins.

Fire Fighting Equipment: Use of extinguishers is very simple if you know how lo operate the extinguishers at the time of fire. Training of persons in fire fighting is necessary. Practical demonstration at the warehouses at least once in three months should be arranged. Important telephone nos. like that of fire brigade, police, ambulance, etc. should he available in the premises and fire brigade should be summoned in case of large fire.

In warehouses where rubber products are stored large quantities of foam will be required. In case of rubber, fire-masks will be required as rubber generates lot of smoke.

For large warehouses, fire hydrant facilities should exist. Fire pump of adequate capacity fire hydrant lines, jet nozzles, fog nozzles should be available.

For small warehouses fire extinguishers, sand buckets and water buckets should be provided.

For flammable products observe safety distances. If explosives are stored take precautions against static electricity, impact of vibrations. Some explosives can explode even if one shouts loudly.

If storing asbestos fibers, take care against inhalation hazards. Use masks.

If storing heavy engineering materials, store in such a manner that heavy equipment cannot fall ovcr somebody and there is no dropping hazard.

Provide sufficient lighting in the warehouse area.

Where fork lifts are used, mark aisles. Train fork lift drivers for reversing or taking turns. At blind corners, provide mirrors at corners for proper vision.

Security: A tremendous amount of materials are lost each year from Indian warehouse because of the absence of proper security arrangements. Losses arising form pilferage or other damage are very common. Such losses can cost severe financial damage and hence the necessity for proper security.

Many kinds of fencing are available. One popular arrangement is to have galvanized or plastic coated chain-link fencing about 2 m high with steel or concrete posts. Sometimes the posts are cranked to carry two or three strands of barbed wire above the chain-link fencing, thus increasing total height and giving more protection against trespassers.

Gates

The number of gates should be kept to a minimum and all gates should be lockable. Railway gates must be provided if required.

Fire Fighting Measures

If large quantities of inflammable materials are held (e.g., timber), permanent fire-prevention equipment should be installed. Where the fire risk is great and the stocks are of high value, it may be worthwhile to have a complete ring main around the stockyard (i.e., a large diameter pipe, usually underground, carrying water for fire fighting). Access roads and the main gangways in the yard should be wide enough to accommodate the local fire engines in case of need. It may be thought desirable to keep a mobile pump on the premises, and there should be adequate provision of standpipes, hoses, chemical extinguishers, and water and sand buckets as necessary. In addition, stacks of noninflammable materials can be arranged in such a way as to provide a fire break to limit the spread of a fire if one does occur.

10.7 TRAINING

The specification, control and assurance of product quality can be carried out only by competent personnel. ISO 9001 therefore requires documented procedures for identifying training needs and for training all personnel performing activities affecting quality. ISO 9004-1 specifies qualifications. training and motivation as the key factors in achieving quality. An enterprise needs to address each of these factors for the effective implementation of a quality system.

Identification of Training Needs

Clearly, when a company is introducing a quality system based on ISO 9000, its stores personnel must be trained in the concept and methodology of implementing quality systems. In addition, the need for organized training can arise in the following situations:

- When it is found that certain processes are being performed unsatisfactorily because of the inadequate knowledge or skills of the task performers;
- When new technology or equipment is being introduced;

- When new products are to be launched;
- When the company is venturing into new export markets requiring the use of another language and familiarity with new product requirement.

Training procedures should cover the identification of training needs, the definition of responsibility for organizing training, and the determination of the knowledge or skill levels to be achieved by various categories of staff.

Training Senior Executives

All executives, including the chief executive officer, should have a clear understanding of the quality system, its operation and the criteria for assessing its effectiveness. To achieve this, they could attend seminars on ISO 9000 or undergo special orientation and appreciation programmes within the company. Executives should be given some exposure to the quality audit and the criteria for evaluating the effectiveness of the system.

Training Middle Management

Second-level engineers and managers in functional areas affecting quality play a crucial role in the implementation of quality systems. Their training should cover two aspects. The first is their professional competence in areas such as design, process engineering, testing stores and purchase management. The second concerns the company's quality policy, quality system, documentation procedures and work instructions as applicable to their areas of responsibility. When training in quality systems is being planned, attention should also be given to training in statistical techniques such as process-capability studies, statistical sampling, statistical process control, data collection and analysis as well as problem-solving techniques.

Training Stores Supervisors and Workers

The basic work elements in all functional areas are carried out by workers under the guidance of their supervisors. Their skill and competence have a decisive effect on the quality of the end-product. These workers and their supervisors should be thoroughly trained in the skills required for their tasks. They need to know how to handle materials and equipment in stores and they should be able to read and understand specifications, drawings and other documentation on quality-related activities. Some training in elementary statistics is also prescribed to create an awareness of the occurrence of variability in there work. This will help the staff to improve their working styles and to become more confident about their work.

Some training can take the form of organized courses, but much of it will on the job, with employees working as understudies to their seniors. A full record of persons trained, the scope and duration of training and qualifications attained should be documented centrally. This record should be made available to various departments so that personnel can be deployed on the basis of their qualifications.

10.8 STORES MANUAL

As the organization grows, the stores also increases in size and more people are recruited for various jobs here. For training such individuals, the best method is to have a Stores Manual which gives all instructions in respect of their duties and responsibilities as well as safety and security requirements.

Some of the advantages and disadvantages of such a manual are:

Advantages

(i) It provides, in readily accessible form, a complete set of standing instructions which have to be observed by Stores personnel.

(ii) It facilitates standardization of procedures and paperwork.

(iii) Because of standardization, Stores personnel can be trained more quickly and efficiently and all of them can become accustomed to the common procedure. Personnel therefore, can be interchanged between one section and the other.

(iv) It aids in supervision as the supervisor has a complete checklist of all the items necessary to be managed.

(v) A systematic procedure will lead to efficient operations.

Disadvantages

(i) A detailed manual is often said to limit local initiative innovation and creativity, restricting new ideas.

(ii) When the organization grows, procedures have to be changed and procedures do not tend to change owing to many reasons, thus inhibiting efficient operations.

A stores manual should basically provide:

(i) The organizational set up of Stores.

(ii) General policy statement on stocking of various materials.

(iii) Control and supervision of storehouses and stockyards.

(iv) Delegation of authority in regard to management of stocks.

(v) Inventory control and determination of maximum and minimum stock levels.

(vi) Custody of records and authorization of issues.

(vii) Standard procedures and forms.

(viii) Instructions in regard to housekeeping, security and safety of Stores, including fire fighting arrangements, etc.

The manual will be useful for training in the matter of safety, security and fire fighting. Everyone should not only to know and understand these provisions but should also ensure very strict observance of them.

Safety is one of the most important aspects of any training programme. For this reason we have collected together the most important safety rules to be complied by Truck operators. Never forget that a safety minded operator protects both himself and others and eliminates the risk of damage to the truck operators and its load.

Such are rules to be learnt thoroughly.

Never - lift loads which exceed the truck's maximum capacity shown on the nameplate.

Never - tilt the mast forward when carrying a maximum capacity load, except when over a stack.

Never - travel forwards with a bulky load obscuring your vision-travel in reverse.

Never - travel on soft ground.

Never - carry passengers.

Never - block fire-fighting equipment by parking the truck or stacking the load in front of it.

Never - attempt to carry out repairs, leave this to a qualified maintenance engineer.

Always - observe floor loading limits - find out what is the unladen weight of your truck.

Always - watch out for overhead obstructions.

Always - ensure the load is not wider than the width of the gangways en route.

Always - when driving on inclines follow these rules: when a load is carried, the load must always face uphill when no load is carried, the forks must always face downhill adjust tilt to suit gradient and raise just enough to clear the road.

Always - travel at a speed consistent with road and load conditions.

Always - sound the horn and slow down for corners.

Always - avoid sudden stops.

Always - travel with the forks lowered - maintaining ground clearance.

Always - ensure that bridge plates are secure and strong.

10.9 SUMMARY

Factories Act, 1948 contains safety provisions which must be observed by the stores management. Stores personnel should understand several factors that cause accidents of materials falling, persons tripping, injuries caused while lifting goods so that preventive action can be taken.

Next, stores personnel operating material handling equipment should be trained in safety measures that must be always observed by them to prevent accidents that cause injuries and damage.

Stores management has to implement appropriate measures to avoid thefts and pilferage by outsiders as well as by employees including stores personnel. Continuous vigilance is essential. It is also necessary for stores management to identify fire hazards and train personnel in preventing fire or explosions. Based on materials handled, prescribed fire fighting equipment has to be installed and religiously checked and maintained. Workers need to be trained in operating this equipment at regular intervals.

All stores security and safety instructions can be consolidated in stores manual for training existing and fresh stores employees.

Stores management has to familiarize itself with various legal provisions applicable with regard to hazardous stores handled and take measures to comply with them.

10.10 SELF ASSESSMENT QUESTIONS

(1) Identify different types of accidents that happen in a stores. How can they be avoided?

(2) What measures are required to prevent thefts by outsiders?

(3) List measures required to control pilferage by employees.

(4) Which aspects the training programme in stores safety, should focus?

(5) Would you recommend use of stores manual to train stores employees in safety and security? Why?

Chapter 11

STORES ACCOUNTING AND RECORD

Objectives

After studying this chapter, you should be able to understand:

- Treatment of excess or short quantity received against Purchase order.
- Stores Records.
- Stock Control
- Methods of Pricing Issues
- Reconciliations

Structure:

11.1 PROVISIONAL PRICING OF RECEIPTS

In case there is a time lag between the details of supply of material and the receipt of supplier's bill the goods receipt cum-inspection note should be priced at provisional vaules based on the prices agreed as per the purchase order due to the fact that it may not be possible to wait till the receipt of supplier's invoice. In such case, provisional pricing may result into a small difference due to other charges billed which are not shown in purchase order fully and correctly. Based on the provisional pricing, issues of materials also are valued accordingly. If the difference between provisional pricing and actual pricing based on supplier's invoice at a later date is small, it may be treated as factory overhead. If it is more the purchase account should be rectified and consequently, the previous issues also require rectification.

Discrepancies in Material Receipts

A. Excess supply of quantity than ordered:

(1) If it is required excess may be retained and taken on charge. Payment has to be made at the agreed price as given in the purchase order.

(2) If it is not required by the organisation, the excess may be returned to the supplier. In such case payment will be released for the accepted (ordered) quantity only.

B. Short supply of quantity than ordered

(1) If the balance quantity is still required the suppliers may be asked to supply.

(2) If he does not supply it may be purchased from alternative source recovering the extra cost and liquidated amages from the original supplier.

(3) If the balance quantity is not required the supplier may be informed accordingly and the purchase order treated as closed.

C. Quality not as per the specifications

(1) If it is required retain them at a price lower than that mentioned in the purchase order, i.e., price mutually agreed upon.

(2) If it is not required return it to supplier requesting him to replace the materials as per the purchase order.

D. Quality above standard;

(1) If it is required. retain them at a higher price mutually agreed upon.

(2) If it is not required, return it to supplier requesting him to replace the materials as per the purchase order.

11.2 PAYMENT FOR RECEIPTS

(A) Supplier should be paid as per the Quantity Accepted (i.e., quantity received minus quantity rejected) multiplied by the price agreed with reference to the purchase order placed on him. While checking the suppliers invoice, the following points also may be looked into:

(1) Trade and Quantity discount as per the terms of purchase order.

(2) Transport charges depending on whether FOR works or FOR destination, etc., i.e., depending on terms of delivery.

(3) Taxes such as sales tax, excise duty, customs duty, octroi and other local taxes, etc., as per the terms of purchase order

(4) Terms of payment.

(5) Charges for containers depending on the non-returnable containers, returnable containers for which there is no charge or optionally returnable containers for which there is a refund at full cost or lower cost.

(6) Packing and other forwarding charges.

(B) It is to be noted that sometimes organisation might have paid the freight charges i.e., carriage inwards but these are to be borne by the supplier as per the terms of purchase order. : Similarly Demurrage 'or wharf age charges might have been incurred by the organisation because of the fault of the supplier for the reasons such as non-dispatch of RR or LR, etc., by him. All these charges paid by the organisation but to be borne by the supplier are to be recovered at the time of passing of supplier's invoice. Cash discount may be availed depending on the management policy and liquidity position.

(C) A cheque for the net amount should be sent to supplier along with debit note for rejected materials and for the charges recovered from supplier indicating reason for the same.

11.3 ACCOUNTING FOR ISSUE OF MATERIAL

After posting of the stores requisition in the issue column of Bin Card, one copy is sent to costing department for necessary posting in stores ledger, pricing of issues and accounting thereof. These stores requisitions may be for Direct Material or for indirect material. If it is for Direct Material. Job No. or work order No. is to be mentioned. If it is for indirect material standing order No. is to be mentioned in case of factory and Cost Account No. is to be mentioned in case of Administration. Selling and Distribution Depts.

Journal Entries :	For Direct Material	: Debit Work-in-progress A/c Credit Stores Ledger A/c.
	(Subsidiary Register)	: Debit Job or process or product as the case may be
	For indirect material	: Debit Factory/Administration/Selling Distribution over head control a/c credit stores Ledger control a/c

Accounting for Material Returns, Transfers, Shortage and Excess.

This has been discussed after pricing of material issues.

Adjustment of Unusual Balances in Stores Ledger.

Some unusual balance are often revealed in the stores ledger because of pricing of issues at average rates and their accounting adjustments are as follows:

NATURE OF BALANCE	TREATMENT	JOURNAL ENTRY
A. Plus Quantity nil or minus value	Quantity on hand should be valued	Debit : Stores ledger Control a/c Creadit : Overhead a/c
B. Minus Quantity	There should not be minus quantity. This may be, due to error. It should be located and rectified,	No. Journal entry.
C. Nil QuantIty Plus value	Value should be wiped out	Debit : Factory overhead a/c Credit : Stores ledger control a/c
D. Nil Quantity minus value	Value should be wiped out	Debit : Stores ledger control a/c Credit : Factory overhead a/c.

Flow Chart-Recording of Material Documents

A. BIN CARD (QUANTITY)

Receipt	Issue	Balance
Goods Receipt and Inspection Note Material Return Note	Stores Requisition Note Materials Returned to Suppliers	Stock Verification Note Note excess or Shortage

B. PRICING OF DOCUMENTS

Document	Pricing
Goods Receipt and Inspection Note	Priced from purchase orders, suppliers' invoices
Materials returned to supplier	-do-
Stores Requisition Note	Priced from stores ledger
Material Return Note	-do-
Stock Verification Note-Excess or shortage	-do-
Material Transfer Note	Priced from Job Ledger

C. STORES LEDGER (QUANTITY, RATE AND VALUE)

Receipt (Debit)	Issue (Credit)	Balance
Goods Receipt and Inspection Note Material Return Note	Stores Requisition Note Materials returned to suppliers	Stock verification Note excess or shortage

D. JOB LEDGER (VALUE)

Debit	Credit
Stores Requisition Note Material Transfer Note (materials received from another job).	Material Return Note Material Transfer Note (materials sent to another job)

11.4 STORES RECORDS

Two sets of records are maintained. They are Bin Card and Stores Ledger. Bin Cards are maintained by Store officer and Stores ledger is maintained in Cost Accounting Department. First has only quantity data, second both quality and value.

(A) Bin Cards

Bin means a rack, container, or space where goods are kept. For each kind of material, an inventory tag is attached to the bin and a bin card is maintained. A bin card is a quantitative record of receipts, issues and closing balance of each item of stores. The bin cards are used not only for entering the receipts and issues but also for controlling the stock by watching the maximum and minimum levels stated on the card. When the ordering level is reached the store keeper has to send the requisition for further supplies. For each entry, whether relating to receipt or issue, the balance quantity is calculated and recorded in the 'Balance' column. It should agree with the physical balance in Bins and Stores Ledger balances.

BIN CARD

Bin No. | Maximum level:
Desc ription : | Minimum level:
Grade : | Ordering level:
Material Code No. | Ordering quantity:
Location:
Unit:

Date	Receipt		Issues		Balance of	Remark
	GRN No.	Qty	SR. No.	Qty	Stock Qty.	

In large concerns, two-bin system is adopted. In the system two bins are maintained for each material. One bin contains the minimum quantity or reserve quantity and no issues are made from this bin except under emergency requirement when the other bin is empty. At this time new Purchase Requisition is released. Another bin contains the balance quantity from which issues are made usually. This system facilitates the physical verification of stores as well as placing the purchase requisitions.

Triple Bin System

While the double bin system is followed for materials control and reduces the risk of shortage of materials under normal circumstances, sometimes necessity may arise in which case the double bin system be modified as triple bin system. It has been shown in the following diagram along with double bin system:

Double Bin System

A	B
Minimum Level	

Triple Bin System

Minimum Level		B
A1	A2	
Danger Level		

The sum of Al + A2 + B is the total stock and the consumption of materials of 'B' portion indicates the minimum level and necessity for fresh supplies. Materials of Al + A2 portions are equal to minimum stock level and Al portion is equal to danger stock level. If fresh supplies have not been received and materials of A2 portion are also consumed, it indicates the danger level and any delay in receiving the materials will lead to interruption in the production with its concomitant evils. Then, the firm should take emergency action to procure materials even paying slightly higher prices so as to keep the production going.

Re-ordering level is useful to know when fresh order is to be placed. While double bin system is useful to know the minimum level and consequential necessity for fresh supplies, triple bin system has the added advantage of identifying an emergency situation for procuring the materials on top priority basis.

Illustration 1

The following information regarding coal is obtained from the Stores Records of a factory: Dec. 1977: (1) Opening Balance-200 tons; (2) Issued on Requisition No. 273-57 tons; (3) Issued on Requisition No. 285-83 tons; (4) Received from supplier by Challan No. 77 of Dec. 5, 1977 ; 120 tons. The supply was expected on this date. (5) Issued on Requisition No. 341-92 tons; (6) Issued on Requisition No. 364-30 tons; (7) Received from supplier by Challan No. 98 of Dec. 17, 1977-100 tons. The supply was expected on this date. (8) Issued on Requisition No. 428-69 tons ; (9) Issued on Requisition No.447-29 tons; (10) Received from supplier by Challan No. 171 of Dec. 30, 1977-125 tons. The supply was expected on this date. Received back by Credit Slip No. 31-10 tons. (11) Issued on Requisition No. 483-85 tons. Examination by the Stock Verifier on Dec. 26, 1977 revealed a Shortage of 5 tons, Maximum 200 tons. Minimum 50 tons. ordering level 100 tons. Draw up the Bin Card (No. 23) for Coal with all the necessary details showing the transactions in Dec. 1977.

Answer:

Bin Card (No. 23) Coal

Description: COAL	Minimum level : 200 tons
Material code Location code	Minimum level: 50 tons
Bin No: 23	Ordering level: 100 tons
Stores ledger folio No	Accounting unit: ton

Date	GRN No. (tons)	Receipts Qty. (tons)	Issues SR No.	Qty. (tons)	Balance of stock Qty. (tons)
1.12.09					200
2.12.09			273	57	143
4.12.09			285	83	60
5.12.09	7	120			180
8.12.09			341	92	88
12.12.09			364	30	58
17.12.09	98	100			158
24.12.09			428	69	89
26.12.09			S.V.	5 (shortage)	84
28.12.09			447	29	55
30.12.09	171	125			180
Credit Slip NO.37	10			85	190
31.12.09			483		105

(B) Stores Ledger:

The Stores Ledger, also called as priced stores ledger is maintained in the cost accounting department and is akin to the Bin cards in all respects except that the rate and values are also shown in addition to the columns given in the Bin Card. For each kind and class of material ledger is maintained. A form of the stores ledger is given below:

STORES LEDGER

PSR No :	Maximum level :
Description :	Minimum level :
Grade :	Ordering level :
Material Code No:	Ordering Quantity :
Location :	
Unit:	

D A T E	Receipt				Issue				Balance of stock		
	GRN No.	Qty	Rate	Amount	SR	Qty.	Rate	Amount	Qyt	Rate	Amount

Generally, it is maintained in a loose leaf ledger form. The number of cards are the same as in case of Bin Cards which are dependent upon the number of kinds and classes of materials. If the new Bin Card is opened or any Bin Card is closed, the information should be sent by the Store Keeper so that similar action is taken in Cost Accounting Department also in respect of opening or closing of stores ledger cards, The posting in the Stores Ledger is the same way as done in the case of Bin Cards. In the large organisations, the line number of Bin Cards is also indicated in the Material document so that the document is valued and posted in the same line number in the stores ledger also. It facilitates the reconciliation between Bin Card and Stores Ledger in such a way that balance after entry in the bin card is tallied with that of balance shown in the stores ledger. By following the system of serial number of documents as mentioned before and the line numbers, missing vouchers, if any, are called for from the Stores Department by the Cost Accounting Department.

11.5 RECONCILIATIONS

Reconciliation is three-folds (A) Reconciliation between physical balance of stores and bin card balance in respect of each material (B) Reconciliation between bin cards and stores ledger in regard to quantities; and (C) Reconciliation between the stores ledger and cost ledger in regard to value.

(A) Reconciliation between physical balance of stores and bin card balances:

Physical balance of material should reconcile with the bin card balance. Normally, there should be no difference between both the balances except due to the causes discussed later under the perpetual inventory system. If the physical balance is less than the bin card balance, the shortage is to be entered in the issue column and the excess, if any, should be entered in the receipt column preferably in red ink.

(B) Reconciliation between bin cards and stores ledger in regard to quantities:

After posting in the bin cards, all the material documents such as goods receipt and inspection note, stores requisition note, material return note, materials returned to suppliers, stock verification note-shortage and excess are to be valued and posted in the stores ledger by following the same order and sequence as followed in the bin cards. Thus, normally there should not be any difference between the quantity balances shown in the two sets of records, But in practice, differences arise due to the following reasons:

(1) Non-posting of a document in Bin Card or stores ledger card.

(2) Posting in the wrong bin card or stores ledger card.

(3) Posting in the wrong column, i.e., posting of receipt in the issue column or vice versa.

(4) Arithmetical errors in working out the balance. The differences should be reconciled and corrected at regular intervals: The differences can be avoided if the following system is adopted :

(a) Serial number of the document:

(b) Line number of the posting in Bin Card; and

(c) Indicating the balance of stock in each and every material document after posting in the Bin Card. This facilitates automatic reconciliation at the time of posting in Stores Ledger Card.

Maintenance of both sets of cards is a duplication of work. However, it became essential because of the following reasons:

(1) Bin cards are maintained in Stores Department.

(2) Stores Ledger cards are maintained in the Cost Accounting Department.

(3) Material, like money, requires second check.

To obviate the above difficulty, it is suggested that a CostAccountant is to be posted in Stores Department and asked to maintain the stores ledger there itself. Then the maintenance of Bin cards can be avoided. Cost Accountant has to post the quantities and values in the usual way. In the same usual way, he has to prepare monthly or periodical journal entries and pass on the information to the Cost Accounting Department for necessary postings in the Cost Ledger. This system of simplification avoids lot of expenditure.

(C) Reconciliation between stores ledger and cost ledger in regard to value :

All the receipts, issues, returns, shortages and excess of materials are to be valued, posted and journalised. All the journal entries are posted in the cost ledger. Then the value of closing stock of all the stores ledger cards together should reconcile with the value of closing stock as shown, in the cost ledger. The differences, if any, due to wrong postings and working out balances, etc., should be reconciled and corrected at regular intervals,

Every organisation in spite of its impeccable system faces discrepancies of stock compared to the physical stock. It requires timely verification for avoiding any gross irregularity in future. Some reasons for discrepancies

(i) Incoming goods placed in the bin but GRN or Materials Return Note not posted in the. stock card.

(ii) Material issued but stock card not posted.

(iii) Incorrect quantities issued, i.e., issue of more quantity or less quantity than what was indented or noted in the bin card or stock card.

(iv) Errors in quantity posted. For example, 20mt is posted as 21mt or 700 is posted as 900

(v) Posting done on wrong stock card.

(vi) Errors in posting, i.e., entry of receipts made in 'issue' column.

(vii) Errors in addition or subtraction while posting.

(viii) Actual shortages due to human element in receipts and issues, e.g. in bulk handling.

(ix) Pilferage. This is a very common reason, especially of costly material.

(x) Natural phenomena evaporation.

Errors of the above nature can lead to several problems. In order to avoid problems arising from shortages or overages, physical checking of stocks or stock checking is very necessary. Of course, apart from this objective, checking of inven.tories is vital from the point of accountabilit.

Some of the important objectives are as follows:

(i) To verify the accuracy of stock records.

(ii) To support the value of stock shown in the balance sheet by physical verification.

(iii) To disclose the possibility of fraud theft or loss.

(iv) To reveal any weaknesses in the system for the custody and control of stock.

Techniques of Stocktaking: Various methods, of stock verificationcan are adopted. The actual technique to be used will depend on the size and value of the stock held and its complexity. Some of the methods generally used are described below:

(i) Annual Stocktaking: This is done at the end of each financial year by closing down the Stores for a certain number of days. As per statutory requirement each item must be physically checked and counted and the auditor must be satisfied that the physical checkings has been satisfactorily carried out.

(ii) Perpetual Inventory Method: If the stores is very big and a very large number of materials are stocked. a year-end stock verification would be a very difficult task unless a large number of stock verifiers are employed. A technique to overcome this problem is the perpetual inventory method. It is also some times called the rotational system of stock checking.

The stock check should be planned in such a way that all the items are checked at least once in a year and the important items checked two, three, or four times a year.

Some companies adopt a system of checking the balances every time a receipt or issue is made. In a small orgnisation, this would be adequate, but it would very difficult where a large number of items are stocked.

(iii) Daily Stock Checking: In this method the stockeepers arc required to check 12 to 15 times a day at random. This enables Stores to locate discrepancies as the storekeepers are conversant with possible areas/items where such discrepancies are likely to occur.

(iv) Checking by Stores-in-charge: This method is similar to the one described above except that the checking is done by stores-in-charge.

(v) Periodic Checking: This is halfway between annual checking and perpetual checking. This checking is done by Accounts and Stores at regular intervals, e.g., in two months.

Investigation of discrepancie, reconciliation, Stock adjustment and write-off.

Minor Discrepancie: For example, in measuring 100 steel bars of random length two people are not likely to get the same result to the nearest foot. If, therefore, discrepancies of small proportions appear to be found in such circumstances, it is advisable to leave the book balance unaltered unless the value involved is significant.

Storekeeper's Agreement: Stocktakers should not declare a diserepancy on any item without first giving the storekeeper concerned the opportunity of investigation. There are several reasons for this:

(i) The storekeeper usually has a better practical knowledge of the stock than anyone else and may be able to correct errors on the part of the stock verifiers, particularly errors of identification.

When the storekeeper is unable to explain a discrepancy, the stock sheet should be signed to indicate an agreement that the discrepancy is genuine.

Investigation of Discrepancies: After the stocktaker and storekeeper have agreed that a discrepancy exists, following steps should be taken in regard to investigation of discrepancy discrepancies:

(i) Examine the stock record since the date of the last check to make sure that there are no arithmetical errors, obvious omissions or duplications in posting.

(ii) Scrutinise the record to see that there has been no mistake over units of issue.

(iii) Examine the items kept in neighboring bins to find out if a balancing discrepancy exists on another item.

(iv) Check the basic documents (i.e., receipt, issue, transfer, return-to-store notes, etc.,) for any exceptionally large or apparently unusual transactions.

(v) Check all basic documents on which action has been taken since the last stocktaking.

(vi) Have the physical stocktaking verified by an independent person.

For any identified loss write of should be done and stock records are to be adjuststed.

B. Methods for Valuation of Issues

B.1. First in First Out (FIFO): Stock Valuation

This method is used under the assumption that the materials which are received first are issued first. Hence, the price of the first batch/lot purchased is charged for all the issues until the stock of that batch/lot is exhausted. In other words, the issues are priced in the chronological order of receipt. In this case, issues to production/maintenance are valued at historical price and stock is valued at latest purchase price.

Advantages

(1) Issues are charged at actual cost and hence no adjustment for profit or loss is necessary.

(2) This method is easy to understand and operate if prices do not fluctuate too often.

(3) The value of closing stock represents the current market price.

(4) This Method is useful in the case of slow moving materials bulk items and the materials of high unit cost.

(5) Issues are priced in the same order in which the materials are issued.

Disadvantages

(1) If the prices fluctuate too often, this method will involve more calculations with resultant clerical errors.

(2) Useful comparison of material cost of one job to another is not possible if the prices fluctuate too often.

(3) The issue prices do not reflect the current market prices.

(a) In case of rising prices. the charge to job is under-priced and profits are unduly inflated

(b) In case of-falling prices, the charge to job is over-priced.

This will result into high quotations thereby losing prospective sales.

(4) Sometimes, more than one price has to be adopted for pricing a single issue of materials.

(5) In case the materials found defective after their issue to Production, credit adjustment will be required when such defective materials are returned to suppliers and it will affect the pricing of next few issues.

(6) When the excess material is returned from Production to Stores, the adjustment will create complications in case of issues with more than one price as in (4) above.

B.2 Last in First Out (LIFO)

This method uses the price of the last batch purchased for all issues until stock of that batch is exhausted. Hence, issues are valued at current prices and stock is valued at historical prices.As the issues are valued at current prices, this method is also called as Replacement Cost method. Here also, the physical flow of materials is not concerned to the Cost Accountant.

Advantages

(1) Like the FIFO system, issues are charged at actual cost and hence no adjustment for profit or loss is necessary.

(2) Issues are valued at current prices and hence charge to production is more appropriate;

(3) Like the FIFO system, the method also is easy to understand and operate, if the prices do not fluctuate too often.

(4) This method is useful when the prices are on the increasing trend,

(5) It obviates the necessity of ascertaining the replacement price of materials.

Disadvantages

(1) Like the FIFO system, this method also will involve more calculations with resultant clerical errors, if the prices fluctuate too often.

(2) Like the FIFO system, useful comparison of material cost of one job to another is not possible if the prices fluctuate too often.

(3) As the stock is valued at historical prices, it will not be reflected in the Balance Sheet at realistic value and thus false working capital position is shown in the Balance Sheet. Secret Reserve will be created.

(4) Issues are not valued in same order in which the materials are issued.

(5) Like the FIFO system, sometimes more than one price has to be adopted for pricing a single issue of materials.

(6) During the periods of falling prices, the issues are priced at lower rates and the stock value will be at higher prices. In such case, it requires some adjustment on the principle of valuation of stock at the cost or market price whichever is lower.

(7) If the latest receipt rate is not finalised the work of pricing of issues will be held up.

B.3 Highest in First Out (HIFO)

Under this method, issues are valued at the highest price paid for a lot/batch of materials until stock of that lot/batch is exhausted and so on. It has the effect of overvaluing production and undervaluing stock i.e. stock should always remain at the lowest value. Thus, the Secret Reserve will be created. This method is complicated to administer and hence it has not become so popular. This method is mainly used in case of monopoly products or cost plus contracts.

B.4 Next in First Out (NIFO)

Under this method, issues are valued at the price estimated or expected for the next purchase. This is similar to replacement price.

The problem will arise if the price ruling at the time of supply differs from the purchase order price.

B.5 Base Stock Price

This usually used with FIFO or LIFO method by assuming a fixed minimum stock of materials which is called as the Base Stock. The minimum stock is not used except under emergency. This method is suitable in smelting, tanning, and oil refining industries where it is necessary to keep minimum stock of basic raw materials because of long period of processing. Issues are valued at actual cost. As this method is used with FIFO or LIFO, all the advantages and disadvantages of FIFO or LIFO will apply depending on the method followed.

C.1 Simple Average Price

Under this method, issues are valued at simple average price which is the average of number of prices. (available at the time of issue) without any regard to quantities. Issues are not, therefore, charged out at actual cost and hence profit or loss may be incurred by adopting this system. It is useful when the materials are purchased in the uniform quantities and prices do not fluctuate.

Advantages

(1) It is easy to operate.

(2) Cost distortion is not much because of adopting an averag price.

Disadvantages

(1) When the prices rise sharply, the closing stock may show a minus balance.

(2) As in case of FIFO and LIFO, the value of closing stock cannot be reconciled.

(3) As the quantities are not considered, the system may produce incorrect results.

(4) As the issues are not valued at actual cost, profit or loss may arise.

(5) Cumulative receipt column and cumulative issue column are to be adopted to ensure the average of number of prices available at the time of issue.

(6) Price has to be calculated at each issue of material made.

C.2 Periodic Simple Average Price

Under this method, simple average price will be calculated periodically (normally a month) and not at each issue of material. A simple average of all the receipts during a month will be arrived at and applied to all the issues during the month. The opening stock does not enter into the calculation because it was not purchased during the current period.

Advantages

(1) As there is only one issue rate for the whole period (normally) a month, it is very easy to operate.

(2) This system can be useful in process industries;

Disadvantages

(1) This system is not useful to jobbing industry.

(2) Though it is only one issue rate, it requires lot of time to calculate.

(3) The disadvantages at 1 to 4 of simple average price will apply here also.

C.3 Moving Simple Average Price

Under this method, the issues are valued at a price which is calculated by dividing the total of the periodic simple average prices of a given number of periods by the number of periods. It takes into account the average price of the current period and also the average prices for a given number of preceding periods; Generally, odd number of months, say 3, 5 or 7 is used. This method evens out price fluctuations over a number of periods and cost distortions from one job to another job are reduced. In case of rising prices, the stock is overvalued. Profit or loss may arise due to approximations.

C.4 Weighted Average Price

Under this method, issues are valued at a price which is calculated by dividing the total cost of material in the stock by the total quantity of material in that stock. This method averages prices after multiplying by their quantities. A new average price has to be worked out on each and every purchase of materials and this weighted average price is to be applied to all the issues till another purchase is made. To achieve accuracy, the issue price has to be calculated up to 4 decimal places.

Advantages

(1) This method is suitable where there are wide fluctuations in purchase prices and it evens out prices over the whole period of accounting because of considering the quantities

(2) Since the receipts are much less frequent than issues, number of calculations are not many as the weighted average price is calculated on the receipt of materials and not on the issue of materials.

(3) Value of closing-stock accepted for the purpose of Balance Sheet.

(4) It is easy to calculate.

Disadvantages

(1) As the issues are not valued at actual costs, profit or loss may arise.

(2) If the receipts are many, this method requires lot of calculations.

(3) Issue prices may be calculated up to 4 decimal points.

(4) Issues may not be at current prices.

(5) Inventory on hand does not represent current economic values.

C.5 Periodic Weighted Average Price

Under this method, the issues are valued at a price which is calculated by dividing the total cost of the materials obtained during tbat period by the quantity purchased. It is the weighted average price of materials purchased during a period. A new average price is calculated at the end of each period, normally a month and is applied to all the issues in that month.

Advantages

(1) Only one calculation is required at the end of the period, normally a month and hence it is easy to operate.

(2) As the quantities and costs are considered, this method is much more accurate than the periodic simple average price.

(3) It is useful in process industries where accounting entries can be made at the end of a period.

(4) It is usefully employed where the prices of materials fluctuate considerably.

(5) It evens out wide fluctuations in a particular period.

Disadvantages

(1) This method is not useful to jobbing industry.

(2) Profit or loss may arise as the issues are not valued at actual cost or current market price.

(3) The value of closing stock does not represent either the actual cost or current market price.

(4) This method involves considerable delay in pricing material issues and a heavy burden of clerical work at the end of the period. This can be avoided if the weighted average price of one period is used in the subsequent period.

C.6 Moving Weighted Average Price

To obtain the Moving Weighted Average Price, the total of the weighted average price of the current period and weighted average prices of given number of preceding periods is to be divided by the number of periods (i.e., current + preceding periods). This price is to be applied to all the issues in the current period. It is more or less similar to moving simple average method excepting that this is a Moving Weighted Average price and hence all the advantages and disadvantages of Moving Simple Average method are applicable here also.

D.1 Standard Price

It is a pre-determined price fixed on the basis of a specification of all the factors affecting price of materials in a future period; such factors include:

(1) The quantity of materials on hand

(2) The quantity of materials to be purchased

(3) Quantity discounts

(4) Prices normally paid or payable

(5) Normal purchasing cost involved.

(6) The likelihood of a rise or fall in prices due to market conditions

(7) Changes in production requirements

(8) Charging of containers, freight and warehousing expenses to the price of materials.

A standard price will be set for each material and is applied for all the issues in a period, normally a year. It is compared with the actual price paid. Profit or Loss may arise under this method also but it is not due to average prices it is on account of variances from a pre-determined price set for each material.

If the actual price paid exceeds standard, it is adverse variance and if the actual price is less than standard, it is favourable variance. All receipts under this method are posted at actual prices and issues at standard prices for each material. The difference between standard and actual is disposed of through price variance account.

This method can be utilised in most of the industries in general and Steel Industry in particular where material transactions are numerous, even though a system of standard costing is not in operation.

Standard price should not be set on a long term basis. It should be determined for short periods only and revised as and when necessary.

Advantages

(1) It is easy to operate because all the issues are priced at the same standard rate.

(2) Efficiency of purchase department can be measured

(3) Useful comparison of one job/process with another job/process can be made.

(4) It reduces the clerical costs as the standard price will be applied to all the issues in a period, normally a year.

Disadvantages

(1) Issues may not be at current economic values and hence profit or loss may arise which has to be adjusted in the accounts.

(2) It is very difficult to fix a standard price during the period of inflation or when prices fluctuate widely from time to time.

(3) The value of closing stock may show absurd figures.

(4) The trend of actual prices may not be reflected.

D.2 Inflated Price

It is a price. which includes a charge designed to cover the cost of contingencies of related costs.. Normally, the invoice price includes the cost, freight, insurance and taxes less discounts. Other Expenses like cost of receiving, inspection, storing and carrying, handling of materials and losses arising out of evaporation and breaking-up bulk, etc., are treated as production overhead. Under this method, all these expenses are added to determine the cost of issues. Hence, inflated price will recover the full cost of materials. This is not a separate method of pricing. Any of the prices — actual average, or notional — may be inflated for the purpose of valuation of issues.

D.3 Replacement Price or Market Price

Under this method, issues are valued at the replacement price prevailing in the market on the date of issue. The method presupposes the determination of replacement cost of material at the time of each issue which may involve considerable work.

Advantages

(1) It is easy to operate as there are no calculations of issue prices. Ascertain the market price and charge the issues accordingly.

(2) The issues are priced at the current market prices.

Disadvantages

(1) It is not so easy to get market quotation.

(2) It is very difficult to get the market prices daily for all the issues made on that day. In such case, current prices are to be estimated.

(3) Issues are not priced at actual cost.

(4) This method causes an element of unrealised profit or loss which has to be adjusted in accounts.

(5) The valuation of closing stock will not be at current market prices. In times of rising prices, the value of closing stock may show a negligible amount or even a negative amount. because of charging issues at higher market prices. In times of falling prices, the stock value becomes alarmingly high.

D.4 Re-Use Price

It is the price which is used to value a material in its re-use. This price is adopted for the issue of materials to other departments for an alternative use. Profit or Loss may arise because the issues are not valued at actual cost and it has to be adjusted in accounts.

11.6 SUMMARY OF PRICING METHODS

The various methods described above may be tabulated as follows:

PRICING OF MATERIAL ISSUES

- Specific Price
- Actual Cost
  - FIFO
  - LIFO
  - HIFO
  - NIFO
  - Base Stock
- Average Price
  - Simple
    - Simple Average
    - Periodic
    - Moving
  - Weighted
    - Weighted Average
    - Periodic
    - Moving
- Notional Price
  - Standard
  - Inflated
  - Replacement
  - Re-use

Impact of Pricing of Material Issues

The impact of pricing on cost of material of closing stock is summarised below :

	Method of Pricing	Effect on cost of materials issued.	Effect on value of closing stock.
(1)	Specific price	Actual cost but not current price	
(2)	FIFO	Actual cost but not current price	Nearer to current price
(3)	LIFO	Nearer to current price	Actual cost but not current price
(4)	HIFO	Actual cost but not current price	
(5)	NIFO	Neither actual cost nor current price	
(6)	Base Stock Price-through FIFO	Nearer to current price.	Actual cost but not current price
	Base Stock Price-through LIFO	Nearer to current price.	Actual cost but not current price
(7)	Simple Average price	Nearer to current price. not current price	Neither actual cost nor current price. It may indicate even negative value.

(8) Periodic Simple Average Price	,,	,,
(9) Moving Simple A verage Price	,,	,,
(10) Weighted Average Price	,,	,,
(11) Periodic Weighted A verage price	,,	,,
(12) Moving Weighted Average Price	,,	,,
(13) Standard Price	Reflects standard cost	Shows standard value. The difference between actual and standard is variance.
(14) Inflated Price	Reflects inflated price	Actual cost but not current price.
(15) Replacement Price or Market Price	Reflects current market price	May be valued at current price with necessary accounting adjustments.
(16) Re-use Price	Reflects re-use price.	,,

Pricing of Returns, Transfers, Shortage and Excess of Materials

A. Pricing of Material Returns from Production Department to Stores Department.

The excess material drawn from the Stores Department may be returned by the Foreman of the Production Department to the Stores Department. The quantity of materials returned should be entered in the receipt column and valued at the price at which the materials were originally issued. If the original issue is not ascertainable, the latest issue price can be adopted for pricing the material returns.

Journal Entry:

Debit: Stores Ledger Control Account

Credit: Work-in-progress account (i.e., job/process/product)

B. Materials Returned to Suppliers

Generally, the accepted quantity only should be entered in the receipt column. Depending on the technical condition of the material, if it is to be inspected over the machines for a certain number of hours and if it is found not acceptable after testing on the machines, etc. The same has to be returned to suppliers. Then the quantity should be entered in the issue column and valued at the price at which it was originally purchased from the supplier.

Journal Entry:

Debit: Sundry Creditors a/c.

Credit: Stores Ledger Control Account.

C. Pricing of Material Transfers

Sometimes, Foreman may not return the excess material drawn and meant for one particular job. Instead, he may use this material for another similar job. In such case, he need not return the material to the Store Keeper but he has to inform the Costing Department by way of Material Transfer Note for valuation and accounting thereof. In Cost Ledger, no transfer entry is required but in the Subsidiary Register of Jobs, the job where these excess materials are used has to be debited by crediting the job wherefrom the material has been transferred.

D. Shortages Found During Physical Verification

The quantity of shortage found during physical verification is to be entered in the issue column and valued at the issue price depending on the method followed, i.e., ***FIFO.*** **LIFO,** Weighted Average, etc., followed by the organisation.

Journal Entry :

(1) Debit: Factory Overhead a/c.

Credit: Stores Ledger Control a/c.

(If the shortage is normal)

(2) Debit: Costing P & L a/c

Credit: Stores Ledger Control a/c

(If the shortage is abnormal)

(3) Debit: Work-in-progress a/c

Credit: Stores Ledger Control a/c.

(If it is ascertained that the shortage was on account of wrong counting or weighing at the time of original issue of materials or a particular job).

E. Excess Found During Physical Verification

The excess quantity found during physical verification should be entered in the receipt column and valued at the latest purchase price or market price. If it is not ascertainable, it should be valued at latest issue price.

Journal Entry:

(1) Debit : Stores Ledger Control a/c

Credit : Factory Overhead a/c

(If the excess is due to normal causes)

(2) Debit: Stores Ledger Control a/c

Credit: Costing P & L a/c

(If the excess is due to abnormal circumstances).

(3) Debit: Stores Ledger Control a/c

Credit: Work-in-Progress a/c.

(If it is ascertained that the excess was on account of wrong counting or weighing at the time original issue).

11.7 INVENTORY VALUATION

Inventory valuation is an important matter in accounting. There are various methods of inventory valuation which are indicated below:

(1) Valuation as per actual cost.

(2) Valuation as per cost or market price whichever is lower.

(3) Valuation as per market price or replacement cost.

(4) Valuation as per anticipated selling price of finished good.

(5) Valuation as per FIFO, LIFO, Average Prices or standard prices as described above in the various methods of pricing of issue of materials.

Illustcation 1

A.T. Ltd. furnishes the following store transactions for September

1-9-09	Opening balance	25 Units value ₹ 162.50
4-9-09	Issues Reg. No. 85	8 Units.
6-9-09	Receipts from B & Co. GRN No. 26	50 Units ₹ 5.75 per unit.
7-9-09	Issues Req. No. 97	12 Units
10-9-09	Returns to 8 & Co.	10 Units
12-9-09	Issues Req. No. 108	15 Units
13-9-09	Issues Req. No.110	20 Units
15.9-09	Receipts from M & Co. GRN No. 33	25 Units @ ₹ 6.10 per unit.
17-9-09	Issues Req. No. 121	10 Units
1 9-9-09	Received replacement from B & Co. GRN No. 38	10 Units
20-9-09	Returned from department material of M & Co. MRR No. 4	5 Units.
22-9-09	Transfer from Job 182 to Job 187 in the Dept. MTR 6	5 Units
26-9-09	Issue Req. No. 146	10 Units
29-9-09	Transfer from Dept. "A" to Dept. "B" MTR 10	5 Units
30-9-09	Shortage in stock taking	2 Units

Write up the priced stores ledger on **FIFO** method and discuss how you would treat the shortage in stock taking.

Date	GRN. No.	Qty. Units	Rate ₹	Amo-unt ₹	SR No.	Qty. Units	Rate ₹	Amounts ₹	Qty. Units	Rate ₹	Amount
1-9-09									25	6.50	162.50
4-9-09					85	8	6.50	52.00	17	6.50	110.50
6-9-09	26	50	5.75	287.50					67		398.00
7-9-09					96	12	6.50	78.00	55		320.00
10-9-09					Return to B & Co.	10	5.75	57.50	45		262.50
12-9-09					108	5	6.50	32.50			
						10	5.75	57.50			
						15		90.00	30		172.50
13-9-09					110	20	5.75	115.00	10		57.50
15-9-09	33	25	6.10	152.50					35		210.00
17-9-09					121	10	5.75	57.50	25	6.10	152.50
19-9-09	38	10	5.75	57.50					35		210.00
20-9-09	(replacement MRP No. 4	5	5.75	28.75					40		238.75
26-9-09					146	10	6.10	61.00	30		177.75
30-9-09					Shortage	2	6.10	12.20	28		165.55

Reconciliation of Balance of Stock

	₹
13 Units at 6.10 =	79.30
15 Units at 5.75 =	86.25
28 Units	165.25

Treatment of Shortage In Stock taking. The shortage in stock taking is to be entered in the Issue Column and valued at the rate as per the method adopted treating as one of the issues, i.e., **FIFO** in this case. If the shortage is normal the amount of shortage is to be debited to production overhead a/c by crediting the stock a/c. If it is abnormal, it is to be debited to costing P & L a/c.

Notes: (1) Materials returned to B & Co., on 10-09 to be entered in the Issue Column and valued at the rates at which they were originally purchased. They have been replaced on 19-9-09 and entered in the Receipt column at the same rate of ₹ 5.75 each.

(2) Materials returned from the department to stores are to be valued at the rates at which they were originally issued to the department. In the absence of information relating to original issue, these are to be valued at the latest issue rate i.e., at ₹ 5.75 in this case.

(3) Transfers from one job to another job and from one department to another department are to be entered in the Subsidiary register of jobs in order to find out the cost of jobs accurately. These items need not be entered in the Stores Ledger as these items do not pass through stores.

Illustration 2

(a) You are supplied with the following information extracted from the budget estimates of a Company:

	₹	₹
Net purchases		
Freight and insurance	10,000	2,00,000
Buying expenses	5,000	
Receiving expenses	4,000	
Inspection expenses	2,000	
Storage expenses	3,000	
		24,000

The company made the following purchases during the budget period:

	₹	₹
Consignment No. 1	30,000	
2	50,000	
3	70,000	1,50,000
Actual costs during the period were:		
Freight and insurance	6.000	
Buying expenses	4.000	
Receiving expenses	3.000	
Inspection expenses	1,000	
Storage expenses	1,000	
		15,500

Compute the applied material receiving and handling rate for the period and determine the amount of receiving and handling cost chargeable to purchases. Also state whether there is any under/or over absorption.

(b) Receipts and issues of an item of stores are made as follows:

There was no balance before 9th January.

Date	Receipts Quantity	Receipts Price ₹	Issues Quantity
9th January	10	17.0	
19th ”	25	10.0	
20th ”	“		10
29th ”	15	8.0	
30th ”			20
13th February	20	12.0	
27th ”	10	16.9	
28th ”			40
30th March	20	20.0	20
31st March			

(i) What is the simple average price of February receipts?

(ii) What are the moving monthly simple average prices for January-February and February-March?

(iii) If a weighted average is used for pricing issues how does the value of the balance in stock change during January?

(iv) If a weighted average price is calculated at the end of each month and is then used for pricing the issues of that month,what will be the value of the month-end balance?

Answer

(a) Budget estimates:

	₹
Net Purchases	2,00,000
Material receiving and handling cost i.e.,	
Freight, Insurance, etc	24,000

Material receiving and handling rate = $\frac{24,000}{2,00,000} \times 100 = 12\%$

Actual purchases:	₹ 1,50,000	
Amount of receiving and handling cost,		
Chargeable to Purchases 1,50,000 × 12%		18,000
Actual cost		15,500
	Over absorption =	2,500

(b) Simple average price of February receipts

$$\frac{12.00 + 16.90}{2} = ₹\ 14.45$$

(ii) Simple average price of January receipts

$$\frac{17.00 + 10.00 + 8.00}{3} = \frac{35.00}{3} = ₹\ 11.67$$

₹

Add: Simple average price of February receipts = 14.45

₹ 26.12

Moving monthly simple average price for January-Februa

$$\frac{26.12}{2} = ₹\ 13.06$$

₹

Add: Simple average price of February receipts = 20.00

₹ 14.45

Moving monthly simple average price for January-Februa

$$\frac{34.45}{2} = ₹\ 17.225$$

(iii) Stores Ledger a/c Weighted average method

Date	Receipts GRN Qty.	Rate	Amount	SRN Qty.	Issues Price	Amount	Balance of Stock Qty.	Rate	Amount
9th Jan.	10	17	170				10	17.00	170
19th "	25	10	250				35	12.00	420
20th "				10	12.00	120	25		300
29th "	15	8	120				40	10.50	420
30th "				20	10.50	210	20	10.50	210
Total	50		540	30		330	20	10.50	210

Value of closing stock at the end of January under simple average price method.

₹

Total purchases 540

Less: Total Issues 30 'units at 11.67 = 350

Value of closing stock		190
Value of Closing Stock under Weighted Average Method =		210
Change in Valuation of Closing Stock =		20

(iv) Weighted average price at the end of January $= \frac{540}{50}$

$= ₹\ 10.80$

	₹
Total purchase during January	540
Less : Value of total issues during January = 30 × 10.80 =	324
Value of Closing Stock at the end of January	216

January Qty $\frac{216}{20}$ ₹ 10.80

	Qty	Value ₹
Value of Opening stock for February	20	216
Add: Purchases during February 240 + 169 =	30	409
Total	50	625

i.e., Weighted average rate at the end of

February : $\frac{625}{50} = ₹\ 12.50$

Less: Value of Issues during February 40 × 12.50 =	40	500
Value of Closing Stock at the end of February =	10	125
Value of Opening Stock for March	10	125
Add: Purchases during March	20	400
Total	30	525

i.e., weighted average at the end of

March: $\frac{525}{30}$ = ₹ 17.50

Less: Value of Issues during March

= 20 × 17.50 | 20 | 350

Value of Closing Stock at the end of March = | 10 | 175

Illustration 3

From the following transactions extracted from the books of accounts of a manufacturing concern as on 31-12-80 work out

(a) consumption value of raw material in the month and

(b) value of closing stock as on 31-12-80, under the following methods of pricing issues :

(i) FIFO:

(ii) LIFO:

(iii) Moving Average Cost;

(iv) Weighted average cost (end of month).

SHOW THE RESULTS IN A TABULATED FORM

1980 December	Quantity in units	Rate per unit in ₹
1 Opening Stock	300	9.70
3 Purchase	250	9.80
11 Issue	400	
15 Purchase	300	10.05
20 Issue	210	
25 Purchase	150	10.30
29 Issue	100	

Answer

(I) STORES LEDGER A/C FIFO METHOD

Date	Receipts Qty. units	Receipts Rate ₹	Receipts Amt. ₹	Issues Qty. units	Issues Rate ₹	Issues Amount ₹	Balance of Stock Qty. units	Balance of Stock Rate ₹	Balance of Stock amt. ₹
1-12-09							300	9.70	2,910
3-12-09	250	9.80	2,450				350		5,360
11-12-09				300	9.70	2,910			
				100	9.80	980			
				400		3,980	150		1,470
15-12-09	300	10.05	3,015				450		4,485
20-12-09				150	9.80	1,470			
				60	10.05	603			
				210		2,073	240		2,412
25-12-09	150	10.30	1,545				390		3,957
29-12-09				100	10.05	1,005	290		2,952
Total	700		7,010	710		6,968			

(a) Consumption value of raw materials = ₹ 6.968/-

(b) Value of closing Stock as on 31-12-80 :

	Qty (units) ₹	Rate ₹
140	10.05	1,407
150	10.30	1,545
290		2,952

(II) STORES LEDGER A/C LIFO METHOD

Date	Receipts Qty. units	Receipts Rate ₹	Receipts Amt. ₹	Issues Qty. units	Issues Rate ₹	Issues Amount ₹	Balance of Stock Qty. units	Balance of Stock Rate ₹	Balance of Stock amt. ₹
1-12-09							300	9.70	2,910
3-12-09	250	9.80	2,450				550		5,360
11-12-09				250	9.80	2,450			
				150	9.70	1,455			
				400		3,905	150	9.70	1,470
15-12-09	300	10.05	3,015				450		4,485
20-12-09				210	10.05	2110.50	240		2,374.50
25-12-09	150	10.30	1,545				390		3,919.50
29-12-09				100	10.30	10.30	290		2,889.50
Total	700		7,010	710		7045.50			

(a) Consumption value of raw materials = ₹ 7,045.50.

(b) Value of closing stock as on 31-12-09 =

Qty (units)	Rate ₹	₹
150	9.70	1455
90	10.05	904.50
50	10.30	515
290		2,874.50

(III) STORES LEDGER ALE-MOVING AVERAGE COST (ASSUMED AS SIMPLE AVERAGE COST)

Date	Qty. units	Rece-ipts Rate ₹	Amt. ₹	Issues Qty. units	Rate ₹	Amount ₹	Balance of Stock Qty. units	Rate ₹	amt. ₹
1-12-09							300	9.70	2,910
3-12-09	250	9.80	2,450				350		5,360
11-12-09				400	9.75	3,900	150		1,460
15-12-09	300	10.05	3,015				450		4,475
20-12-09				210	9.90	2,079	240		2,396
25-12-09	150	10.30	1,545				390		3,941
29-12-09				100	10.05	1,005	290		2,941
Total	700		7,010	710		6,989			

(a) Consumption value of raw materials = ₹ 6,989

(b) Value of'closing stock as on 31-12.80 = ₹ 2,941

(IV) STORES LEDGER WEAGHTED AVERAGE END OF MONTH METHOD

Date	Qty. units	Rece-ipts Rate ₹	Amt. ₹.	Issues Qty. units	Rate ₹	Amount ₹	Balance of Stock Qty. units	Rate ₹	amt. ₹
1-12-09							300	9.70	2,910
3-12-09	250	9.80	2,450				350		5,360
15-12-09	300	10.05	3,015				850		8375
25-12-09	150	10.30	1,545				1000	9.92	9920
11-12-09				400	9.92	3968	600		5952
29-12-09				210	9.92	2,083.20	390		3,868.80
29-12-09				100	9.92	992.00	290		2,876.80
Total	700		7,010	710		7,043.20			

Note: Weighted average cost (end of month)

Opening 300 units at ₹ 9.70	=	₹ 2,910
Purchasing during Dec.09 700 units	=	₹ 7,010
Total: 1000 unit		₹ 9,920

Weighted average cost (end of month) per unit = $\frac{9920}{1000}$ ₹. 9.92

(a) Consumption value of raw materials = ₹ 7,043.20 (i.e., 710 units at ₹ 9.92).

(b) Value of closing stock as on 31-11-80 = ₹ 2,876.80.

RESULTS IN A TABULATED FORM

Particulars	**Method**			
	FIFO	**LIFO**	**Moving Average (simple average)**	**Weighted average (end of month)**
(a) Consumption value of raw materials	6,968.00	7045.50	6989.00	7043.20
(b) Value of closing stock 31-12-09 as on	2952.00	2874.50	2,941	2876.80

Illustration 4

The following transanctions took place in respect of a material item :

		Qty:	Rate ₹
Jan.	1 Received	1000 units	20.00
,,	10 ,,	260 ,,	21.00
,,	20 Issued	700 ,,	
Feb.	4 Received	400 ,,	23.00
,,	21 ,,	300 ,,	25.00
,,	28 Returned to suppliers defective items (originally received on Jn. 1st)	10 ,,	
March	16 Issued	620 ,,	
April	12 ,,	240 ,,	
May	10 Received	500 ,,	22.00
,,	25 Issued	380 ,,	

Prepare sores ledger a/c

(i) Using the standard price of ₹ 22/- per unit. Show the price variance at the end of May 31st and its treatment in Cost Accounts.

(ii) On replacement price basis-replacement price on 20th Jan. ₹ 22/- 16th March, ₹ 24/- 12th April, ₹ 23/- and May 25th ₹ 22/-

Answer

(I) STORE LEDGER A/C- STANDARD PRICE METHOD (₹ 22/- PER UNIT)

Receipts					Issues				Balance of stock		
Date	GRN. No.	Qty. Units	Rate ₹	Amount ₹	SR No.	Qty. Units	Rate ₹	Amounts ₹	Qty. Units	Rate ₹	Amount
1st Jan.		1000	20	20000					1000	20	20000
10th Jan.		260	21	5460					1260		25460
20th Jan.						700	22	15400	560		10060
4th Feb.		400	23	9200					960		19260
21th Feb.		300	25	7500		10 (Returned to supplier)	20	200	1250		26560
16th March						620	22	13640	630		12920
12th April						240	22	5280	390		7640
10th May		500	22	11000					890		18640
25th May						380	22	8360	510		10280

Note: (1) Generally, materials should be entered into the receipt column after their acceptance. Rejected materials should be kept separately in the stores. But in the case, the materials were found defective and returned to suppliers on Feb.28th, though they have been received on Jan. 1st and entered in the receipt column accordingly. Hence these are valued at the rate at which they were purchased originally, i.e., 10 units at the rate of ₹ 20/- per unit:

(2) The stock valuation at the end of May should be at standard price of ₹ 22/- i.e., 510 units × ₹ 22 = 11220. Hence Material price variance = Standard minus Actual = 11220-10280 = 940 (Favourable)

This should be transferred to Costing P& L a/c

(II) STORES LEDGER ALE-REPLACEMENT PRIEE METHOD

Receipts					Issues				Balance of stock		
Date	GRN. No.	Qty. Units	Rate ₹	Amo-unt ₹	SR No.	Qty. Units	Rate ₹	Amo unts ₹	Qty. Units	Rate ₹	Amo unt
1st Jan.		1000	20	20000					1000	20	20000
10th Jan.		260	21	5460					1260		25460
20th Jan.						700	22	15400	560		10060
4th Feb.		400	23	9200					960		19260
21th Feb.		300	25	7500		10	20	200	1250		26560
16th March						620	24	14880	630		11680
12th April						240	23	5520	390		6160
10th May		500	22	11000					890		17160
25th May						380	22	8360	510		8800

Illustration 5

The stores ledger accounts of a manufacturing Co. reveal the following entries of a particular material.

Date	Receipt			Issue		
2009	Qty. in unit	Rate ₹	Amt. ₹	Qty. in unit	Issue price	Amt. ₹
Jan						
2	4,000	1.80	7,200			
5	2,000	1.75	3,500			
18				10,000		19,500
Feb						
3				5,000		9,750
14	3,000	1.85	5,550			
18	3,000	1.90	5,700			
20				10,000		19,200

Opening stock as on 1.1.09 was 20,000 units valued at ₹ 40,000. Closing stock as per physical verification on 28.2p was 6,950 units.

Work out the method of pricing the issue which you consider to have adopted for the issue of the material and show the working of tbe issue rates (correct to 2 places of decimal). Complete the accounting of the mterial and work out the value of the closing stock as on 28.2.09 the basis of valuation adopted and also nnder any other method of valuation, you are familiar.

Answer

STORES LEDGER CONTROL A/CWEIGHTED AVERAGE METHOD.

Receipts					Issues				Balance of stock		
Date	GRN. No.	Qty. Units	Rate ₹	Amo-unt ₹	SR No.	Qty. Units	Rate ₹	Amo unts ₹	Qty. Units	Rate ₹	Amo unt
1.1.09									20000	2.00	40000
2.1.09		4000	1.80	7200					24000	1.97	47200
5.1.09		2000	1.75	3500					26000	1.95	50700
18.1.09						10000	1.95	19500	16000		31200
3.2.09						5000	1.95	9750	11000		21450
14.2.81		3000	1.85	5550					14000	1.93	27000
18.2.81		3000	1.90	5700					17000	1.92	32700
20.2.81						10000	1.92	19200	7000		13500
28.2.81	(shortage)					50	1.92	96	6950		13404

(i) Value of closing stock as on 28.2.09 ₹ 13,404 (Qty. 6950 units) on the basis of weighted average method.

(ii) Value of closing stock under any other method, i.e., FIFO method :

Qty. units.	Rate ₹	Amt. ₹
950	1.75	1662.50
3000	1.85	5550.00
3000	1.90	5700.00
6950		12912.50

(iii) The issue rate in weighted average method' should be calculated to the place of 4 decimals.

11.7 SUMMARY

If an organisation receives materials in excess or short of ordered quantity, management has right to take suitable action of retaining or returning excess and demanding or leaving shortage.

Suppliers are to be paid for accepted quantity of receipts based on Goods Receipt Note and Purchase Order.

Materials are to be issued against authorized stores Requisition Notes.

Control over Materials in stores is maintained through Bin Cards (Which contain data related to quantity) and stores ledgers (Which contain data related to quantity and value.) Bin cards are written by store keepers and Ledgers by Cost Accountant.

These documents need to be reconciled on a regular basis to correct errors caused by incorrect entries or counts. The discrepancies identified are to be accounted for immediately and reviewed for correcting root causes.

Different methods are used for physical verification of stocks some periodic others continuous.

There are various ways for pricing issues using actual prices paid for receipts or estimated prices like standard or replacement price. Organisations should select the one that suits their business as some methods reflects current prices in issues while some in closing stocks.

11.8 SELF ASSESSMENT QUESTIONS

(1) Which documents are used for approving payments to suppliers? Draw a specimen of one.

(2) What are features of Bin Card and Stores Ledger?

(3) If proper stores Ledgers are maintained for each material, Bin Cards are not required for stores control. Do you agree? Why?

(4) Describe methods of physical verification of stocks. Which do you recommend? Why?

(5) Demonstrate how value of closing stocks depend on method used for pricing issues.

(6) How is LIFO method for pricing issue operated?

Chapter 12

INVENTORY CONTROL

Objectives

After studying this chapter, you should be able to understand:

- Cost effects of excessive and insufficient inventory.
- ABC analysis as a tool of inventory control.
- Various inventory levels.
- MRP – Materials Requirement Planning.
- Methods of inventory control.

Structure:

12.1 INTRODUCTION

Every business must have inventory of some kind. In fact, no business can exist. without inventory. The manufacturing enterprise must have inventory of raw materials, purchased components, in-house fabricated sub assemblies, etc., needed to operate and produce a finished product. It also has to maintain an inventory of finished products in anticipation of demand for them. Thus, to conduct any business, there must be inventory of some kind.

Inventories act as a protective cushion for the continuous operation in any manufacturing enterprise. Inventory represents a cash investment by top management, which:, as with any investment, desires to realize a profit from it. This investment can cause a cash-flow problem when inventory levels are poorly managed due to inability to forecast the actual need for materials.

Improvement in inventory management reduces inventory levels releasing money for other areas of the business. When anticipated demand is not realized, the result is excessive inventory with added carrying costs. When the forecast is much less than actual demand, there is usually insufficient inventory with possible loss of business.

12.2 EFFECT OF INVENTORY SIZE ON COST OF OPERATION

The cost of operation is greatly affected by both excessive and insufficient inventories, as summerized below.

AREA OF COST	EXCESSIVE INVENTORY	INSUFFICIENT INVENTORY
(1) Material Cost	Greater risk of loss because of: (a) devaluation of inventory on hand due to reduction in supplier's prices (b) inventory becomes obsolete (c) inventory deterioration due to increase or no usage (d) more pilferage	Higher cost for materials and higher manufacturing costs due to increase of "small quantity" rush-orders needed to maintain continuous production.
(2) Factory Cost	Increased cost due to need for additional storage space, results in overcrowding in storage area causing inefficient working conditions and delays.	Increased cost due to : (a) work stoppage (b) temporary layoffs and rehiring (c) training new employees (d) additional machine set ups (e) emergency (overtime) operation
(3) Overhead Cost	Increased cost due to: (a) additional carrying cost (b) increased cost for borrowing needed money (c) outside rental of space as needed	Increased cost due to : added clerical cost for extra help or overtime in purchasing receiving in spection, etc., as result of additional "rush orders".

Purpose of Inventory

Inventory was created for two primary purposes: protection and economy.

(1) Protection: To have adequate supply of materials available to meet requirements for continuous operation. This would ensure that the inventory of finished products would be available to meet the demand, thus permitting marketing and sales to function with the knowledge that their sales can be delivered as requested.

(2) Economy: To effect the lowest product cost through the best economical order quantity to purchase at a given time. Savings can sometime be realized from longer production runs, thereby, permitting larger quantities to be purchased at one time.

12.3 NEED FOR INVENTORY

The inventory manager must anticipate the company's need at every stage of production. Inventories protect the inventory manager against unforeseen failures in supply or a sudden increase in demand. Materials are transported thousands of miles before they arrive at a plant, and while in transit they are some one's inventory the legal owner of that material. Even a flat tire on the carrier's truck could interrupt the manufacturing process with a late delivery.

For these reasons every manufacturing company carries a certain minimum amount of inventory. In practice, almost every manufacturer carries an inventory that is substantially greater than the minimum amount because:

(1) The marketing, sales and production departments all find it more convenient to have a supply on hand that is more than ample.

(2) The market indicates a rise in price of the raw material and therefore increases the inventory levels.

(3) There is a lack of skills necessary to control inventory levels, and top management is unwilling to pay for controls and is willing to carry extra inventory.

12.4 OBJECTIVES OF INVENTORY CONTROL

The primary function of inventory is to make supplies available when needed to maintain continuous operation. The primary objectives of inventory control are:

(1) To have a stock of goods when needed by production and by sale

(2) To keep capital investment at the lowest level possible

(3) To institute controls for the protection and distribution of inventory

To achieve these objectives, inventory control must have the cooperation of the production and purchasing and must coordinate activities with them. When considering the goal that inventory control seeks to achive — the lowest cost and the minimum inventory necessary for continuous operation — one must define the different classifications of industrial inventory assets (inventory is a company asset), which include:

(1) Production Inventory: This includes raw-materials, purchased parts and components that enter the finished product.

(2) Work-in-Progress Inventory: This is composed of materials at all production processes at various stages of production prior to being incorporated into the finished product. Also includes any material released from stores.

(3) Finished-Product Inventory: This is the end product ready for shipment to the consumer.

(4) Maintenance, Repair and Operating Supplies (MRO): This includes all expendable items that are required.

12.5 INVENTORY MANAGEMENT BROAD FUNCTION

Inventory Management has two board function;

(1) Inventory Accounting

(2) Stock control or stores inventory control

Inventory Accounting is concerned with the book keeping aspect of Inventory Management. This function deals with the entry, processing and distribution of inventory stock, which, in turn, provides a history for all inventory transactions. This accounting will also provide data for the comparison of "book" inventory to the actual physical count of stock control.

Stock control consists of planning, ordering and scheduling the release of materials used in manufacturing process. The inventory control manager is concerned with all types of inventory in the company, while the purchasing manager is concerned with the acquisition of materials.

12.6 ABC INVENTORY CONTROL

One of the first steps in organizing an effective **Inventory Control System** is to know something about each item stocked. An analysis, tabulation and classification of the characteristics of all commodities is made and listed in the catalog, which is issued to all departments so that all know what items are carried in stock. The catalog should list all items, completely described and identified by manufacturer's product number and cross referenced to the company's own stock number. This will also serve to reducc the number of duplicate items (same item from several suppliers with their stock number)

The catalogue listing with annual consumption values, when totaled in cumulative fashion, will indicate to the inventory manager which items account for the bulk of capital investment. In most manufacturing firms, we find that 10 percent of the items account for about 75 percent of the capital investment. At the other end we find that 75 percent of the items account for only about 10 percent of invested capital, leaving about 15 percent of the items to account for out 15 percent of capital investment. While the figures may vary fiom company to company the magnitude of the variation is not great. This type of **inventory analysis is** known by several names the most common being the **ABC Analysis** system (Exhibit 12.1)

The ABC system is one of the keys to inventory control. It applies to the few items (10 percent) accounting for 75 percent of capital investment. These are classified as **"A items"** and require close security and distribution control. At the other end, we have 75 percent of the items representing 10 percent of capital investment classified as **"C items"**, which can be controlled by any means that provide an **economical order frequency**. Class **"B items"**, consisting of 15 percent of items representing 15 percent capital investment, require normal control supported by good record.

EXHIBIT 12.1: ABC SYSTEM

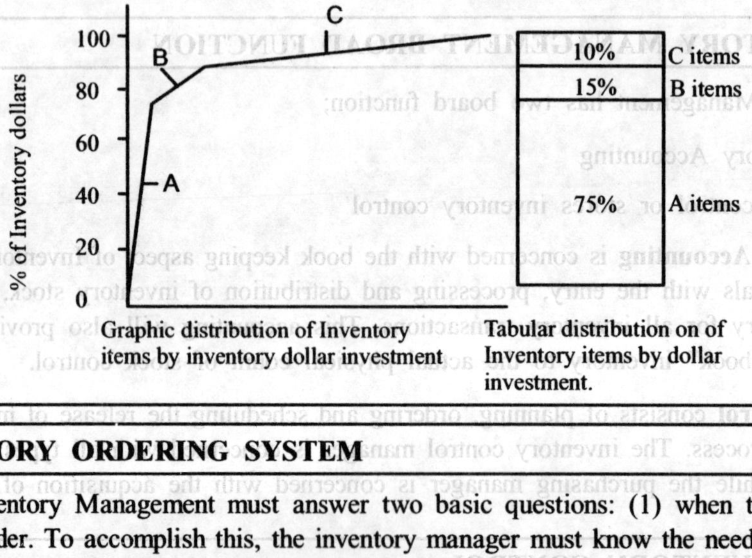

Graphic distribution of Inventory items by inventory dollar investment

Tabular distribution on of Inventory items by dollar investment.

12.7 INVENTORY ORDERING SYSTEM

Sound Inventory Management must answer two basic questions: (1) when to order and (2) how much to order. To accomplish this, the inventory manager must know the need and application for each item stocked, whether the item is a" dependent-demand" or an "independent demand" item.

A **dependent demand** item, also known as an internal-demand item, is that item whose use is directly related to or derived from the demand of other items or end product.

An independent demand item, also called external-demand item, is an item that is unrelated to the demand of items entering the finished product. The demand for lubricating oil for machine operation is independent from the demands of items entering the manufacturing process itself. MRO supplies have an independent demand and their need must be forecast.

There is the **cyclical ordering system,** which is a time-based system and relies upon scheduled periodic review of stock levels for initiating a purchase request if stock is below a certain level. Its disadvantage is that not all items have the same usage rate and not reordering in time makes this system inefficient and can cause production problems.

The **fixed-order quantity system,** which is based on the order quantity factor rather than the time factor, operates smoothly when the items exhibit stable usage and lead time. When these factors change, a new order quantity is again predetermined.

Another system is the two-bin System as the name implies, has inventory stocked in two bins, and when one bin is emptied and the second is used, order is placed for one bin of material.

Still another system for controlling inventory levels is the **maximum-minimum system**,. This system is used when the items are comparatively standard in character and used in steady quantities and there is an established minimum level, maximum level and fixed-order point. Theoretically the minimum level would be reached when the last unit was used and new shipment arrives. This makes the minimum level at zero and the quantity delivered as the maximum level. However, this theoretical policy becomes inoperative when there are unforeseen contingencies, such as a sudden increase in demand, late delivery, or receipt of non conforming goods.

In the real world, manufacturers maintain a **safety reserve** to take care of any contingency that may arise. The amount of safety reaserve or **safety stock** depends on the rate of consumption, importance of time to production and the lead time to obtain replacement. **Safety stock** is essential to prevent production interruption or loss of revenue. The order quantity should take into consideration the **maximum and minimum levels** of the active stock plus the safety stock. In Exhibit-2, we have the following facts: (l) the normal use is 100 units per month, (2) the maximum level is 300 units, representing three months' supply (200 units for active stock and 100 units safety stock); (3) the order point is at the average inventory stock level of 150 units, with the reorder quantity of 200 units (the active stock quantity); and (4) the lead time is one half month. If the production rate is steady, using 100 units per month the safety factor could be reduced or entirely eliminated. That is, when the last unit of the active stock is at its minimum level (at zero), the new stock arrives to boost the stock level to its maximum and there is no need for safety stock. .

The constant threat of that unknown contingency, however, demands that we carry a safety stock. In exhibit 12.2 we see that in July there arose a contingency due to delay in delivery, and without the safety factor there would have been a temporary slow down, or even a shutdown, causing loss to the company. We also see that during October there was a sudden increase in demand, and the November delivery would not arrive in time to meet this increased demand. Again the safety stock prevented disruption of the manufacturing process. The safety factor is a safeguard against such occurrences.

EXHIBIT 12.2: GRAPHIC ILLUSTRATION 01' SAFETY FLOW UNDER MAXIMUM MINIMUM INVENTORY CONTROL

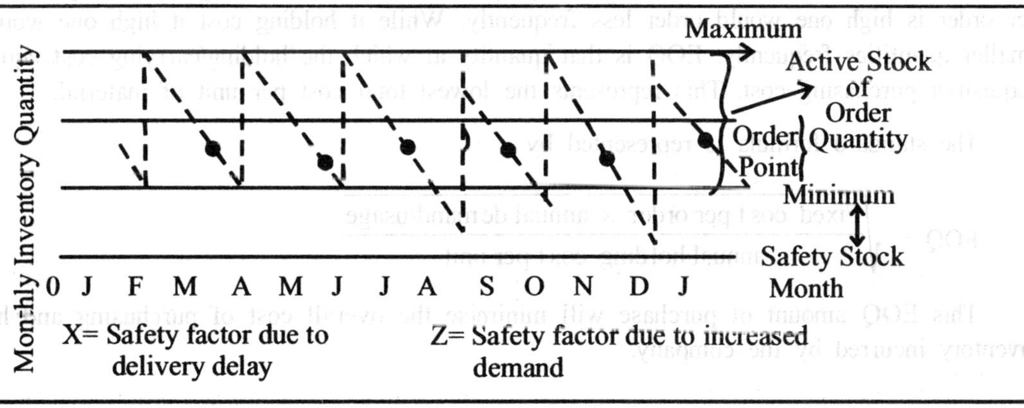

The active inventory stock is that portion of the total inventory supply intended to meet normal expected requirements for the material. This is directly related to the order quantity. Calculation of the economic **order quantity** is the expected annual requirements divided by the number of purchase orders per year, which proves to be the most economical quantity based on the acquisition, the cost of carrying the inventory and total costs. The **most economical order quantity** is the point at which the acquisition cost equals the carrying cost, and this represents the lowest total cost.

The cost of acquisition includes the cost of issuing a purchase order, the cost of receiving, inspection and handing of materials, plus the cost of the accounting procedure to pay for such materials. The cost for issuing a purchase order takes into account the total cost of operating the purchasing department on an annual basis divided into the number of the purchase orders issued annually, which indicates the average cost per order.

The **cost of carrying inventory** also involves multiple activities: (I) These is the cost of capital investment in that inventory. The investment of X rupees in inventory leaves that much less for other investments or expenditures, and the cost of interest for needed capital. (2) There is the cost of insurance needed to protect inventory against loss from fire or some other mishap. (3) The storage building or area is depreciable and must have the various services such as heat, light, security, etc. Storage cost represents space that could be used for other activities. (4) In any operation there is a certain amount of inventory that becomes obsolete or deteriorates, and there is always the occurrence of "shrinkage". The larger the inventory, the greater is the potential loss at its source. The average carrying cost for inventory is about 20 percent of the average inventory value. The inventory carrying cost is a variable percentage based on the actual costs all the activities relating to the charges for carrying inventory.

12.8 ECONOMIC ORDER QUANTITY (EOQ)

EOQ is a mathematical formula used by buyers as a tool in their purchase decisions. The economic order quantity determines the appropriate number of product to order based on a number of variables like annual demand of the product, purchase cost per unit, fixed cost per purchase order, the order quantity and inventory carrying or holding cost of the product. If purchase cost per order is high one would order less frequently. While it holding cost it high one would buy smaller quantities frequently. EOQ is that quantity at which the holding/carrying cost equals the acquisition/purchasing cost. This represents the lowest total cost per unit of material.

The standard formula is represented by

$$\text{EOQ} = \sqrt{\frac{\text{Fixed cost per order} \times \text{annual demand/usage}}{\text{annual holding cost per unit}}}$$

This EOQ amount of purchase will minimise the overall cost of purchasing and holding inventory incurred by the company.

EXHIBIT 12.3: ECONOMIC ORDER QUANTITY

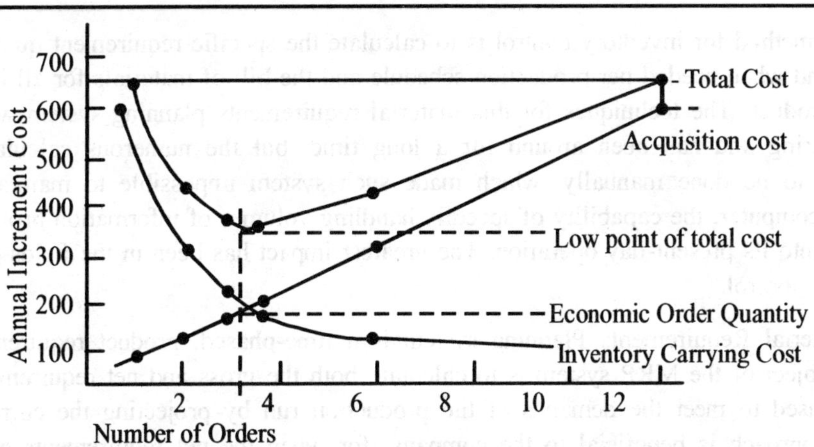

12.9 TOP MANAGEMENT'S VIEWPOINT - STOCKLESS BUYING

The above mainstays of conventional inventory management systems (stock replenishment, reorder point techniques and economic order quantity) have always been subject to review and revaluation. This restoration of inventory to the maximum level was to have inventory always available when needed. This maximum level of inventory is the exact opposite of what top management wanted from inventory management. They want the lowest capital investment in inventory with sufficient stock available for continuous operation.

Striving towards this goal has many purchasing agents using a stockless buying system whereby the responsibility for the inventory is shifted to the supplier. The buyer draws up a purchase agreement or a contract with as many supplier as needed for the many items required. When entering such program, the buyer must be extra careful in his selection of suppliers who can meet the delivery requirement of such program. A blanket order is issued to the supplier, against which requests for shipments are made. This reduces the paper work for the purchasing department.

Supplier arranges shipment when material is needed for production. Carrying costs are eliminated because the supplier stocks the goods. This arrangement is of equal importance to the supplier, for he knows what his customer will require over a specific period of time and can schedule his own production rate.

Then there is on-consignment inventory, which is another stockless buying method. In this situation, the supplier ships goods to your plant, at no charge when shipped, for your company to provide secured storage space with the expectation that your company will eventually use the product, whereby such action becomes a "sale of goods" for which you pay. You are acting as a custodian of property- "to hold property in trust for some purpose." This method is used primarily by retailers. Supplier is paid when goods are used. Suppliers want to expose their product to the consumer. The retailer does not want to invest in a new product, but will handle such product without investment. Some non-profit hospitals have entered into such on-consignment agreements.

12.10 MATERIALS REQUIREMENT PLANNING (MRP)

Another method for inventory control is to calculate the specific requirement quantity for each item needed and when needed per production schedule and the bill of materials for all items entering the finished product. The techniques for this material requirements planning system was developed for manufacturing and has been around for a long time, but the numerous calculations for its operation had to be done manually, which made such system impossible to maintain. With the advent of the computer, the capability of speedily handling volumes of information brought the MRP concept back into its present-day operation. The greatest impact has been in the fields of production and inventory control.

The Material Requirements Planning system is a time-phased, product requirement oriented system. The object of the MRP system is to calculate both the gross and net requirements for each items time-phased to meet the demands of the production run by projecting the correct inventory action. This approach is beneficial to the company, for when the net requirements are calculated with exactness, there is always a lower capital investment needed for inventory.

The MRP system relies on the current information being entered into the computer regarding the production schedule, the bill of materials, the inventory status, and the lead times for each items. This information" explodes" to provide the gross-to-net requirements by time period and permits the buyer to make the correct action. One of the beneficial features of the MRP system is the "re-exploding" capability as it is updated, usually weekly. This lets the buyer have continuous updated information to take prompt corrective action, if needed.

The calculations are quite simple, and with the aid of the computer all items can be calculated with rapidity. The net requirements consist of allocating existing inventories (quantity on hand plus quantity on order) against the gross requirements.

Gross requirements		150 Unit
Less on hand	30 units	
on order	75 units	
		105 units
Net Requirements		**45 units.**

If a safety stock is planned (due to company policy or some market 'condition forecast), the net requirements would be increased by the safety stock desired. Under normal conditions, there would be no need for a safety stock with the MRP system.

Application of MRP

Consequently, if a manager wants to hold down material acquisition costs, MRP is best suited for the control of purchased materials that exhibit the following characteristics:

(1) Materials that can be purchased on long-term contracts or blanket y order with frequent releases for shipment in relatively small quantities.

(2) Raw materials or standard items for which lead time requirements are relatively short and seldom vary appreciably.

(3) Materials that can be purchased repetitively without requiring much creative purchasing analysis or which value analysis, purchasing research and vendor studies have previously been completed.

12.11 JUST-IN-TIME INVENTORY METHOD

Just-in-Time manufacturing is based on zero inventory management, a concept introduced and effectively used by the Japanese to reduce inventorie and boost productivity. In a JIT, manufacturing, materials are not stockpiled and must be carefully scheduled and delivered into production as they are needed in just the right quantities at just the right time. Materials never arriver early, which would add to inventory carrying costs, or late which would seriously slow or halt production.

The success of Japanese companies in cutting manufacturing costs is attributed in part to their use of the **just-in-time** (JIT) **inventory method**— the practice of having inputs to the production process delivered precisely when they are needed, thereby assigning to suppliers the responsibility for keeping inventories to a minimum. McDonald's uses a system of just-in-time delivery for its raw materials, such as hamburger patties and paper goods. Traditionally, U. S. factories attempted to manage inventories internally. More and more, however, they are using the just-in-time method. The use of this method can even result in "Zero" inventory. Zero inventory may seem unrealistic. Nevertheless, JIT can reduce inventory considerably. In the United States, the automobile manufacturers have led the way in adopting this method.

Automobile makers are not alone in efforts to improve inventory control. To win back customers in the apparel market, America's textile companies are mounting a Just-in-time delivery campaign. Each morning, Swift Textiles Inc. ships just enough denim for a day's production at the near by Levi Strauss plant in Valdosta, Georgia. With Swift certifying the quality of denim, Levi closed its warehouse and quality testing lab and gained a competitive advantage.

Evidence suggests that just-in-time purchasing has produced substantial benefits for U.S. companies. One survey showed that when companies moved to JIT purchasing, inventory turnover increased by an average of 97 percent, delivery promises kept increased from 67 percent to 83 percent, and scrap cost declined 40 percent. However, some problems exist in Just-in-time systems. For example, a number of managers are concerned about how dependent they should be on their suppliers. The level of trust between firms and their suppliers may be higher in Japan than it is in the United States.

Inventory control is the "Life-system" control needed for continuous operation in all businesses. Inventory can be compared to the lifc blood of the human body in the correct quality and quantity at the right time, so too, the replacement of used-up inventory is needed in correct quality and quantity at the right time for continuous operation.

Much of the resources of many major companies is locked in inventory, so failure to control inventory can mean the difference between profit and loss.

Inventory permits the relative independence of operations between two activities. Inventory also provides for continuous operations when demand for the product is not consistent. Another purpose of inventory is to allow the filling of orders quickly, thereby maintaining customer satisfaction. If orders come in at a constant rate, there may be no need to maintain inventory.

Sometimes, it is impractical to monitor evey item in inventory with same degree of intensity. In such cases, it is useful to categorize the items in inventory according to the degree of control needed. The success of Japanese companies in cutting manufacturing costs is attributed in part to their use of the Just-in-time (JIT) inventory method.

12.12 STOCK CONTROL/STORES INVENTORY CONTROL

A. Need for Stock Control

Stock control is a system which ensures the availability of the right quantity of material of the right quality at the right time with the minimum amount of capital by purchasing them at right price from the right source.

The system includes the following steps:

(1) Purchase requisition.

(2) Inquiry; tenders and quotations.

(3) Purchase orders and follow-up action.

(4) Receipt and inspection of materials.

(5) Payment to suppliers.

(6) Storage and maintenance of records.

(7) Issue of materials.

Since material cost forms major portion or the total cost. That is to say 50% of the total cost, it is essential that the materials should be controlled to a large extent so that they are purchased properly, safeguarded and correctly consumed and accounted for. Thus, the material control contributes to the efficiency of a business. By exercising the material control, the following advantages are obtained by the organisation:

(1) Minimum investment.

(2) Reduced cost of production through efficient buying and controlled consumption of materials.

(3) Prevention of production delays due to supply of right quantity of right quality of materials at right time.

(4) Minimum wastage.

B. Requirements of Stock control System

(1) Material control is a matter of coordination among the various departments concerned, viz., purchase, production, maintenance inspection, stores, accounts and cost accounting departments.

(2) Use of standard forms and documents in all the stages.

(3) Classification, codification, standardization, rationalization and simplification of materials.

(4) Planning of requirement of materials.

(5) Centralization of purchasing under an efficient purchase department.

(6) Budgetary control of purchases and standards/norms for consumption of stores.

(7) Planned storage of materials.

(8) Demand and supply method of stock control, i.e., control through fixing maximum, minimum and danger levels, reorder point and economic ordering quantity, etc.

(9) Control through ABC analysis according to value of materials and value analysis.

(10) Perpetual inventory system and continuous physical stock verification.

(11) Efficient system of internal audit and internal checks.

(12) Reporting to the management regularly regarding material purchases, inspection, storage, consumption, returns to suppliers, slow-moving, non-moving, dormant, surplus and obsolete stocks, etc.

C. Levels of Inventory

(1) Maximum Stock Level: The maximum stock level is that quantity above which stocks should not normally be allowed to exceed. The following factors are taken into consideration fixing the maximum stock level:

(1) Average rate of consumption of material.

(2) Lead time.

(3) Re-order level.

(4) Maximum requirement of materials for production at time.

(5) Storage space available, cost of storage and insurance.

(6) Financial consideration such as price fluctuations, availability of capital, discount due to seasonal and bulk purchases, etc.

(7) Keeping qualities, e.g., risk of deterioration, obsolescence. Evaporation depletion and natural waste, etc.

(8) Any restrictions imposed by local or national authority in regard to materials, i.e., purchasing from small scale industries and public sector undertakings, price preference clauses import policy, explosion in case of explosive materials risk of fire, etc; and

(9) Economic ordering quantity is also considered:

Formula

Maximum Level = Re-order level - (Minimum consumption × Minimum lead time) + Reorder quantity

(2) Minimum Stock Level: The minimum stock level is that quantity below which stocks should not normally be allowed to fall. If stocks go below this level, there will be danger of stoppage of production due to shortage of supplies. The following factors are taken into account while fixing the minimum stock level:

(1) Average rate of consumption of material.

(2) Average lead time. The shorter the lead time. the lower is the minimum level.

(3) Reorder level.

(4) Nature of the item.

(5) Stock-out cost.

Formula

Minimum Level = Re-order level - (Average usage × Average lead time)

(3) Re-order Level (When to Purchase): This is. the point fixed between the maximum and minimum stock levels and at this time, essential to initiate purchase action for fresh supplies of the material. In order to cover the abnormal usage of material or unexpected delay in delivery of fresh supplies; this point' will usually fixed slightly higher than the minimum stock level. The following factors are taken into account while fixing the re-order level:

(1) Maximum usage of materials.

(2) Maximum lead time.

(3) Maximum stock level.

(4) Minimum stock level.

Formula

Re-order level = Maximum usage × Maximum lead time.

(4) Re-ordering Quantity (How Much to Purchase): It is also called as Economic Ordering Quantity (already discussed in chapter - 4)

(5) Danger Level: This is the level below the minimum stock level. When the stock reaches this level. immediate action is needed for replenishment of stock. As the normal lead time is not available, regular: purchase procedure cannot be adopted resulting in higher purchase cost. Hence, this level is useful for taking corrective action only. If this is fixed below the re-order level and above the minimum level, it will be possible to take preventive action.

Formula

Average rate of consumption × urgent supply time.

(6) Reserve Stock: It is the extra quantity of stock kept in order to take care of the abnormal usage of materials during the lead time and/or unexpected delay in delivery of fresh supplies as mentioned above while discussing the re-order level.

D. Continuous Stock Taking

(A) The control of materials while in storage is effected through the perpetual inventory system. The two main functions of perpetual inventory system are:

(1) It is a method of recording stores balances after each receipt and issue, i.e., recording stores balances after each and every entry in Bin Card.

(2) This facilitates regular checking of stock verification physically which obviates the stopping of the work for stock taking. There will not be stoppage of production in case of continuous physical stock verification.

(B) This continuous physical verification of stock is an essential feature of the perpetual inventory system. Certain number of items should be counted, weighed or measured daily and compared with the Bin Card balances. For example, an organization is possessing 3,000 items of stores. In a year of 300 working days, 10 items should be counted, weighed or measured daily so that all 3,000 items are verified physically once in a year and compared with the Bin Card balances. The programme for physical stock verification should be chalked out for the whole year and a copy of such programme should be sent to the Stores Department. The stock-verifiers should take up the different sections of the store in rotation. All the items should be completely verified in a year so that each item is covered once in a year under the physical stock verification programme and the results of stock verification should be recorded suitably.

(C) There are three methods of recording the results of stock verification as described below:

(1) Inventory Tags: Inventory Tags are most suitable for stock verification. The tag consists two portions. The upper portion attached to the particular bin to indicate that the item has been verified. The lower portion serves the purpose of records of stock verification and shortages or excesses, if any, from these lower portions are entered in the Bin Card in the issue or receipt column. Then, the balance in Bin Card will represent of physical balance of stores.

INVENTORY TAG NO:

Bin Card No.	Unit:
Material Code No.	Location:
Quantity:	Stock verifier :
Nomenclature:	Date:

INVENTORY TAG NO.:	
Bin Card No :	Unit:
Material Code No.	Location:
Nomenclature:	Stock Verifier
Quantity:	Date:

(2) Record in Bin Cards: Instead of maintaining the separate inventory., tags, the stock verifier will enter in the bin card the balance found on physical verification, preferably in red ink in the line after the last entry in bin card. The difference between the bin card balance and the actual physical balance should be treated as shortage or excess and it should be entered in the issue or receipt column of the bin card preferably in Red ink as to be distinct from the normal issues or new receipt of the materials.

(3) Stock Verification Sheets: The stock verification sheets are maintained by the Stock verifier in a chronological order. The balances as per the physical verification are entered by the stock verifier and one copy of the stock verification sheet is sent to the store keeper for entering in the bin cards in regard to the correct balances, shortages or excesses.

STOCK VERIFICATION SHEET NO:								
DATE	Material Code No	Nomen clature	Unit	Physical Balance	Bin card Shortage Balance	Shortage	Excess	Adjustment
								Signature of Stock Verifier

It is also essential that one copy of all such stock verification particulars should be sent to Cost Accounting Department so as to enter the shortage, or excesses, if any, in the Stores Ledger Cards after necessary valuation.

Illustration 1

Two components A and B are used as follows:

Normal usage : 50 per week each.

Minimum usage : 25 per week each.

Maximum usage : 75 per week each.

Re-order quantity : A : 300 ; B ; 500.

Re-order period : A : 4-6 weeks; B: 2-4 weeks.

Calculate' for each component (i) Re-order level, (ii) Minimum level (iii) Maximum level and (iv) Average stock level.

Answer

	Component. A'	*Component 'B'*
(i) Re-order level= Maximum usage × Maximum Re-order Period	75 × 6 = 450 Units	75 × 4 = 300 Units
(ii) Minimum Level = ROL - (Average usage × Average Re-order Period) =	450 - (50 × 5 weeks) = 200 Units	300 - (50 × 3 weeks) = 150 Units.
(iii) Maximum Level = ROL - (Minimum usage × Minimum Re-order Period).	450 (25 × 4) + 300 = 650 Units	300 - (25 × 2) +500 = 750 Units
(iv) Average Stock Maximum Level + Minimum Level ÷ 2	$\frac{200+650}{2}$ = 425 Units	$\frac{150+750}{2}$ = 450 Units,

Note: Average Re-order period lies between 4 & 6 weeks, i.e., 5 weeks in case of component A and 3 weeks in case of B

Note: There are other alternatives to calculate Average stock level depending on the Maximum Usage, Minimum Usage and Average Usage vis-a-vis various lead times as follows:

(iv) Average Stock Level	Component 'A'	Component 'B'
(a) ROL - (Max. Usage × Max. lead time) + 1/ 2 ROQ.	= 450 - (75 × 6) + 150 = 150 Units	300 - (75 × 4) + 250 = 250
(b) ROL - (Min, Usage × Min, Lead Time) + 1/ 2 ROQ.	= 450 - (25 × 4) + 150 = 500 Units	300 - (25 × 2) + 250 = 500
(c) ROL - (average usage × Average Lead Time) + 1/ 2 ROQ.	= 450 - (50 × 5) + 150 = 350 Units	300 - (50 × 3) + 250 = 400 Units.
(d) Minimum Level + 1/ 2 ROQ	= 200 + 150 = 350 Units.	150 +250 – 400 Units

Illustration 2

A manufacturing cnncern is having 1,000 units of materials valuing ₹ 1,00,000 in total. Prepare the statement showing the stock according to ABC Analysis.

Category	Quantity		Value		
	% No. of items		%	Amount ₹	Average Value ₹
A (High value items)	10%	100	70%	70,000	$\frac{70,000}{100} = 700$
B (Medium value items)	20%	200	20%	20,000	$\frac{20,000}{200} = 100$
C (Low value items)	70%	700	10%	10,000	$\frac{10,000}{700} = 14$
Total:	100%	1000	100%	1,00,000	

For the sake of simplicity, the above percentages have been considered. But in practice, the percentages may vary between 5% to 10%, 10% to 20% and 70% to 85%.

In foreign countries, Bin Cards and Stores Ledger Cards are not maintained for 'C' class items. These are issued directly to the production foreman concerned and controlled through norms of consumption based on production targets. By doing this, 70% of the effort required for maintaining the Bin Cards and Stores Ledger cards is eliminated. With 30% of the effort, an organization will be able to exercise control on the 90% of the closer control on costly items in which large amount of capital is invested.

The general procedure for classifying A, B or C items is as follows

(1) Ascertain the cost and consumption of each material over a given period of time.

(2) Multiply unit cost by estimated usage to obtain net value

(3) List out all the items with quantity and value,

(4) Arrange them in descending order in value, i.,e ranking according to value.

(5) Ascertain the monetary limits for A, B or C classification.

(6) Accumulate value and add up number of items of A items. Calculate percentage on total inventory in value and in number.

(7) Similar action for B and C class items

Illustration 3

From the following details, draw a plan of ABC selective control

ITEM	UNITS	UNITS COST ₹ P.
1	7,000	5,00
2	24000	3.00
3	1,500	10,00
4	600	22.00
5	38,000	1.50
6	40,000	0.50
7	60,000	0.20
8	3,000	3.50
9	300	8.00
10	29,000	0.40
11	11,500	7.10
12	4,100	6.20

Answer

STATEMENT OF TOTAL COST AND RANKING

Items.	Unit	Unit' Cost	Total Cost	% of Total Cost.	Ranking.
1	7,000	5.00	35,000	9.84%	4
2	24,000	3.00	72,000	20.24%	2
3	1,500	10.00	15,000	4.22%	7
4	6 C	22.00	13,200	3.71%	8
5	38,000	1.50	57,000	16.02%	3
6	40,000	0.50	20,000	5.62%	6
7	60,000	0.20	12,000	3.37%	9
8	3,000	3.50	10,500	2.95%	11
9	300	8.00	2,400	0.67%	12
10	29,000	0.40	11,600	3.26%	10
11	11,500	7.10	81,650	22.95%	1
12	4,100	6.20	25,420	7.15%	5
			3,55,770		100.00

BASIS FOR SELECTIVE CONTROL (ASSUMED)

₹ 50,000 & above	-	'A' items.
₹ 15,000 to 50,000	-	'B' items.
Below ₹ 15,000	-	'C' items.

On this basis, a plan of ABC selective control is given below

Ranking	Item Nos.	% of Total Items	Cost ₹	% of Total Cost	Category
1	11		81,650		
2	2		72,000		
3	5		51,000		
Total	3	25%	2,10,650	59,21%	A
4	1		35,000		
5	12		25,420		
6	6		20,000		
7	3		15,000		
Total	4	$33\frac{1}{3}$	95,420	26.82%	B
8	4		13,200		
9	7		12,000		
10	10		11,600		
11	8		10,500		
12	9		2,400		
Total	5	$41\frac{2}{3}$ %	49,700	13.97%	C
Grand Total	12	100	3,55,770	100	

INVENTORY CONTROL

Stock Control Purchase Control	Issue Control	Consumption Control	Quantity Control	Value Control	Others
1 Right Quality 2 Right Time 3 Right Quantity 4 Right Price	1. Issue against proper authorisation 2. Proper classification and Job Number 3. Proper Records Bin cards & Stores Ledger. 4. Issue of right quantity as per bill of materials	1. Standard to be set in respect of consumption scrap, wastage spoilage & defectives having regard to the nature of process, working conditions. 2. Forms for reporting to be standardised. 3. Remedial action based on reports.	1. Maximum stock level. 2. Minimum stock level 3. Reordering level 4. Danger level 5. E O Q	A B C Analysis and other selection technics	1. Perpetual inventory system 2. Physical Stock verification. 3. Slow moving, non-moving obsolete and surplus items. 4. Disposal of surplus items 5. Reports.

12.15 SUMMARY

Both excessive and insufficient inventory have adverse effects on cost of operations. Excessive inventory results in blockage of capital, increased storage cost and loss through pilferage and obsolescence. Insufficient inventory causes interruptions in operations, missed deliveries and loss of potential sales.

Inventory control ensures that right materials are available at right time and place in right quantities with minimum capital locked in inventories.

ABC analysis of inventory allows management to exercise greater control on vital but few items of inventory with least efforts. Different ordering systems including Economic order Quantity allow management to procure materials in required quantity at required times.

Materials Requirement Planning is another tool effectively used for control of inventory with use of computers. Maximum, Minimum, order, Danger are different levels of stocks that are determined to control inventory. Physical verification of stock is undertaken on periodic or continuous basis to retain control over inventory held.

12.16 SELF ASSESSMENT QUESTIONS

(1) How does excessive inventory affect costs or operation?

(2) What are various consequences of insufficient inventory?

(3) Describe ABC analysis. How is it used to control inventory.

(4) What are different stock levels determined to control inventory? How are they calculated?

(5) What is the role of physical verification of inventory in its control?

Chapter 13

AUTOMATION OF STORES RECORD SYSTEM

Objectives

After studying this chapter, you should be able to understand:

What is ERP.

Advantages of ERP for stores management.

Initial configuration for implementing ERP.

Various reports available to users under ERP.

Structure:

13.1 INTRODUCTION

Ours is a very interesting country. For years, we resist or remain ignorant of radical and significant concepts, which evolve around us and in the rest of the world. Nevertheless, when we do decide to take the plunge, the momentum with which the concept takes off is truly phenomenal. This is obviously supported by the inherent huge volume of potential which exists in our developing economy, wherein the current scenario is rapidly changing with the arrival of a new breed of trained and informed executives.

ERP seems to be the present day moksha that has completely taken over the IT related media, ie the print as well as electronic. There is a sudden credibility attached with this concept which is revered by all and sundry. The question is how many people really know the concept what is really being talked about when we discuss ERP.

To most people ERP stands for big names like Oracle, BaaN and ASP which in turn also connotes huge investments in terms of both time and money. This, coupled with the fact an ERP means an essential change in one's way of working, seems to be the major deterrent for a large section of the Indian business enterprises, who seem to think that the ERP concept is relevant only to multi- the "nationals or big corporate houses with turnover in the range of ₹ 500 to ₹ 2,000crore. But what about the corporate sector in the ₹ 25 crore to ₹ 500 crore range, which is the most densely populated industrial segment in India? Can it benefit too?

13.2 WHAT IS ERP?

In the strict sense of a definition, Enterprise Resource Planning is a strategic software tool, which equips any enterprise with the necessary capabilities to integrate and synchronies the isolated function into streamlined business processes in order to give a competitive edge to the organization in a turbulent business environment.

The name ERP itself states that the entire concept is about optimization of the resources available within an organization. The present day environment is a sea change from what it was three years ago. Today to survive, an enterprise has to be globally competitive, qualitative and sensitive as well as responsive not only to customer feedback but also to the entire marketplace.

The competitive environment ensures that a business remains close to its customer and delivers the best possible product within the shortest possible time with maximum possible value-addition. This in turn demands integration and synergisation of the business processes of an enterprise. This also demands that in order to produce goods tailored to customer requirements and provide faster deliveries, the enterprise must be closely linked to both suppliers and customers. For achieving this, we need efficient planning and control systems that enable very good synchronization and planning in all the processes of the organization.

ERP Software is an integrated uniform system which helps an organization get a competitive edge by integrating all business processes and optimizing the resources available.

13.3 AN ERP VS. OTHER APPLICATIONS

Liberalization, globalization and exploration of business opportunities by the West in the emerging and developing Indian economy leads us to a scenario where decision-makers are forced to travel extensively, handle complex business relationship on a global plane and constantly take decision, which are best for the company. More than anything else time is of essence.

Most organizations find this difficult if they do not have a fully-intergrated, uniform system in place. In other words, when the organization is people-dependent, instead of people facilitated process dependent, the decision making is either delayed or not at best. The fast paced 90's thus have seen the emergence of a new, virtual world of business, where the need of the hour has been a new breed of people who can evolve the system of management from an art to a science.

This science of business management, through management of not the isolated function, but with the overall perspective of the organization, paved the way for the corporates towards ERP as the inevitable option for management of business.

The Evolution of ERP has been a very gradual process. It started long ago when we used to talk about EOQ (Economy Order Quantity). This was reactive management. We were talking about only one step further from MRP was MRP II which also covered production scheduling and machine capacity planning.

Today the concern of the management is optimum use of all four resources ie Man, Machine, Money and Materials thereby leading to the need for ERP systems. An effective and properly implemented ERP Software will create an ability to respond to new customer needs by providing a high level of integration of the functional areas within the organization. This in turn will help an organization to seize the market opportunities at the right time.

Standardization of System

Despite the need and trend for globalization, a majority of Indian business continue to exist in an environment wherein standardization of systems, procedures and methodology is a distant reality. This as well as a wide disparity in management perceptions, attitudes and commitment both in terms of time and finance towards IT related issues creates the need for easily adaptable and cost-effective ERP.

Modules/Producers

Impelx, an implementation methodology for Movex, is an ERP product from Sweden-based Intentia. The Implex model describes how project should be organized, carried through and followed up. Each project is divided into five phases: Position, Design, Configure, Plan, Implement and Start-up. Intentia also offers a number of products to enable efficient execution of each of these phases.

> The distribution channel for spares and replacement parts for autos is highly complex, comprising lakhs of outlets around the world, with supply chains extending across national boundaries and continents. Launched in early 1998, BPCS client/Server Aftermarket has features that include flexible and direct order entry by buyers.

In 19977 In Denver, Colorado, three men left the accounting world to from a software company that would specialize in mid-range computing solutions. The three founders-Jack Thompson, Dan Gregory, and ED McVaney – each lent a small portion of his name for the company moniker.

J D Edwards with sites in 100 countries signed up with customers over 9500. They include Bassett Furniture Industries, Nordic Track Autoliv ASP, AFC Cable Systems, City of Orlando, Mail Well Envelope, SE Johnson Companies, Daewoo Motors, Magyar Aluminum in Hungary and Employee Solutions In Arizona.

BaaN Data Navigator Suite, a new component in BaaN Series, is a navigational tool that makes use of Top Tier software's hyper-relational technology to information contained in BaaN Series applications.

'One World', introduced in 1996 by J D Edwards, is one of the first network-centric, object-oriented ERP architectures, providing customers with the flexibility to quickly adapt business processes to meet market demands, as well as the ability to capitalize on the latest functionality and lower costs offered by emerging technologies One world provides a true distributed object architecture and a business rules engine that transcends traditional client/server technology.

ERP vendor Cincom Systems has launched a sales automation software that helps corporations deliver complex, customized products and services. Called Cincom Acquire, it empowers sales personnel with product engineering knowledge and eliminates bottlenecks in the selling chain, thus supporting the concept of mass customization. Cincom Acqire comprises three integrated solutions: Configutator Workbench, Sales Configuratuior and Bid Management

One of the most important decisions that a senior executive will have to make is related to the selection and implementation of an enterprise resources planning (ERP) package. It is one of the investments that will contribute to every aspect of business from the operations and transactions of a company to its product and services. However, many managers are ill equipped to make a sound decision on these issues.

The Concept of Enterprise Resources Planning Systems

There have never been commensurate gains accruing to an enterprise corresponding to the level of its investments in IT. This has also come to be known as the productivity paradox of IT. It has been a reality that all of us in the IT industry have lived unmfortably with for the major part of our professional lives.

In the past few decades, all of us have witnessed a procession of different methodologies, tools, and techniques emanating from this industry that have had tremendous impact on the very nature and operations of business enterprises. But in midst of all this turmoil, one fact has remained constant, and that has been the lack of productivity improvements, irrespective of the extent and nature of computerization.

But right from the start, there was an even more basic problem in terms of the number of software applications that were actually completed and implemented successfully. Much has been written on the software crisis that was engulfing information service groups in the' 80s. The reasons were multifold:

With the advent of PC-like functionalities, users were becoming more complex and demanding.

Consequently, applications were becoming bigger and more complex.

Correspondingly, productivity was reducing rather than increasing.

Software development times were increasing, and cost and time overruns were fairly routine.

Quality, trained professionals were always in short supply, resulting in increased costs for programmers; hence, systems development costs were ever-increasing.

Mortality of systems was very high.

On average, out of the total number of IT systems under development, more than half used to be cancelled; out of the remaining half, only about two-thirds was delivered. Half of the delivered systems never got implemented, whereas another quarter were abandoned midway through the implementation. Out of the residual quarter of the delivered systems, half failed to deliver the functionality required by the Management and, therefore, were scrapped. Only the remaining half of the systems were used after great modifications, which entailed further delays and costs in an almost never-ending process.

One of the root causes identified for these problems was the inherent weakness of the phase in which requirements were captured and analyzed. This phase never seemed to get the correct and complete requirements. As a result, completed projects never seemed to deliver promised functionality and had to be recycled for more analysis and development. Maintenance and enhancements were called for indefinitely and became harder to achieve as time passed by. Because individuals changed midway both on the development and user sides, system requirements changed and the whole process continued indefinitely. This is primarily because there is a fundamental disconnect between the business and the ITI/IS people. Notwithstanding how much both the parties try to bridge the gap, there is a fundamental gap between the perception of a business user and what is understood by the systems staff; both classes of people speak different languages. Even if the systems personnel tried to increase precision by using methodologies and specification tools, because users were unfamiliar with these tools, they were never able to ratify the documented requirements completely.

Typically, surveys found that 50% to 80% of the ITI/IS resources were dedicated to application maintenance. The return on investments in IT was abysmally low by any standard of measurement and expectations. With ITI/IS budgets stretching beyond the capabilities of most organizations, there was a compelling need for a radically new approach that could result in actual usable functionality that was professionally developed, under control, and on time.

This is the post modern version of C. P. Snow's 'two cultures'. which he had initially mooted to talk meaningfully about the worlds of art and science in the middle of the last century.

The traditional software implementations involving the development of applications were characterized by:

Requirement-driven functional decomposition

Late risk resolution

Late error detection

Use of different languages or artifacts at different phases of the project

Large proportion of scrap and rework

Adversarial stakeholder relationship with non-IT users

Priority of techniques over tools

Priority of quality of developed software rather than functionality per se

Great emphasis on current, correct, complete and consistent documentation

Great emphasis on testing and reviews

Major effort on change control and management

Large and diverse resource requirements

Schedules always under pressure

Great effort on projected or estimated target performance

Inherent limitations on scalability

Protracted integration between systems

The increased time spent on requirements definition with the users was envisaged to lead to systems that were closer to the users' actual requirements. On the other hand, prototyping was designed to address the requirements capture issue by making the users directly participate in the process of defining the requirements. This was focused mainly on the screen and reports design because these were the elements that could be visualized directly by the user. But, none of these strategies really resolved the problem. ERP packages adopted a totally different approach by providing the most comprehensive functionality within the package. Company personnel were only expected to pick and choose whatever was required by the company actually using the package. Thus, ERP packages effectively short-circuited the whole issue of capturing requirements. The traditional project life cycle-consisting of analysis, design, development, testing, and implementation-was transformed to the ERP implementation. This is the main reason for its success.

13.4 WHY USE ERP?

The implementation of ERP engenders the following business and technical advantages:

Reconciles and optimizes the conflicting goals of different divisions or departments.

Standardizes business processes across all constituent companies and sites thus increasing their efficiencies.

Provides the ability to know and implement global best practices.

Alters the function-oriented organization toward a more team-based, cross-functional, process-oriented organization, thus leading to more flexible, flatter, and tightly integrated organization.

Provides a responsive medium for undertaking all variants on process improvement programs and methodologies, including process innovation, process improvement, business process, and so on.

Provides a responsive medium for quality improvement and standardization efforts including QC, QA, and TQM.

Is process-oriented, and therefore is fertile ground for implementing Activity Based Management (ABM) efforts be they for budgeting, costing, efficiency, or quality.

Provides the best conduit for measuring the benefits accruing to an organization by monitoring the Return on Investment (ROI) of not only money, but also manpower. materials, time, and information. This could be in terms of various parameters like cost. quality, responsiveness, cycle time, and so on. Thus, ERP could assist in the implementation of, for instance, the balanced scorecard within the enterprise.

Customarily implements best-of-class practices and provides the best means for benchmarking the organization's competitiveness.

Enables an enterprise to scale up its level of operations drastically, or even enter into different businesses altogether, without any disruption or performance degradation.

Enables real-time creation of data directly during the actual transaction or processes by the persons who are actually responsible for it.

Pushes latest data and status to the operational-level persons for better and faster decisions, at least on routine issues; empowers and gives ownership to the operational personnel at the level of actual work (this automatically does away with problems associated with collection of voluminous data preparation, entry, corrections of inaccuracies, backups, and so on).

Integrates data of the organization into a single comprehensive database. Provides online availability of correct and up-to-date data.

Provides the most current, correct, consistent, and complete operational data that could be populated into the enterprise data warehouse for analysis and reporting.

Greatly reduces the cost of maintaining systems.

Interface to Other Functions

The interfaces of this module with other modules are as given below:

Materials Management (MM): Availability checking, scheduling deliveries, credit checking, material shipments, transfers of inventory between plants, material determination, material exclusion and material substitution, reorder points, and returns

Production Planning (PP): Availability checking, SOP forecasting, sales order, requirements transfer to PP

Finance (FI): Credit checking, material shipments, material returns, billing, taxes and pricing, outstanding balances, profitability analysis

Application of MM Material Management models

Materials Management (MM)

The MM module functions with complete integration with other modules such as logistics and financial accounting. The MM module business processes include POs, goods receipts and invoice verification. and supplier payments. MM is a multisite inventory management system and can handle consignment stocks as well as processing of subcontract orders.

Core Business Processes

The various core processes that are available within SAP that companies may implement depending on their requirements are

Purchase requisition inquiry

Request for quotation

Quotation

Purchase order

Goods receipt

Invoice verification

Payments

Outstanding payments

Vendor evaluation

Quality control

13.5 INITIAL CONFIGURATION AND MASTER DATA

There are certain enterprisewide (client-independent as well as client-dependent) parameters that need to be defined initially depending on the business requirements of the company. Some of these prerequisite parameters are as follows:

Purchasing organization

Plant

Storage location

Conditions for pricing (gross, net, and effective price), taxes, discounts, surcharges, and so on

Vendor master (general, purchasing, and accounting data)

Vendor-material information records

Material master (basic, purchasing, MRP, forecasting, storage, accounting, costing, job preparation, and quality management data)

Quality information records

Scheduling agreements

Special Features

A partial list of features and facilities provided by the MM modules is as follows:

Provides for three major sources of requirement: production planned orders, purchase requisitions, and schedule lines. These sources arise from the stock requirement list prepared by MRP.

Provides for international calendars, sizes, and unit of measurement, as well as country-specific requirements such as taxes, postal codes, banks, currencies, and so on.

Provides for defining various types of material, such as raw material, trading goods, product, non valuated material, and so on.

Has facilities to handle vendor consignment stocks and subcontract orders, as well as processing of consumable materials.

Provides multisite inventory management system

Provides for MRP to release scheduling line against a long-term scheduling agreement with a vendor, without going through the requisition and purchase order process every time. Has provisions for maintaining a source list for such items for the MRP run to generate the scheduling lines automatically.

Provides for maintenance of source list of vendors (including other plants), material vendor relationship information, and quota arrangements for allocation of purchases.

Provides for creating purchase requisitions manually or automatically through MRP or PM module or from networks in the PS module. Flexible release strategy for approving purchase orders.

Provides preparation of RFQs for items not having a source of supply, including a delivery schedule.

Permits vendors responses to the RFQs to be stored as quotations along with specifics such as pricing.

Provides for outline agreement for long-term agreements with vendors that 'Could be either scheduling agreements, or quantity and value contract agreements that require a release order (that is, a PO) for every delivery.

Provides for creation of POs, either manually or automatically, by using outstanding requisitions with exact delivery quantity and dates.

Provides the facility to prepare the goods receipt on the basis of the corresponding PO. Provides for the goods to be received at different locations or directly as unrestricted stock, blocked stock, or stock in quality inspection if dictated by the corresponding PO.

Permits for management of quality planning, execution and improvement activities resulting in the usage decision of acceptance in unrestricted stock, blocked stock, scrapped, return to vendor etc.

Has a powerful facility for inventory movements, identified by the corresponding movement type, on account of goods receipts, goods issues, stock transfers, and transfer posting. The latter might occur after quality inspection, and so on.

Enables each movement type to trigger a material document and if required, an accounting document for reflecting the inventory and accounting impact of these movements. Achieves the latter through predefined automatic account determination for posting into the general ledger accounts, based on the movement type and the material type.

Provides many facilities for tracking inventory involving monitoring stock levels and the status of materials at various locations.

Provides different procedures for material valuation (FIFO, LIFO, and standard price).

Provides facilities for ascertaining a physical inventory of goods to validate the accuracy of inventory data in the system through procedures such as periodic inventory, continuous inventory, inventory sampling, and cycle counting.

Permits the definition of different cycle counts for different materials or groups of materials. Provides facilities for any reported differences in quantity and amount to be posted for updating stock, as well as the corresponding G/L account, respectively.

Permits proper reflection of all deliveries by vendors, vendor invoices, and payments to vendors in the corresponding G/L accounts.

Provides a powerful facility to set up a payment program for processing, as well as printing. the payments for open items selected into the program at the time the payment program is defined.

Permits decentralized procurement and centralized inventory control simultaneously.

Allows a three-way matching process whereby a payment is made only when the invoice received matches the price on the purchase order and the correct quantity in the goods receipt. Can also allow a two-way matching process or other business process based on your business requirements.

Can be set up to allow different tolerances for quantity received against purchase order quantity, price invoiced against purchase order price, and so on.

Has automatic update capabilities that immediately update previous documents when a new activity has occurred. For example, the purchase order will keep track of undelivered amounts and immediately be updated when a goods receipt has been made and when an invoice has been received.

Has helpful information and warning messages that will inform you when a duplicate in voice has been received, or if a duplicate purchase order is being created,

Interface to Other Functions

In an integrated installation, the interface of this module with other modulaes are as given below:

Finance and Controlling (FI-Co): Purchase orders,supplier invoice, payments to suppliers, inventory movements, quality inspection, stock inventory,phaysicl inventory differences,payment programs, and so forth

Sales and Distribution (SD): Availability checking,scheduling deliveries, credit checking material shipments, transfers of inventory between plants, material determination, material exclusion, material substitution, recorder points, and returns

Production Planning (PP): Stock requirement list, MRP-run-generated schedule lines, back flushing via confirmation and production order, and so forth

Quality Management (QM): Quality info records usage decisions, and so forth

Plant Maintenance (PM): Purchase orders, external services management, and so forth

13.6 AUTOMATED PROCUREMENT AND INVENTORY MANAGEMENT

Material Management (MM) Module

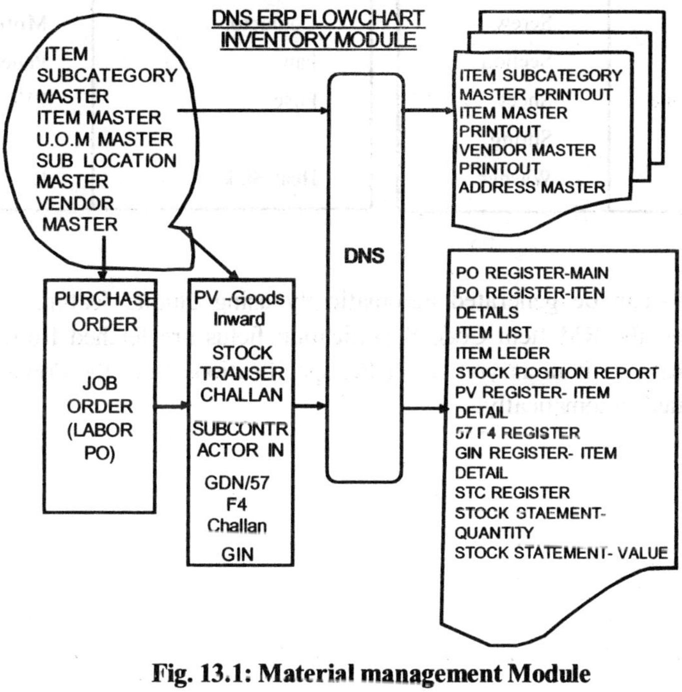

Fig. 13.1: Material management Module

Material Management Module: This is also referred as Inventory module.

Material Management module optimizes all purchasing processes workflow driven processing functions, enabling automated procure storing with accurate inventory management and integrates purchase as well as quality check of material at the time of receiving the same stores. ERP gives real-time inventory report quickly for JIT (Just inventory management.

Inventory Master

First,classify items into major categories such as: Finished Goods, Semi Finished Goods (or sub-assemblies, raw material, consumables, packing material, etc.

Second, classify further each category into sub-category. For instance, say raw or bought out items can be classified into sub-categories as follows:

Example of 'Mechanical items' (bought out items or raw meterial grouping)	
Angle	Nut
Bar	Paint
Bearing	Pipe
Bolt	Plate
Channel	Rivet
Circlip	Rod
Handle	Screw
Hinge	Section
Hydraulic & Pneumatic	Sheet
Ink	Spring
Insulation	Washer

Example of 'Electrical items' (bought out items or raw meterial grouping)	
Actuator	Indicator
Blower	Insulation Metirial
Cable	Junction Box
Ceramic Bead	Lighting Lamps
Circuit Breaker	Lug
Connector	Meter
Contactor	Motor
Fan	Panel Meter
Fuse	PVC Channel
Heat Sink	Relay

Item Code Generator

In ERP, item code can be generated automatically using unique feature - auto itemicode generator. In item master, the RM Item Code Specification fields are fetched from masters. While entering any new raw material item as you select the specifications from the down list one by one the item code is generated automatically.

Item Master

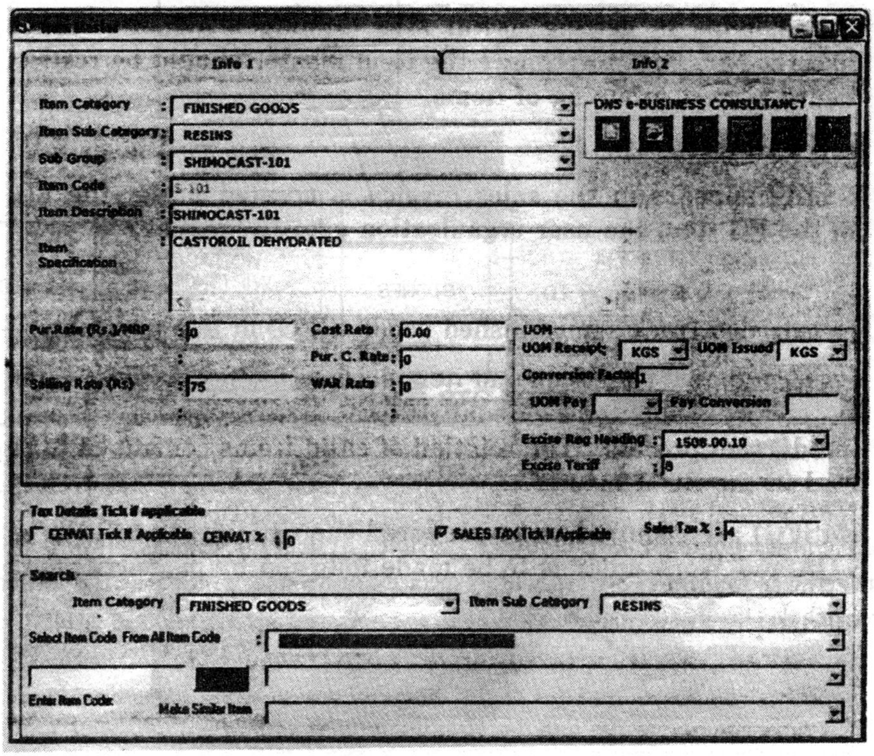

Fig. 13.2: Item Master: Master Database Containing Information about All Kinds of Material.

Everyone in the organization must call any material by this code only. Proper classification or categorization of material is must for ERP. This discipline helps in getting useful MIS (Management Information System) reports. Access/secret password to prepare the item master should be with authorised people only, to ensure correct grouping of items.

Finished Goods (Products)

The item that usually appears in the sales invoice is created under the FG Finished Goods Category.

Semi-finished Item

The ERP software can also track semi-finished goods (SFG) or sub assemblies.

For this, it is necessary to give item code and item description for such materials which can be classified as factory made items. Usually these items are produced (assembled) as a result of some production process. The relation of child items consumed to produce the SFG item is defined in the BOM master.

Location Concept

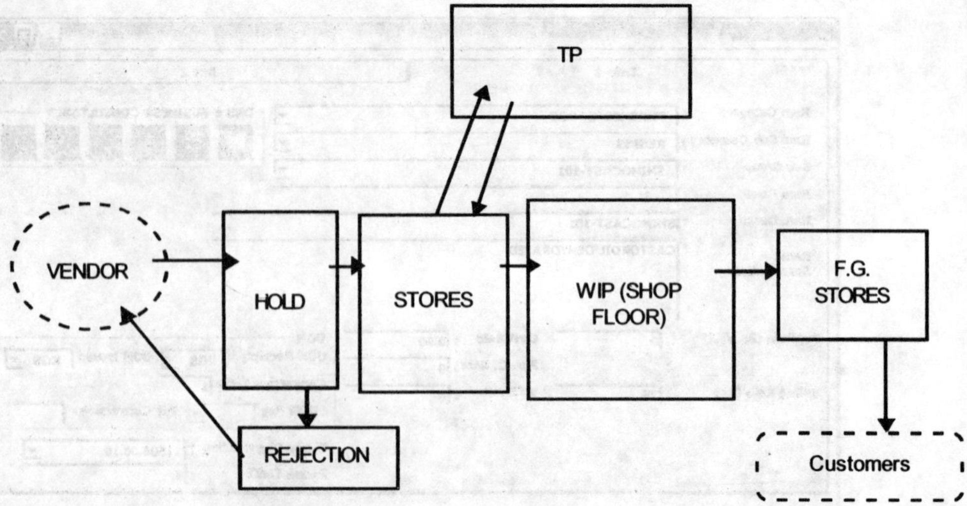

Fig. 13.3: Make Logical Locations and if Possible Physical Location as Shown

Any material movement is always with respect to an inventory location. The location and sub-location are included in master database.

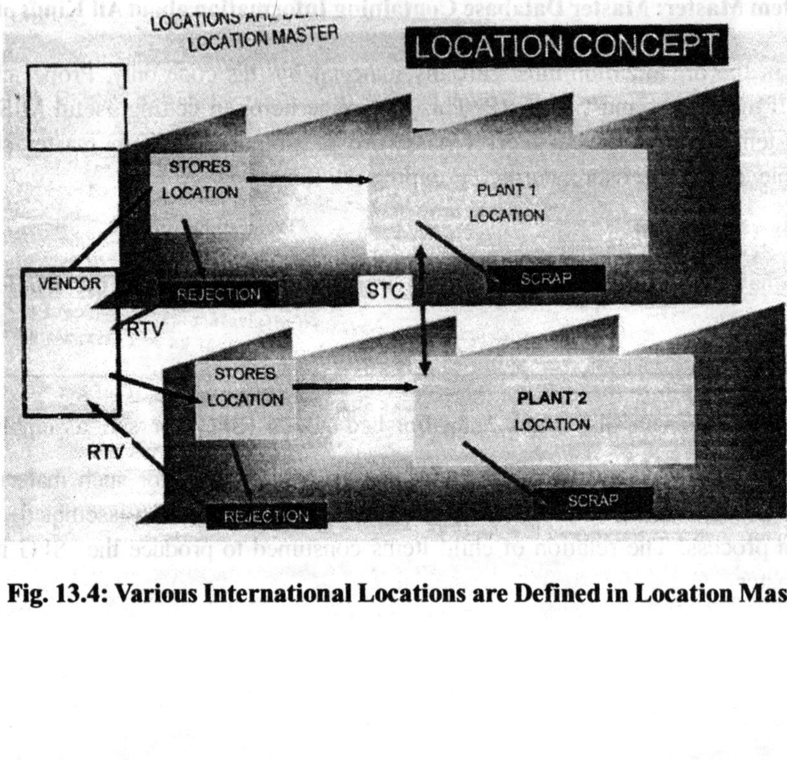

Fig. 13.4: Various International Locations are Defined in Location Master

Subcategory Master

There are two important flags (tick marks) provided on the Item sub-category master.

Activate Serial Number: When ticked, ERP will keep track of serial number of the item.

Excess Received Percentage: When material is received, the PO quantity is defaulted automatically. The stores person cannot receive quantity exceeding PO quantity. However, for some items it may not be practically possible for vendor to supply the exact quantity. When ticked, ERP will allow excess by percentage to be defined for a given sub-category.

UOM (Unit of Measurement) Master

It displays various units of measurement, which are regularly used, e.g., Kg, Each, Pair, Set, etc. This is 'accounting unit' required while creating item master.

EACH
KG
MTR
MT
SET
NO

GIN/RM/Bought out: Goods Inward Note cum Inspection or GRN is used when material is being received in the stores. PO is a parent document to make a GIN or GRN. When the user selects the vendor name, all pending PO will default automatically. User will enter Quantity information and save the GIN or GRN. This document is active document. In ERP, user does not have to enter documents twice.

GRN [or GIN] does the following:

GIN or GRN will add material into stock.

Credit the Vendor (Supplier): Automatic posting in creditor ledger ensures that both ledgers - item and account - are updated instantly after the material is accepted QC inspector/Quality Assurance will enter accepted quantity. This will automatically add item into main stores and if item is rejected, it is added into Rejection Location.

Note: This GRN option can be seen under the Inventory menu -> Inventory Transaction sub menu. The GRN is a unique transaction that is integrated with purchase order, inventory as well as creditor account.

Stock Transfer Challan (STC)

STC is used to transfer material from one location to another. This does not consume material. User has to select 'From' location and 'To' location.

Purchase Return

Prepare Excise invoice when material is returned back to vendor. For non-excisable material user can prepare RTV or Return-To-Vendor. Reference of GIN OR GRN is required.

Sales Return (RGN - Return Goods Note)

It is prepared when material is received back from customer (e.g., Rejected by customer). This scenario can be taken care of in ERP by following way:

(1) Let us assume that material sold to customer through Challan cum Invoice is say, 1000 Qty FG.

(2) Partial FG are rejected at customer's end, e.g., 100 Qty

(3) Customer sends back the material through his Challan cum Invoice

(4) To receive this material back, a logical location will be created in ERP called 'Sales Return' Location.

(5) Rejected Material will come in ERP by a transaction called RGN (Return Goods Note)/

(6) In RGN customer is selected first.

(7) Then Sales Invoices made for that customer is selected.

(8) Here entire Sales Invoice will be defaulted in RGN.

(9) By double clicking on the invoice, the rejected qty e.g. 100 is entered.

(10) RGN with all taxes details are saved. This will add the material in the 'Sales Return' Location and gives credit to the customer for rejected amt.

(11) 100 qty will reflect in 'Sales Return Location' in Item ledger.

(12) Then after inspection, it will be known whether to do rework on the same material or replace with new FG.

(13) Once 100 qty FG of acceptable quality are ready, that will be dispatched through Sales Invoice with different series.

(14) This sale Invoice posting will NOT come in DSA register (Daily Stock Account - Excise related records) and separate register will be maintain for these invoices.

Stock Adjustment Note

SAN is used to add or remove item from the stock. Access to SAN is given to authorize responsible person only. This is useful to correct the stock balance in case of difference in the ERP book-stock and physical-stock.

Inventory Reports

(A) GRN OR PV Register

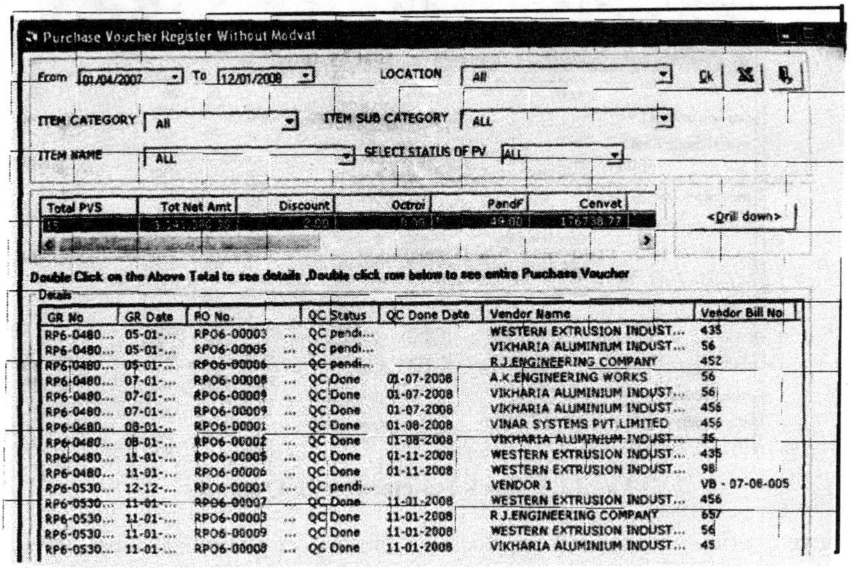

Fig. 13.5: Grods Receipt Note (GRN) Register

GRN register is also called Purchase Register. Some users refer the same as 'Purchase Voucher Register'. This gives details of item received in the stores. GRN register can be prepared for a given location, say stores and for a given period by giving 'From' date and 'To' date in ERP.

The following columns display important information in the GRN register:

(1) GR No	(2) GR Date	(3) PO No.	(4) QC Status	(5) QC Done Date
(6) Vendor Name	(7) Vendor Bill No	(8) Vendor Bill Date	(9) Net Amt	
(10) Discount	(11) Octroi	(12) P & F Amount	(13) CenVAT	(14) Cess
(15) Sh Cess	(16) VAT	(17) CST	(18) Freight	
(19) Insurrance	(20) Other Chg.	(21) Grand Total	(22) Location	(23) ACCT. Status

There are TWO parts:

The first part gives document level detail, that is vendor bill amount information, whereas on drilldown user can get item level details, that is quantity information.

(B) STC Register: This gives list of Stock Transfer Challan.

(C) Item Ledger

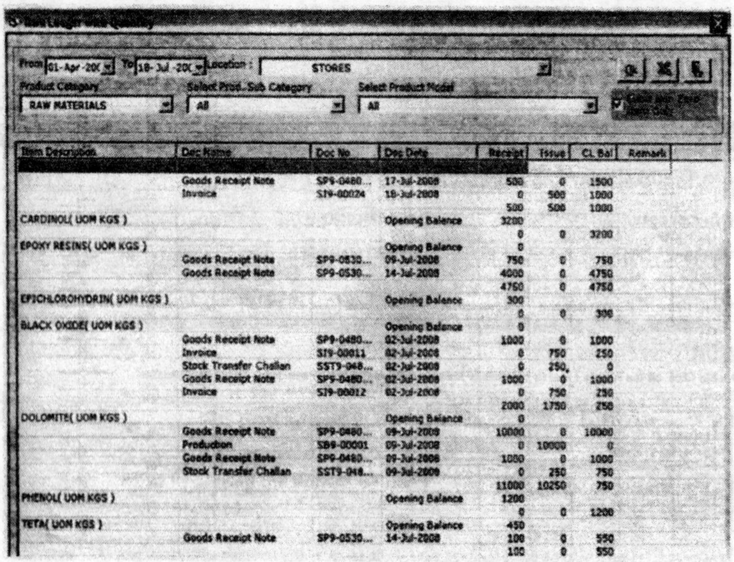

Item Description	Doc Name	Doc No	Doc Date	Receipt	Issue	CL Bal	Remark
	Goods Receipt Note	SP9-0480...	17-Jul-2008	500	0	1500	
	Invoice	SI9-00024	18-Jul-2008	0	500	1000	
				500	500	1000	
CARDINOL(UOM KGS)			Opening Balance	3200			
				0	0	3200	
EPOXY RESINS(UOM KGS)			Opening Balance	0			
	Goods Receipt Note	SP9-0530...	09-Jul-2008	750	0	750	
	Goods Receipt Note	SP9-0530...	14-Jul-2008	4000	0	4750	
				4750	0	4750	
EPICHLOROHYDRIN(UOM KGS)			Opening Balance	300			
				0	0	300	
BLACK OXIDE(UOM KGS)			Opening Balance	0			
	Goods Receipt Note	SP9-0480...	02-Jul-2008	1000	0	1000	
	Invoice	SI9-00011	02-Jul-2008	0	750	250	
	Stock Transfer Challan	SST9-048...	02-Jul-2008	0	250,	0	
	Goods Receipt Note	SP9-0480...	02-Jul-2008	1000	0	1000	
	Invoice	SI9-00012	02-Jul-2008	0	750	250	
				2000	1750	250	
DOLOMITE(UOM KGS)			Opening Balance	0			
	Goods Receipt Note	SP9-0480...	09-Jul-2008	10000	0	10000	
	Production	SB9-00001	09-Jul-2008	0	10000	0	
	Goods Receipt Note	SP9-0480...	09-Jul-2008	1000	0	1000	
	Stock Transfer Challan	SST9-048...	09-Jul-2008	0	250	750	
				11000	10250	750	
PHENOL(UOM KGS)			Opening Balance	1200			
				0	0	1200	
TETA(UOM KGS)			Opening Balance	450			
	Goods Receipt Note	SP9-0530...	14-Jul-2008	100	0	550	
				100	0	550	

Fig. 13.6: Stock Statement with Quantity

For a given period and for a given location this report gives date wise, item wise details of quantity with Opening Balance, Receipt, Issue, and Closing Balance. This is inventory ledger in detail, showing posting of each inventory related transactions.

(D) Stock Statement

For a given period and for a given location this report gives item wise details of quantity with Opening Balance, Receipt, Issue, and Closing Balance. This is item ledger summary.

There are two types Stock Statements

(1) Stock Statement with Quantity

(2) Stock Statement with Value.

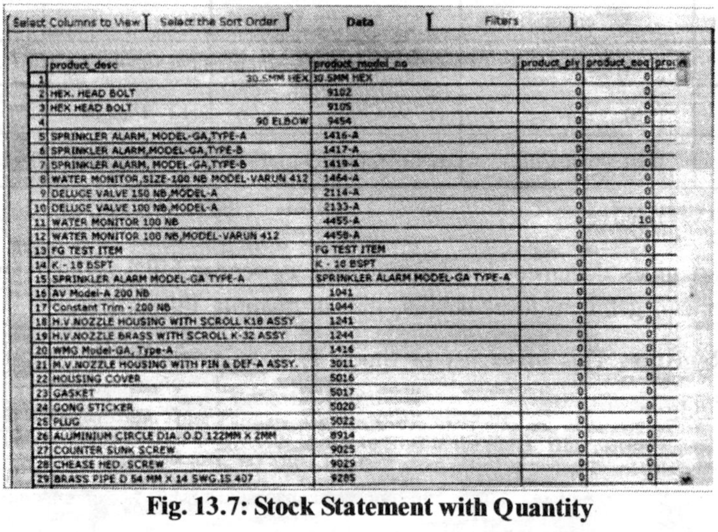

	product_desc	product_model_no	product_ply	product_eoq
1	30.5MM HEX	30.5MM HEX	0	0
2	HEX. HEAD BOLT	9102	0	0
3	HEX HEAD BOLT	9105	0	0
4	90 ELBOW	9454	0	0
5	SPRINKLER ALARM, MODEL-GA,TYPE-A	1416-A	0	0
6	SPRINKLER ALARM,MODEL-GA,TYPE-B	1417-A	0	0
7	SPRINKLER ALARM, MODEL-GA,TYPE-B	1419-A	0	0
8	WATER MONITOR,SIZE-100 NB MODEL-VARUN 412	1464-A	0	0
9	DELUGE VALVE 150 NB,MODEL-A	2114-A	0	0
10	DELUGE VALVE 100 NB,MODEL-A	2133-A	0	0
11	WATER MONITOR 100 NB	4455-A	0	10
12	WATER MONITOR 100 NB,MODEL-VARUN 412	4458-A	0	0
13	FG TEST ITEM	FG TEST ITEM	0	0
14	K - 18 BSPT	K - 18 BSPT	0	0
15	SPRINKLER ALARM MODEL-GA TYPE-A	SPRINKLER ALARM MODEL-GA TYPE-A	0	0
16	AV Model-A 200 NB	1041	0	0
17	Constant Trim - 200 NB	1044	0	0
18	H.V.NOZZLE HOUSING WITH SCROLL K18 ASSY	1241	0	0
19	H.V.NOZZLE BRASS WITH SCROLL K-32 ASSY	1244	0	0
20	WMG Model-GA, Type-A	1416	0	0
21	M.V.NOZZLE HOUSING WITH PIN & DEF-A ASSY.	3011	0	0
22	HOUSING COVER	5016	0	0
23	GASKET	5017	0	0
24	GONG STICKER	5020	0	0
25	PLUG	5022	0	0
26	ALUMINIUM CIRCLE DIA. O.D 122MM X 2MM	8914	0	0
27	COUNTER SUNK SCREW	9025	0	0
28	CHEASE HED. SCREW	9029	0	0
29	BRASS PIPE D 54 MM X 14 SWG.IS 407	9285	0	0

Fig. 13.7: Stock Statement with Quantity

It displays a list of all inventory items. User can prepare this category wise or sub-category wise. The column heading is a sorting button to prepare the list in desired sequence. The report can be automatically saved, instantly as an MS Excel Sheet.

(E) **MIN Register:** Material issue Note is MIN. List of material issue note is shown in the MIN register.

(F) **Stock Adjustment Note Register:** Adjustments to stock quantity are listed in this Register.

13.7 BOM MODULE

BILL OF MATERIAL is master database giving relation of child item and father item for a given finished goods or semi-finished goods. The semi-finished goods is also called 'Factory made item'.

What is the use of BOM in ERP?

The BOM is used in the following business process:

(1) **MRP:** material requirement planning.

(2) **Creating the Work Order Automatically:** This is communication to production what to produce and from what, because work order will automatically explode the BOM and show the child items required.

(3) **Cost Sheet:** This gives material cost for a given FG.

(4) **BOM can be used for stores issue to shop floor:**

   (a) Material issue note (MIN) link to BOM for stores issue to shop floor. Material is consumed at stores location.

   (b) Or stock transfer challan (STC) link to work order for stores issue to shop floor - (recommended) -> production entry will consume the material from shop floor.

(5) **Production Entry to Consume Raw Material:** This is linked to the work order that is in turn linked to the BOM.

The following is a procedure to prepare Bill Of Material of factory made item and finished goods:

(1) Prepare the BOM of a factory made item, which will be made by R & D (or Design) department (competent user).

(2) Using factory made item prepare the BOM of finished goods. When factory made item in finished goods is dragged & dropped, all child item of factory made item will be displayed automatically in this BOM. While making BOM of finished goods you cannot edit the factory made item BOM.

Note: Only few selected users are given access to the BOM master menu for security reason. Only specially trained ERP user is allowed to use the BOM. This is not for sundry users. Here the word bill should not be confused with the account bill. Here, bill simply means list. BOM is list of material required to make another item.

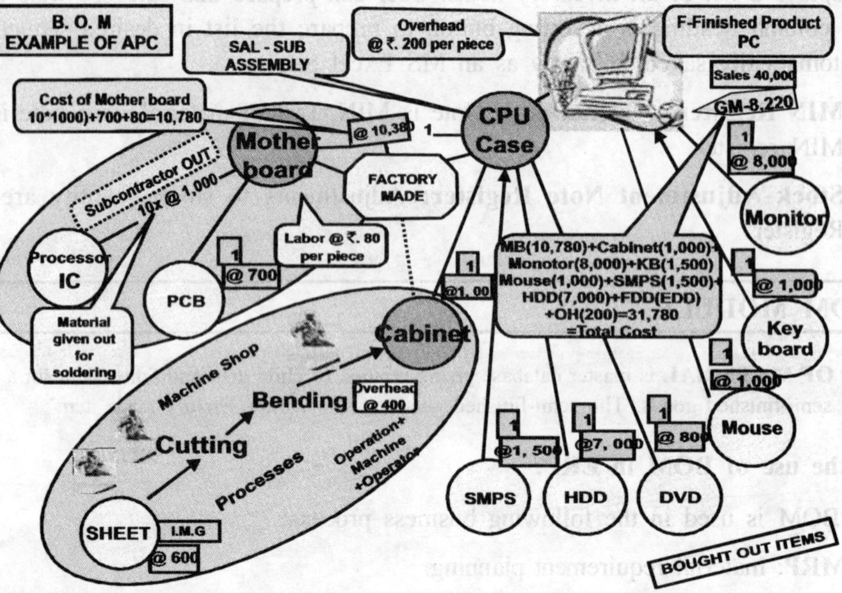

Fig. 13.8: Bill of Materials Example. Child Items Required to Make a PC

Microsoft Excel - BOM_GLASS_WINDOW_ASSEMBLY_CONSTRUCTION

D2 BOM Master Listing prepared from DNS ERP Software

	A	B	C	D
1				
2				BOM Master Listing prepared from DNS ERP Software
3				
4			GLASS WINDOW CONSTRUCTIONS COMPANY	
5				
6			Finished Goods – Father item	Production consumables / bought out / child items
7				
8		1	BOM Listing for item name : SLIDING WINDOW - 4 GLASS SHUTTERS ON 2 TRACK - 19MM RNo : 1R	
9			SLIDING WINDOW - 4 GLASS SHUTTERS ON 2 TRACK - 19MM, SL-19-2T4S, , 0, 0, ALL, Rate : 0, UOM : SQMTR, RNo : 1, DATE : 01-Feb-2008)	
10				HANDLE 18X50- 1200 MM (ALUMINIUM SECTION Gross Quantity : 2 Rate : 0 UOM : KGS)
11				INTERLOCK 18X50-1200 MM (ALUMINIUM SECTION Gross Quantity : 2 Rate : 0 UOM : KGS)
12				TOP BOTTOM 18X50 - 1500 MM (ALUMINIUM SECTION Gross Quantity : 1 Rate : 0 UOM : KGS)
13				TWO TR TOP 19MM-1200 - 1.2 MM (ALUMINIUM SECTION Gross Quantity : 2 Rate : 0 UOM : KGS)
14			MS EXCEL SHEET EXPORTED FROM	TWO TR TOP 19MM- 1500 1.2 MM (ALUMINIUM SECTION Gross Quantity : 1 Rate : 0 UOM : KGS)
15			DNS BOM MASTER DATA	SLIDING BUSH BLACK (BUSH Gross Quantity : 8 Rate : 25 UOM : NOS)
16				CON. LOCK 105 NO. (LOCK Gross Quantity : 2 Rate : UOM : NOS)
17				UM4 EPDM 4MM (GASKET Gross Quantity : 8.4 Rate : UOM : KGS)
18				CLEAR GLASS 4MM 1500*1200 (CLEAR GLASS Gross Quantity : 1 Rate : 0 UOM : SQMTR)
19				ROLLER 18*50 (ROLLER Gross Quantity : 6 Rate : UOM : NOS)
20				RAWAL PLUG 10*35 (RAWAL PLUG Gross Quantity : 14 Rate : 0 UOM : NOS)
21				SCREW SM 4X13 CSK (SCREW Gross Quantity : 4 Rate : 0 UOM : NOS)
22				SCREW STAR 6X9.5 PAN (SCREW Gross Quantity : 14 Rate : 0 UOM : NOS)
23				WOOD SCREW 10*60 (SCREW Gross Quantity : 14 Rate : 0 UOM : NOS)
24				WOOL 18MM (GASKET Gross Quantity : 21.6 Rate : UOM : RMTR)
25				
26		2	BOM Listing for item name : SLIDING WINDOW - 2 GLASS SHUTTERS ON 2 TRACK - 19MM RNo : 2R	
27			SLIDING WINDOW - 2 GLASS SHUTTERS ON 2 TRACK - 19MM, SL-19-2T2S, , 0, 6, ALL, Rate : 0, UOM : SQMTR, RNo : 2, DATE : 01-Feb-2008)	
28				ANGLE CUT 38*38 -56MM (ALUMINIUM SECTION Gross Quantity : 4 Rate : 250 UOM : NOS)
29				HANDLE 18X50- 1200 MM (ALUMINIUM SECTION Gross Quantity : 2 Rate : 0 UOM : KGS)

Fig. 13.8: Bom Master Listing

Bom Master Listing: Alpha Blue Colour Pigment

	BOM Master Listing prepared from DNS ERP SOFTWARE
	DNS BOM for Chemical Industry - Color Pigmnets
Finished Goods = Father Item	**Production Consumables / bought out / child items**
	BOM Master For item name ALPHA BLUE (FG 56.0 Rate 655 UOM : KG RNo : 1)
Father Item	**ALPHA BLUE (PB 15.0 Rate : 35 UOM : KG RNo : 1 DATE : 23-Jun-2006 TIME : 0)**
Raw Material - Child Items :-	CAUSTIC SODA FLAKES (Net Wt.: 0.025 Wastage Per.: 0 Rate : 19 UOM : KG Time :)
	COPPER PHTHALOCYANINE BLUE (Net Wt.: 1.052 Wastage Per.: 0 Rate : 163 UOM : KG Time :)
	FATTY ACID (Net Wt : 0.015 Wastage Per.: 0 Rate : 56.75 UOM : KG Time :)
	F.SALT (Net Wt.: 0.17 Wastage Per.: 0 Rate : 2.5 UOM : KG Time :)
	V. POWDER (Aqua AC-303) (Net Wt.: 0.0025 Wastage Per.: 0 Rate : 9.4 UOM : KG Time :)
	ORTHA XYFGDFJ (Quantity 1: 0.035 Quantity 2: 0 Rate : 70 UOM : LTR Time :)
	PHOSPHORIC ACID 454 (Quantity 1: 7.368 Quantity 2: 0 Rate : 3000 UOM : MT Time :)

BOM master data entry screen is shown below. The BOM or Recipe for making Pickle. Note the packing material, plastic bag, is also included in the BOM master of 200-Gram pouch product,

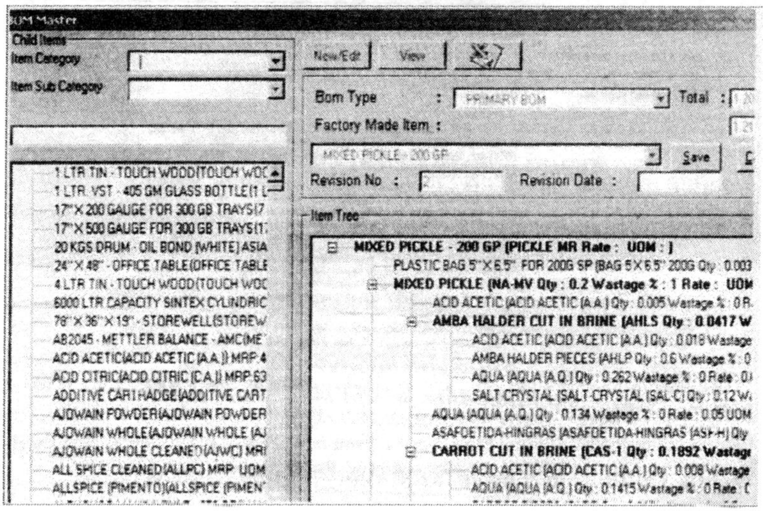

Fig. 13.9: Bom Master for Making Pickle

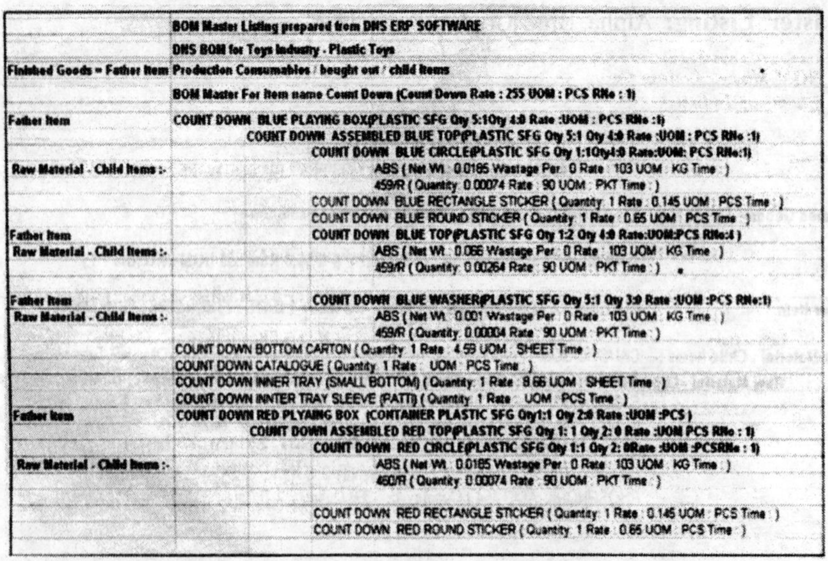

Fig. 13.10: Bom Master for Making Safety Value

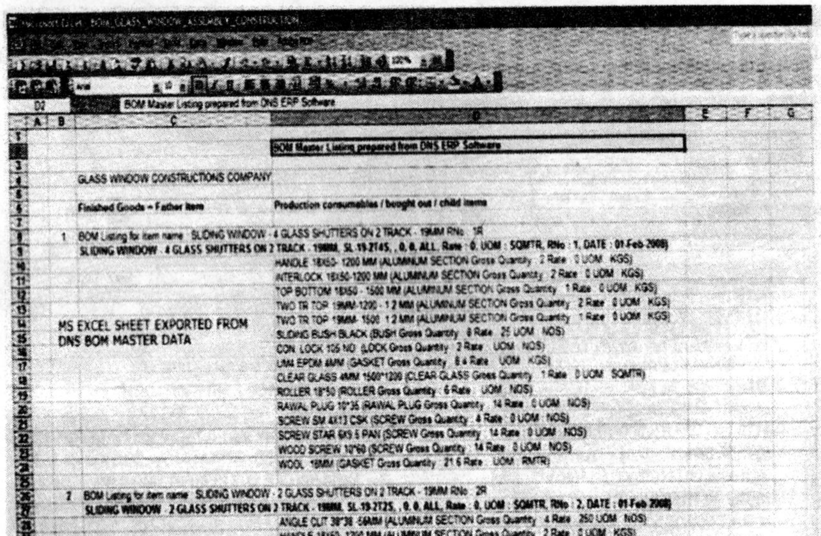

Fig. 13.10: Bom Master for Making Sliding Glass Window

BOM Master Reports

User can print the BOM using BOM reports menu in MS Excel sheet format, The Excel sheet can be saved as soft copy or user can print the excel sheet from Excel.

The item in bold is the father item and the child item below (raw material) which will be consumed to produce the father item.

Example of BOM of a Special Purpose Machine. Instantly exported to MS Excel Sheet.

Note that some child items are itself a father item, it has its own child item, and so forth. The last leaf of the BOM tree is the bought out item or the raw material. The BOM master data also clearly captures the quantity and Unit of Measurement of each child item.

13.11 SUMMARY

Enterprise Resource Planning or ERP is a strategic software Tool that is very effective for automation of stores record system. ERP is not meant only for industrial giants but for all business organisations.

Earlier software applications were not as successful as ERP because of complexities involved in determination of user requirements, software design, acceptance and implementation. ERP packages adopted a totally different approach by providing the most comprehensive functionality within the package. User company was only expected to pick and choose whatever was required for its operations.

ERP reconciles and optimizes different goals of the departments of the company and makes the organisation team based, cross functional, process oriented organisation.

Materials Management module of the ERP is applicable for stores management. The module has many useful features and once initial master data is generated, it provides all required reports to managers immediately online.

13.12 SELF ASSESSMENT QUESTIONS

(1) List main factors that were responsible for failure of traditional business automation attempts.

(2) How does ERP resolve Typical Problems faced by organisations wanting to automate materials management?

(3) Describe different reports generated under ERP for use by different functions.

NOTES